Beyond Debt

Beyond Debt

Islamic Experiments in Global Finance

DAROMIR RUDNYCKYJ

THE UNIVERSITY OF CHICAGO PRESS   CHICAGO AND LONDON

The University of Chicago Press, Chicago 60637
The University of Chicago Press, Ltd., London
© 2019 by The University of Chicago
Published 2019
Printed in the United States of America

28 27 26 25 24 23 22 21 20 19   1 2 3 4 5

ISBN-13: 978-0-226-55192-0 (cloth)
ISBN-13: 978-0-226-55208-8 (paper)
ISBN-13: 978-0-226-55211-8 (e-book)
DOI: https://doi.org/10.7208/chicago/9780226552118.001.0001

Portions of chapter 1 were previously published in "Wall Street or *Halal* Street? Malaysia and the Globalization of Islamic Finance," *Journal of Asian Studies* 72, no. 4 (2013):
831–848. Copyright © 2013 by the Association of Asian Studies. Portions of chapter 6 were
previously published in "Debating Form, Consuming Substance: Halal Authenticity in
Malaysian Islamic Finance," *Practical Matters* 10 (2017): 1–14. Copyright © 2017 by Emory
University. Portions of chapter 8 were previously published in "Subjects of Debt: Financial
Subjectification and Collaborative Risk in Malaysian Islamic Finance," *American Anthro-
pologist* 119, no. 2 (2017): 269–283. Copyright © 2017 by the American Anthropological
Association.

Library of Congress Cataloging-in-Publication Data

Names: Rudnyckyj, Daromir, 1972– author.
Title: Beyond debt : Islamic experiments in global finance / Daromir Rudnyckyj.
Description: Chicago : The University of Chicago Press, 2018. | Includes bibliographical
    references and index.
Identifiers: LCCN 2018009775 | ISBN 9780226551920 (cloth : alk. paper) |
    ISBN 9780226552088 (pbk. : alk. paper) | ISBN 9780226552118 (e-book)
Subjects: LCSH: Finance, Public—Malaysia. | Finance, Public—Islamic countries. |
    Finance—Religious aspects—Islam. | Bonds (Islamic law)—Islamic countries. |
    Debt equity conversion—Islamic countries.
Classification: LCC HJ70.7 .R83 2018 | DDC 332/.042091767—dc23
LC record available at https://lccn.loc.gov/2018009775

♾ This paper meets the requirements of ANSI/NISO Z39.48-1992 (Permanence of Paper).

Contents

Abbreviations

AAOIFI	Accounting and Auditing Organization for Islamic Financial Institutions
APB	Asian Participation Bank
BBA	bai bithaman ajil
FDI	foreign direct investment
FDIC	Federal Deposit Insurance Corporation
GCC	Gulf Cooperation Council
GIC	government investment certificate
GTP	Government Transformation Program
IAS	International Accounting Standards
IFI	Islamic financial institution
IFSA	Islamic Financial Services Act
IFSB	Islamic Financial Services Board
IMF	International Monetary Fund
IIFA	International Islamic Fiqh Academy
INCEIF	International Centre for Education in Islamic Finance
ISRA	International Shari'ah Research Academy for Islamic Finance
JPIT	Jabatan Perbankan Islam dan Takaful (Department of Islamic Banking and Takaful)
KLSI	Kuala Lumpur Shariah Index
LME	London Metal Exchange
MAIWP	Majlis Agama Islam Wilayah Persekutuan (Federal Territory Islamic Religious Council)
MGS	Malaysian Global Sukuk
MSC	Multimedia Super Corridor
NEP	New Economic Policy

NKRA	National Key Result Area
NSAC	National Shariah Advisory Council
PAS	Partai Al-Islam Se-Malaysia (Malaysian Islamist opposition party)
PSIA	profit-sharing investment account
SC	Securities Commission
SPTF	Skim Perbankan Tanpa Faedah (Interest-Free Banking Scheme)
SPV	special purpose vehicle
UMNO	United Malays National Organization (Malaysian ruling political party)

Pious Finance in the Islamic Global City

In early 2009, as citizens around the world reeled from the reverberating effects of a vast and unruly economic tempest, a small group of about thirty Islamic finance practitioners, shariah scholars, and Islamic economists met in the comparative calm of a closed-door forum at the Kuala Lumpur Hilton to discuss recent events in Islamic finance. When his turn to speak came, dressed in his customary Arab robe and checkered head covering, Sheikh Nizam Yacuby wasted no time in urging his colleagues to seize the historical moment: "In the current financial crisis, everybody is asking us, what is the role of Islamic finance?" His colleagues shifted uncomfortably in their chairs in the muted conference room as he derided them for failing to aggressively make the case for Islamic finance as the remedy to the crisis. The McGill-trained and Bahrain-based shariah expert exclaimed, "Instead of presenting to the world that we are the solution and a better alternative, we are still discussing and disputing." He castigated his colleagues, intoning that the failure to forcefully present Islamic finance as a solution would make Muslims "the *ummah* of lost opportunity."[1] Sheikh Nizam urged them to "seize the moment" because people around the world were being "hurt by the money they are losing" and "are looking for some relief. Instead of seizing this opportunity, we are still in our general and learned forum debating about things that should have been ended" (*ISRA Bulletin* 2009b, 10).

In the wake of what was called the worst economic downturn since the Great Depression, Sheikh Nizam's outburst reflected concerns that went well beyond discussions among Islamic finance experts. As citizens around the world searched for alternatives to existing financial arrangements, Islamic principles found appeal in unexpected quarters. *L'Osservatore Romano*, the Vatican newspaper and tacit mouthpiece of the pope, wrote that the "principles on which Islamic finance is based may bring banks closer to their clients and to the true spirit which should mark every financial service" (Totaro 2009). Some time later, a photograph that circulated with great fanfare on many Islamic finance blogs during the Occupy Movement of 2011 showed a protestor at an Amsterdam march carrying a boldly lettered sign that read "Let's bank the Muslim way?"[2] Although the question mark indicated less than a full-throated endorsement, it also opened up the possibility of a different view of Islam a decade after George W. Bush initiated the so-called war on terror. Indeed, in the years after the financial gyrations of 2008, citizens and states appeared eager to find a resolution to the seemingly interminable series of economic calamities that periodically afflicted capitalism. The near collapse of the global economy had inspired interest in Islamic financial possibilities from the unprecedented endorsement of Islamic conventions by an influential organ of the Catholic Church to the protest discourses of the Occupy Movement. The time seemed ripe for Islamic finance to move from the margins to the mainstream of global finance.

This book documents both the debates among experts about the authenticity of Islamic finance and the alternative it offered in the wake of the 2008 crisis. Focusing on the Southeast Asian nation of Malaysia, it describes steps the state, mainly at the initiative of the country's central bank, has taken to transform the country's capital into what one of my interlocutors called the "New York of the Muslim world." State planners seek to make Kuala Lumpur into an Islamic global city: a central node in a transnational network of Islamic financial hubs that will eventually rival the conventional financial network and its hubs in New York, London, and Hong Kong. This book describes the efforts to cultivate the infrastructure—the institutions, laws, education, human resources, and contracts—that are intended to enable an alternative to what Islamic finance experts term "conventional finance." The challenge of creating a global alternative to conventional finance was a dominant preoccupation among Islamic finance experts in Malaysia and beyond during the years after the crisis. However, while the experts with whom I interacted in Malaysia were seeking to create an alternative financial system, they were simultaneously confronted by a fundamental set of questions. What exactly *is* Islamic finance? What makes it Islamic? What kind of alternative does Islam's restrictions on interest and debt pose to conventional finance? Is debt a necessary feature of capitalism?

While conducting fieldwork for this book in Malaysia between 2010 and

2015 I found that there was no single answer to these questions. My goal is to show how they were addressed by four primary groups of experts in this field. In so doing, I shed some light on assumptions about economic action that are taken for granted in the countries of the North Atlantic, and I further explore the solution that those seeking to reform Islamic finance believe it offers to the global economic predicament. The book seeks to achieve these goals by describing the debates in which Islamic finance experts are engaged as they scale Islamic finance up from a disconnected set of discrete national systems to a functioning transnational system. As this process unfolds, a pressing problem for Islamic finance experts concerns the centrality of debt to contemporary economic practice. This is an especially vexed concern for Muslims because both paying and collecting interest is viewed as a grievous sin. As Bill Maurer has noted, the Qur'an refers to *riba*—which literally means "increase" but also refers to the interest owed on a debt—more than twenty times (Maurer 2005, 27). Moneylending without interest is permitted in Islam under a contract known as *qard al-hasan*, but such "benevolent loans" cannot produce profit.

To solve the problem of making capital available for commerce, contemporary Muslims resort to two main techniques. The first technique involves the sale and repurchase of an asset at a markup on a deferred payment basis. There are a number of different ways this can be structured, but they are all involve price premiums and deferred payments. The most common version of this technique in Malaysia is called *bai al inah*. In this contract a party with surplus capital sells an asset to a second party in need of capital on a deferred payment basis. The second party then immediately sells the asset back to the first party for a lower cash price. In so doing, the two parties effectively circumvent the Qur'anic prohibition on interest through the two sales, the deferred payment, and by fixing the price increase to prevailing interest rates. Most Islamic finance experts acknowledge that these contracts obey the letter of religious injunctions but do not conform to their spirit. Because they effectively replicate interest-bearing loans through the deferred payment and marked-up price, they are often referred to as "debt based."

The second method of financing is less common, but most Islamic finance experts view it as more true to the spirit of Islamic law. They seek to increase its use to amplify the distinctiveness of Islamic finance from its conventional counterpart. Experts refer to this set of techniques as "equity based," as they entail the provision of capital through investment. Drawing on passages from Islam's history and sacred texts, critics and reformers *ownership* ↗

argue that the true essence of Islamic finance is the sharing of risk between contracting parties, which is most effectively achieved through equity-based instruments (Ng, Mirakhor, and Ibrahim 2015, 161). "Equity" refers to the ownership share of an asset and is equivalent to the value of an asset minus any liabilities due. For example, if someone owns a home worth $100,000 but owes $80,000 to a bank, the owner's equity in the home is $20,000.

Proponents of equity-based Islamic finance contend that it emphasizes "risk sharing," namely partnership and profit and loss sharing, rather than lending at interest. There are different versions of equity-based devices, but the one most often invoked by those seeking to reform Islamic finance is called a *mudaraba*. In this type of contract a party with surplus capital invests with an entrepreneur in need of capital for a business concern. The two parties form a partnership in which they agree to share in any profits (or losses) generated by the company. The investor accepts the risk that the enterprise may not produce any returns but also offers his or her guidance and advice to the entrepreneur. Advocates of the partnership dimension of Islamic finance argue that it creates greater collective solidarity (through yielding collaborative partnerships) than debt (which yields individualized and self-interested economic actors). This book details the religious and economic debates over these two forms of financing, the problems they present as mechanisms for the provision of capital, and the relative promise that they hold as alternatives to prevailing economic norms.

BOX 1. **Student Loans and Islamic Equity Finance**

The distinction between debt-based devices and equity-based contracts can be illustrated in the different ways each type of contract might be used to finance a university education. An equity investment in education under Islamic principles would operate much differently from the interest-based loan financing that is common in many developed economies, such as the United States, Canada, and Europe. Over the past thirty years there has been a massive increase in the portion of undergraduate education expenses that are financed through debt in the United States as states have withdrawn investment in public higher education (Brown 2011). Central to these changes has been an effort to make students individually responsible for the costs of their own education (Ross 2014, 107–108). For many undergraduates, student debt is now a taken-for-granted aspect of student life, but it has also constrained the fiscal well-being of recent graduates and become the focal point of political action (McKee 2013).

BOX 1. **(Continued)**

In a typical student loan, a borrower receives a loan to finance a portion of his or her education, and then after graduation the student repays the principle plus interest in periodic installments. In their essential features student loans resemble other debt arrangements, such as the loans that might be obtained to start a small business, finance the expansion of an existing enterprise, or purchase a home or car. An obligation to repay and the rate of interest on the repayment are core features of the contract.

In contrast, a college degree financed through an equity-based Islamic contract would operate in a radically different manner. Rather than a loan, the student and the financing body form a partnership that provides the student with funds to support his or her education, with the financer obtaining a share of the student's future income, agreed in advance, as the return on his or her investment. In such an equity-financing scheme the knowledge and skills that a student obtains are redefined as equity: an asset that produces a revenue stream. This framing closely resembles the neoliberal conceptualization of "human capital" (Foucault 2008, 229–230). Of course, students that become bankers or medical doctors would likely yield a far greater return on investment than those that become schoolteachers or social workers. Some proponents of equity financing for education contend that state regulation may be required to ensure that all students have equal access to financing. Furthermore, there is the potential for a moral hazard: if repayments are linked to income, some have argued that there may be a disincentive among graduates to work (*Economist* 2015). Nonetheless, equity financing for education has been suggested in non-Islamic contexts as well, including by magazines such as *Forbes* and by the intellectual godfather of American neoliberalism, Milton Friedman (Friedman 1955; Leaf 2014).

Global Experiments

In describing these global experiments in Islamic finance this book makes three central arguments. First, I contend that during the period of my fieldwork Islamic finance was in an experimental moment in which the norms and forms of Islamic finance were subject to debate and up for revision. In this moment, old truths about Islamic finance were being questioned and new definitions were proposed. Those in favor of reforming the industry often attributed the 2008 global financial crisis to the proliferation of debt in conventional finance. They argued that equity-based forms of finance were more economically stable, were more authentic to Islamic religious

risk-sharing

experiments around risk-sharing ①

principles, and offered a clearer alternative to prevailing financial norms. However, shifting from a financial system heavily reliant on debt to one centered on equity is no simple task. I describe experimental efforts to create new, more authentic Islamic financial devices—from home mortgages to government bonds to ways in which stress tests are executed on banks.

a around debt ②

Second, I argue that efforts to reform Islamic finance offer an incisive diagnosis of and potential solution to debt as a theoretical and practical problem—a solution that is scarcely known in North America and Europe, even in literature critical of the global financial system. While an extensive social scientific literature critical of debt has emerged in recent years (Kar 2013; Lazzarato 2012; Schuster 2014; Stout 2016), there is little understanding of what to do about it or what kind of alternatives might exist. For example, in his widely-lauded book *Debt: The First 5,000 Years*, David Graeber, proposes a "biblical-style Jubilee" for both "international debt and consumer debt" (Graeber 2011, 390). Debts would be relieved through an institutionalized program of forgiveness. However, the only substantive change that Graeber's proposal makes to the cycle of overconsumption-indebtedness-default that characterizes debt-intensive economies, is to add forgiveness to the chain. Rather than challenging the premise that debt is necessarily a central feature of economic life, Graeber's "Jubilee" simply institutionalizes debt forgiveness, while taking the other aspects of the debt cycle for granted.

In contrast, Islamic finance promises a more radical corrective to the predominance of debt in contemporary capitalism. Posing equity investment in contrast to interest-based lending, Islamic finance experts identify the instability created by leverage as the central culprit in precipitating financial instability and crisis. "Leveraging" refers to the practice of purchasing assets with a combination of equity and borrowed funds, under the presumption that the income generated by the asset will exceed the cost of borrowing those funds (the interest). During the rapid escalation of real estate values in the early 2000s, many Americans "leveraged up" by using the equity in their homes to take out a second mortgage and sometimes used these borrowed funds to purchase additional property. During an economic boom leveraging can be an enormously profitable strategy, as it was for homeowners who used debt to purchase rapidly appreciating properties. However, during a downturn, leverage can lead to devastating losses. This was evident during the 2008 crisis when real estate values suddenly suffered acute drops. In several cases this left homeowners and other real estate investors owing more to banks than the value of their properties. Forced sales of real estate led to further declines in property prices, pushing more homeowners underwater.

Islamic finance experts argue that redesigning capitalism to be centered on equity investments will lead to greater economic stability. They argue that promoting equity investment will eliminate leverage because, in the words of one interlocutor, "You can't invest what you don't already own." In the economy they envision, investors will not be able to leverage the equity they already have to borrow even larger sums. For example, during the 2008 crisis an equity-based Islamic financial system would have inhibited the volume of capital available for leverage. Such a limit would have constricted the rise in property values and inhibited the formation of a real estate bubble. Those seeking to reform Islamic finance hope to delink debt and equity. In advancing this position these experts find allies among prominent economists and other social scientists who have likewise identified leverage as the root of recent economic crises (Appadurai 2016, 151–153; Reinhart and Rogoff 2009). As several of my interlocutors were eager to point out, economists such as Reinhart and Rogoff also posed equity finance as an antidote to economic turmoil, albeit in decidedly secular terms.[3]

Third, I argue that the ambitious effort to make Kuala Lumpur an Islamic global city by transforming it into an international hub for Islamic finance reveals an alternative configuration of globalization. In this new, transnationally integrated financial system, historical centers of economic and political power in Europe and North America are marginalized in favor of new centers in the Muslim world. Building on thirty years of extensive development in its national Islamic financial system, the Malaysian state has invested heavily to create the infrastructure to make the country's capital a central hub in global Islamic finance. Planners have sought to advance the so-called Malaysian model as the main international standard for the organization and practice of Islamic finance. I argue that dedicating extensive resources has been an explicit part of a state development policy that is simultaneously seeking to find a niche for Malaysia to thrive in the global economy and to create an alternative global financial network where financial centers are not isomorphic with the metropoles on the old map of colonial political and economic power. These twin aims make Malaysia quite possibly the best site to conduct research on contemporary Islamic finance.

Deliberations over the present and future of Islamic finance entail a search for alternatives to debt. Islamic contracts based on debt largely replicate the lending mechanisms of conventional finance. Those seeking to reform Islamic finance object to these contracts because payments on debt

risk-taking journey

subject to change

deposit

are specified at the moment the contract is written and because these payments are not dependent on the financial outcome of the venture being financed. In contrast, the reformers favor equity-based instruments because they involve contingent payments to investors based on the actual profits (or losses) generated by an enterprise. They prefer investments in equity over those made in the form of debt because they believe the assumption of risk is truer to both economic and Islamic principles. They view guarantees such as collateralized debt, deposit insurance, or government bailouts (e.g., for institutions that are "too big to fail") as contrary to Islamic injunctions. Reformers actively seek to reduce debt-based instruments and to make ones based on equity central to a new form of capitalism. Hence the title of this book: *Beyond Debt*.

Debates over the norms and forms of Islamic finance were in some respects a reflection of its rapid growth. By the end of 2016 the total assets held by Islamic financial institutions around the world was over $1.89 trillion, and the annual growth rate of those assets averaged 10 percent per year (IFSB 2017, 7–11). The experts with whom I interacted while conducting research for this book recalled that during its initial stages, in the 1970s and 1980s, there was little discussion regarding what made Islamic finance Islamic. Although some recalled that there was skepticism toward Islamic finance by some consumers, Islamic scholars and academics, key experts such as Islamic finance professionals and regulators working at the central bank, seldom if ever reflected long on the claim to religious authenticity that was implied through adding the appellation "Islamic" to the noun "finance." As Daud Vicary, the former CEO of a major Islamic bank, candidly explained in 2014,

> Today we're now questioning how different is Islamic finance from conventional finance. And the answer today is, of course, it's not that different. And the reason is because [at first] we copied conventional products and, I won't say made them shariah compliant, but worked at "how is this shariah compliant?" The point I'm making here is that, at that time . . . had we been perhaps a little bit smarter, we could have said, "No, we have to come from an Islamic base. Let's throw away the rule book; let's throw away everything the conventional world does and start from scratch and figure out what we can do as an industry." Now that would have been very nice; it also would have been very naïve, because my belief is we never would have got going had we decided to do that.

Vicary's reflection on the history of Islamic finance demonstrates the tension between pragmatism and idealism that characterizes current disputes over the religious authenticity of its practices and structures. For years the industry had adapted conventional financial instruments and used a diverse range of strategies to make them appear genuinely Islamic. However, by the 2010s the industry had reached the point where questions regarding the authenticity of Islamic finance could no longer be deferred.

Recharting Anthropologies of Economy

Malaysia's Islamic finance project presents an ethnographic and conceptual challenge to how the discipline of anthropology has approached economic questions in the past. Work in economic anthropology has emphasized two major tropes. First, it has argued that economic action is embedded in society and culture. It has sought to show how relations of production, consumption, and exchange, especially outside the West, have not been exclusively, or in some cases even partially, guided by material interests but have been instead dedicated to cementing social relationships (Mauss [1925] 1990; Polanyi 1944; Scott 1976). Second, it has sought to show how capitalism breaks down preexisting social relations and introduces individualization and alienation (Nash 1979; Stoler 1985; Taussig 1980). Recourse to the social as necessarily in conflict with the economic remains an assumed position in much anthropological work (Comaroff and Comaroff 2000; Goodale and Postero 2013; Graeber 2012; Klima 2004). In contrast, I seek to show how reformers in Islamic finance seek to remake society through reconfiguring the economy. In this sense they seek to create an *ummah* (Islamic community) through a new set of market devices.

Marcel Mauss presented economic practices that were contained by social relations, arguing that in most human communities exchange was based on gift giving rather than market transactions. Indeed, although he notes that gift giving still plays an important role in modernity, Mauss suggests the West is peculiar insofar as it is one of the few historical examples in which exchange is based on exclusive property rights and cash sales (Mauss [1925] 1990). Polanyi followed Mauss, arguing that prior to the emergence of capitalism, economic exchanges were "embedded" in social relations. However, following the introduction of market transactions, the economy was progressively divorced from society (Polanyi 1944). Scott documented how precolonial economic formations in Southeast Asia were characterized by reciprocal relations in which clients accepted unequal exchanges with the implicit expectation that their subsistence needs would

be guaranteed by a patron in times of calamity (Scott 1976). These patron-
client ties were the basis for a social and moral order during the early modern period prior to the onslaught of colonial capitalism, which ultimately
dissolved these networks and precipitated widespread rebellion.

The historical narrative illustrated in the work of Mauss, Polanyi, and
Scott, in which societies characterized by embedded market relationships
give way historically to disembedded capitalism, has become the common
sense of anthropology and has served as a sort of unstated set of assumptions for anthropological work. Further, it has often been hitched to an
origin story with an implicit morality. In general, so the argument goes,
human life was more humane and cohesive when the economy was embedded in society because people were less competitive and more communal.
In contrast, the progressive disembedding of the market has created individualization and alienation and a consequent decline of sociality. Indeed,
the opposition between the moral economy with its positive associations
and the ills of market society has framed a great number of anthropological research projects.

My approach to economic anthropology departs from these common
tropes. Rather than presuming a necessary opposition between society
and economy, in my work I have sought to show how new forms of subjectivity and collectivity are produced *through* economic action (Rudnyckyj
2004, 2009, 2016, 2017a). In so doing, I build on a different scholarly lineage that does not presume a subject prior to discursive practice but
rather examines how ethical practices, market devices, and calculative
techniques form subjects and groups. The germinal figure in this vein is
Max Weber, who documented how "intense worldly activity" as a means
of attaining conviction in one's salvation gave rise to capitalist subjects
(Weber [1920] 2001).

This line of analysis also draws on the work of Michel Foucault, who documented the redefinition of the word "economy" in modernity. In ancient
Greece, "economy" referred to the management (*nomos*) of the household
(*oikos*). With the emergence of the modern state, the term was used to denote a discrete domain and set of techniques through which citizens were

produced and administered. Statistics (the "science of the state") consisted
of calculative techniques that could be applied to produce a new object, the
population (Foucault 1991, 96). The modern definition of "economy," as
Foucault points out, served as a means of creating "continuity" between
individual conduct, the government of the family, and the administration
of the state (Foucault 1991, 92). In this formulation, society, understood

as simultaneously referring to the collective of individuals, families, and populations, was constituted through conceptualization of an economy. The key intervention here was to show that society and economy are not necessarily in conflict but rather emerge in dialogue with one another.

Building on these approaches, I seek to show that efforts to globalize Islamic finance represent an effort to foster a new configuration of sociality elicited *through* capitalist economic action. In other words, rather than presuming that the capitalist market necessarily corrodes society, this book demonstrates how economic configurations can produce different forms of social organization and belonging. Indeed, although some of those involved in Islamic finance argued that this form of finance should advance social values of justice, equality, and mutuality in the face of market isolation, perhaps more interesting was the fact that many Islamic finance experts saw the market as a means of fostering a new social configuration (Rabinow 1996; Rose 1999). Indeed, they sought to use finance to achieve an ummah commensurate with the discursive tradition of Islam. In this respect, Islamic finance was a means of enhancing the ability of Muslims to live in a pious manner.

Rather than presuming a definition of capitalism at the outset and then documenting its effects, this book seeks to document the formation of a distinctive type of capitalism. Through an ethnographic exploration of Islamic finance I seek to understand how this economic formulation actually operates in practice and how its proponents imagine it will work in the future. This approach builds on recent work on finance in the human sciences. As finance has become an increasingly powerful force in modern life, scholars in anthropology, sociology, science and technology studies, and allied disciplines have demonstrated how finance poses critical social scientific questions pertaining to the resolution of difference across space, time, and value (Maurer 2005; Miyazaki 2013; Riles 2011). Relatedly, others have shed light on how transparency and opacity both figure into finance as a political undertaking (Hertz 1998; Holmes 2014; Lepinay 2011). Other scholars have examined the exclusions that characterize the everyday politics of finance (Fisher 2012; Ho 2009). A germinal body of work, drawing on studies by the French sociologist of science Michel Callon, has sought to show the performative nature of economics and finance, insofar as the theories deployed in these domains of thought shape the very markets that they seek to model (Callon 1998; MacKenzie, Muniesa, and Siu 2008).

Building on recent work in anthropology, a central focus of this book is on contractual forms and the promises that they entail (Appadurai 2016; Davis 2013; Pietz 2002; Riles 2010). In so doing I follow Jane Guyer's call for anthropologists to focus ethnographic attention on documents as the "fetish of the modern economic era" (Guyer 2004, 159). I refer to the contracts that Islamic finance experts seek to deploy to enable Islamic financial action as Islamic market devices. This formulation builds on the notion of "market devices" understood as "the material and discursive assemblages that intervene in the construction of markets" (Muniesa, Millo, and Callon 2007, 2). These include things such as analytical techniques, pricing models, merchandising tools, trading protocols, and aggregate indicators. As Muniesa, Millo, and Callon note, "Devices do things. They articulate actions; they act or they make others act" (2). In debates over the authenticity of Islamic finance and the extent to which it offers solutions to the predicaments of conventional finance, contracts are a specific type of documentary device. A central story in this book is the opposition that Islamic finance experts in Malaysia draw between two contracts: debt-based devices (of which the most often invoked is the bai al inah contract) and equity-based devices (of which the most prominent example is the mudaraba contract). In what follows, by focusing on these devices I seek to show how they represent different visions of what authentic Islamic economic action is and what distinguishes it from conventional finance.

This book documents debates within Islamic finance, efforts to position it as an alternative to its conventional counterpart, and the experimental ethos that characterizes it. In so doing, I build on Hiro Miyazaki's observation that finance professionals are "not simply decision makers but also thinking subjects engaged in dialogue with a variety of broader intellectual debates and projects" (Miyazaki 2013, 6). Like professionals in the Tokyo financial world who work to transform the financial system that they have in part created, I approach Islamic finance experts as reflective subjects who constantly seek vantage points from which to reflect critically on their own technical practices. ⌐a good position/point affording a good point

In taking this approach I build on contemporary work in the anthropology of finance that has shown how financial practices and technologies shape both subjects and selves (Miyazaki 2013; Riles 2010; Schwittay 2011; Zaloom 2006). The sociologist Maurizio Lazzarato makes the compelling observation that debt is a technology of subjectification and that contemporary debt contracts are "part of a long process in which we have witnessed techniques for making a debtor 'subject'" (Lazzarato 2012, 131). Lazzarato refers to the subject of debt as "homo debtor" (or the indebted human) (Lazzarato 2012, 127) and connects the emergence of this subject to the broader dismantling of the welfare state and to the deployment of neoliberal technologies of government. As I demonstrate in this book, Islamic finance experts in Malaysia are keenly aware of the mobilization of debt as a technology of subjectification. Their efforts to substitute equity and investment for debt offers a different vision of economic subjectivity than what has been characteristic of conventional finance.

In so doing, this book documents how experts are engaged in experimental projects to create new forms of capitalism. As Douglas Holmes has shown, conventional financial regulation is characterized by an "experimental ethos" in which central bankers constantly adjust regulatory devices to meet the ongoing changes of the object they seek to manage: the economy (Holmes 2014, 26–27). I found a similar experimental ethos evident in Islamic finance as experts debated devices and sought to simultaneously make Islamic finance meet authentic religious principles and present itself as a viable and distinct alternative to conventional finance. It would be a grand overstatement to consider Islamic finance a revolutionary project that will ultimately supplant contemporary capitalism, but those seeking to reform Islamic finance have the more modest goal of making a capitalism that is less destructive and more humane. → religion attempts this too

In making these interventions this book addresses Islamic finance from a perspective that differs from most recent scholarly work on the subject. This work is, in large measure, framed primarily by two disciplines: Islamic sciences and conventional economics and finance. Most scholars researching and writing about Islamic finance at universities in Malaysia and elsewhere are credentialed in either of these two areas but rarely in both. Islamic law as it pertains to Islamic finance is most often narrowly defined as *fiqh*, or Islamic jurisprudence. Ironically, this definition has its origins in colonialism, as fiqh was institutionalized as the authoritative approach to Islamic law by European scholars during and after the colonial period and has become the dominant form of applied religious knowledge in contemporary Islamic finance. The Islamic sciences in Southeast Asia have typically been divided into subjects such as *tawhid* (theology), fiqh (jurisprudence), *tasawwuf* (spiritual knowledge), *tafsir* (interpretation of the Qur'an), *mustalah al-hadith* (methodology of the hadiths), *tajwid* (recitation of the Qur'an), and Arabic language and grammar (Abdul Hamid 2005, 171). These are typically the core subjects of instruction taught at *pesantren* (Islamic boarding schools, equivalent to *madrassah*), which are widely spread across Muslim Southeast Asia and provide the basis of Islamic education for students who subsequently study at Islamic universities in the region (Abdullah 1986; Dhofier 1999). Despite the diversity of specializations within Islamic education, fiqh has

theory or philosophy if law
Islamic
⊢ jurisprudence ↓ human understanding of the sharia

Sharïa

become the dominant scholarly frame for determining religious authenticity in Islamic finance. As I describe below, the predominance of fiqh in Islamic finance has led to criticism that Islamic scholars are overly literal in their application of Islamic law and tend to emphasize the letter of the law rather than its spirit. This formalist approach to Islamic finance has taken religious knowledge as a blueprint rather than an ongoing process of interpretation.

While most scholarly work in this field has been written with the goal of either improving the economic performance or bolstering the religious credentials of Islamic finance, there is a growing social scientific literature that approaches Islamic finance within broader social, political, and historical contexts (Pitluck 2008; Pollard and Samers 2007; Tobin 2016; Warde 2010). This literature is characterized by two main themes. First, scholars have criticized Islamic finance for its failure to achieve the moral prescriptions of Islam, such as greater equality and social justice. These scholars point to the implicit and explicit values of Islam and show how Islamic finance has, in many cases, failed to meet them (Asutay 2012; Tripp 2006). Second, scholars have argued that it is little more than a second-rate imitation of conventional finance adorned with an Islamic veneer (El-Gamal 2006; Kuran 1997). Arguably, the prevailing question in qualitative approaches to Islamic finance in the human sciences has been the extent to which Islamic finance offers a genuine alternative to conventional finance or merely a superficial façade (Bassens et al. 2013; Malik, Malik, and Mustafa 2011; Maurer 2005; Pitluck 2013; Pollard and Samers 2013). These approaches disparage Islamic finance for replicating conventional finance while using Arabic terminology and Muslim religious symbols to conceal this underlying orientation (Kuran 2004). This has precipitated what El-Gamal calls "shariah arbitrage": obtaining approval from an Islamic jurist for a financial instrument superficially altered to be shariah compliant and charging a premium for it (El-Gamal 2007). The orienting frame of this work has been to assert that Islamic finance is insufficiently Islamic and only deploys Islamic religious symbols and Arabic language to lend credibility to what is essentially conventional finance. Even less derisive scholarly appraisals contend that Islamic finance differs only in the most superficial of ways from its conventional counterpart (Rethel 2011).

This book moves existing scholarship beyond the question of Islamic finance's religious authenticity by showing how Islamic finance experts *themselves* are posing the problem of the alternative potential of Islamic finance and by documenting some of the concrete experiments in which they are engaged to do so. In making this move I build on work that has shown how contemporary Muslims are actively working to adapt modern institutions and practices to the imperatives of Islamic action (Fernando 2014; Hoesterey 2016; Rudnyckyj 2010; Silverstein 2011; Walton 2017). My goal here is not to come to a conclusion about what constitutes authentic Islamic finance but rather to show how this object is subject to debate and in formation. The financial crisis of 2008 was a pivotal historical moment in which the problem of the alternative potential of Islamic finance was posed with heightened urgency. Yet it simultaneously raised the related problem of what makes Islamic finance Islamic.

Presented with these problems, Islamic finance experts generally relied on two foundational binaries in articulating their vision of Islamic finance: one between what they identified as conventional finance and Islamic finance, and one between debt- and equity-based finance. While these binaries were useful heuristic devices for my interlocutors and produced a grid of intelligibility through which they understood and represented Islamic financial forms and practice, like virtually all binaries they deteriorate when subjected to rigorous interrogation. These binaries idealized an equity-based Islamic finance against a debt-based conventional finance. My interlocutors granted that equity-based financing was present in conventional finance as well, visible, for example, in devices such as stock markets and profit-sharing contracts. Furthermore, Islamic finance experts were freely willing to admit that at some level both systems were bound up with one another, as was most evident when confronted with the reality of state-issued fiat money. Many experts noted that so long as such national currencies were used as the medium of exchange in commercial transactions, Islamic and conventional finance would be inextricably entangled. For this reason, the most radical proposals in Islamic finance involved completely dissociating from the international currency system and adopting precious metal as a medium of exchange, unit of account, and store of value through the gold dinar and the silver dirham. However, as I describe below, even given its experimental ethos, such a radical rethinking of money itself was a bridge too far for the Malaysian Central Bank. Abandoning state-issued currency for precious metal was, for many, beyond the limits of financial thought.

Islamic finance experts, especially those seeking to reform the industry, often drew a second binary distinction between equity and debt. This distinction was morally weighted, with equity viewed as a more ethical alternative that fostered values such as partnership and equality, whereas debt was negatively associated with individualism and inequality. Of course, in conventional finance, debt and equity are often mutually constitutive, and there are a number of products and practices that combine them, such as leveraging. Indeed, Islamic finance practitioners often criticized reformers who drew such a stark opposition between debt and equity. As the CEO of one Islamic bank told me, "We've got to be clear about what is debt and what is equity. . . . There are structures that might have debt with convertible equity. . . . I think it is too naïve . . . to say we've got to convert from debt to equity. Equity has a lot of classes as well." Indeed, practitioners were often eager to point out that the division between equity and debt is not as clear cut as some of the participants in my research made it out to be.

Fieldwork in an Islamic Global City

Political leaders in Malaysia have long sought to foster the compatibility of the country's majority Muslim population with modern economic norms and forms. As a key part of this project, Malaysia's position in the global network of Islamic finance cannot be understated. Saskia Sassen has developed the concept of "global cities," which identifies urban areas that contain the infrastructure and expertise that undergirds economic globalization (Sassen 1991). In her words these cities are the "command centers" of global capitalism. Taking Aihwa Ong's caution regarding the universalism implicit in Sassen's formulation (Ong 2011, 6), I argue that Malaysia's Islamic finance project represents an attempt to create an Islamic global city. In Sassen's model there is an elite network of global cities, prominently featuring New York, London, and Tokyo, that dominates the global economy. Islamic finance planners and practitioners seek to create a network of Islamic financial centers linking cities such as Kuala Lumpur, Dubai, and Istanbul (see figure 1).

The effort to create this alternative network dates to an earlier moment of fiscal calamity, the Asian financial crisis of 1998, when Malaysian planners greatly accelerated their efforts to forge an integrated Islamic alternative to the conventional financial system. At times competing and at other times collaborating with sites in the Middle East, the architects of Malaysia's Islamic finance project have recently sought to create an "Islamic Wall Street" in Kuala Lumpur. However, this project is no recent fancy or passing fad. Indeed, as I describe below, it is the outcome of thirty years of state efforts to promote Islamic finance as an economic and political strategy.

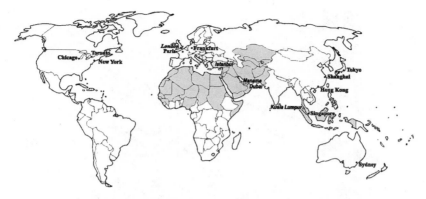

FIGURE 1. World map depicting financial centers. Centers in the global Islamic financial network are italicized. Conventional financial centers are in Roman type. London is a key center
for both conventional and Islamic finance. Nations with Muslim-majority populations are
shaded.

Ambitious plans to make Malaysia into what planners envision as a
"global hub" for Islamic finance are evident not only in government planning documents, such as the state's Ninth Malaysia Plan, which provided the
blueprint for economic development in the country (Kassim, Majid, and
Yusof 2009, 16), but also in Kuala Lumpur's booming cityscape. Amid the
construction cranes and new building projects, advertisements by Islamic
banks, offering everything from home financing to wealth management services, line many key boulevards and highways. In the 2010s Bank Islam,
founded in 1983 and Malaysia's oldest Islamic bank, aggressively promoted
a platinum credit card that was "accepted worldwide." Inside KL Sentral,
Kuala Lumpur's massive ultramodern train station, eye-catching advertisements for a Saudi firm that bills itself as the world's largest Islamic bank encouraged potential customers to "Get There Fast" with "Al Rajhi Personal
Financing." On the other side of the station, the mainly Qatari-held Asian
Finance Bank boldly proclaimed that it is "moving the world to Islamic
banking" (see figure 2). During prime shopping hours, customers queued
at the numerous ATMs owned by one of the over twenty Islamic banks operating in the country. Inside the cars of Kuala Lumpur's fully automated,
driverless light rail system, Bank Rakyat (which literally means "People's
Bank") billed itself as "100% Islamic banking" to differentiate itself from
other banks, such as CIMB, one of Malaysia's largest banks, that offered
both conventional and Islamic financial services.[4] On city streets it was not

FIGURE 2. An advertisement for Asian Finance Bank, a Qatari-controlled Islamic bank, reflects the optimistic spirit of Islamic finance in Malaysia during the 2010s. Photo by author.

uncommon to find promotions for Islamic mortgages depicting scenes of domestic idyll with frolicking children and smiling mothers piously attired in brightly colored headscarves. These ads sought to attract bystanders with various kinds of home financing contracts that substitute shariah-compliant contracts for financial devices premised on the payment of interest. Downtown, the government's Economic Planning Unit was developing the Kuala Lumpur International Financial District, intended to compete with Singapore as a global financial center for Southeast Asia but with a special focus on assembling a critical mass of Islamic financial institutions and expertise.[5]

Islamic finance is but one facet of efforts to make Kuala Lumpur an Islamic global city. Johan Fischer has described how Malaysian planners have sought to make Malaysia a hub for the global *halal* food industry, with many of the standards-setting and regulatory offices for halal food in and around Kuala Lumpur (Fischer 2011).[6] These efforts build on a longer history in which senior officials have sought to make Malaysia play a prominent role in the Organisation of Islamic Cooperation by seeking to host key international Islamic institutions, such as the International Islamic University of Malaysia, which was founded in 1983, the same year as Malaysia's first Islamic bank (Milne and Mauzy 1999, 135). In sum, Malaysia in general and Kuala Lumpur in particular offer the opportunity to understand the intellectual and practical ferment in Islamic finance as practitioners seek to scale it up from a disconnected set of systems based in individual nation-states to a transnationally integrated system that might someday rival its conventional counterpart. This emerging Islamic global city proved to be an advantageous site from which to document the increasing complexity of Islamic finance and the deliberations and debates occurring as this ambitious effort unfolded.

The Book

In describing debates over the role and status of debt at an experimental moment in contemporary Islamic finance, the first section of the book examines the key Islamic financial institutions in Malaysia, describes the individuals that occupy these institutions, and documents debates over the definition of Islamic finance. The goals are to illustrate conflicting ideas about what makes Islamic finance Islamic and to track efforts to make Kuala Lumpur an Islamic global city by creating an Islamic financial infrastructure. I also describe the four main groups of Islamic finance experts who both work in Islamic finance on an everyday basis and are engaged in polemics over what it should be in the future.

The second section of the book describes the everyday practices of Islamic finance in its current iteration. I seek to show how, in many respects, contemporary Islamic finance is framed by the knowledge practices of its conventional counterpart. It ends up replicating many of the central features of the financial status quo rather than offering a convincing alternative. I then describe debates over what exactly would constitute an Islamic alternative to conventional finance. I argue that these debates hinge on a distinction between form and content by describing the methodological differences between what experts call "shariah-compliant" Islamic finance, which applies formal rules to test financial devices for complicity with religious directives, and what they refer to as "shariah-based" Islamic finance, which seeks to synthesize new financial forms based on

Islamic texts and grounded in Islamic history. Their methodological disagreement rests on whether Islamic finance is conceived of in formal or substantive terms.

The third section of the book turns to how the religious authenticity of Islamic finance is problematized in Malaysia. It documents how the different approaches to Islamic finance described at the outset of the book are put into practice. Those seeking to reform Islamic finance claim that their project will both be more religiously authentic and lead to greater economic benefits. I then describe the steps that Central Bank officials and others tasked with oversight of Islamic finance in Malaysia have taken to address the concerns of reformers. I argue that although the Central Bank's reforms in some cases were contrary to the desires of Islamic banks, these reforms fit into broader state development efforts and the politics of religion and race in Malaysia while also, somewhat surprisingly, converging with certain principles characteristic of neoliberalism.

This study of Islamic finance might be broadly framed, following Marcus and Fischer, under the rubric of anthropology as financial critique (Marcus and Fischer 1986). I adopt the classic anthropological strategy of seeking to make the familiar strange and enhance "comprehension of the self through the detour of the comprehension of the other" (quoted in Rabinow 1977, 5). Since the financial crisis of 2008 there has been a widespread sense among the public and activists that finance is important but limited understanding of how finance works and what alternatives might exist to dominant financial practices and models. This book addresses these problems by describing how Islamic finance experts are developing a response to the global financial predicament that differs from that offered by both Wall Street and Occupy Movement activists. In the wake of the crisis, major financial institutions requested loans and other financial guarantees from government to maintain the solvency of the financial system (Sorkin 2009). Occupy activists called for forgiveness for those mired in debt and those adversely afflicted by the sharp decline in the value of real estate (Juris 2012). In contrast, this book argues that experts seeking to reform Islamic finance challenge the epistemology of finance by posing investment rather than debt as the central mechanism for the mobilization of capital.

In contemporary Malaysia, experts assert that Islamic finance offers a more stable, just, and sustainable alternative to conventional finance. By the time the crisis erupted, the Islamic financial industry had reached a scale by which it could be plausibly imagined as an alternative to its conventional counterpart. Simultaneously, however, a vociferous debate raged over the extent to which Islamic finance adequately conformed to religious prescriptions for economic action. Much of the initial growth of Islamic finance has come from "reverse engineering" debt agreements using "paper sales" of tangible assets to create contracts that comply with the letter of Islamic law. However, as these methods have come under increased scrutiny and criticism, reformers have sought to substitute them with investment-oriented contracts less prone to the risks of leveraging as a financial strategy. Indeed, reformers pose an economy without leverage as a more stable and sustainable alternative to debt-based capitalism. Insofar as these experts draw on religious logics to question some of the presumed instruments that undergird our financial world, *Beyond Debt* demonstrates how Islamic finance is an anthropology of finance: it asks how finance might be thought of, and practiced, differently.

PART I
Infrastructure

FIGURE 3. Logos for Islamic financial services firms adorn buildings adjacent to Kuala Lumpur City Centre. Photo by author.

The key institutions developed by the Malaysian state to provide the infrastructure for Islamic finance include special offices within the Central Bank, research centers and think tanks, and educational institutions. In addition, the Malaysian government successfully lobbied to have the Islamic Financial Services Board, an international standard-setting organization that develops global standards and guiding principles for Islamic financial institutions, located in Kuala Lumpur. Furthermore, the state has offered incentives to conventional banks to establish Islamic operations, thus encouraging private firms located both inside and outside Malaysia to establish an Islamic banking infrastructure.

Challenging the Secularity of Development

After Malaysia's independence in 1957, the country's extant political, legal, and financial systems had all been inherited from the British (Peletz 2002, 38–47). The absence of any alternative to conventional interest-based finance precipitated a moral quandary for those saving to embark on the hajj pilgrimage. Due to the Qur'anic prohibition of interest, pious

Muslims in Malaysia had refrained from participating in the interest-based banking system. The hajj is one of Islam's five core rituals alongside the confession of the faith, daily prayer, fasting during Ramadan, and paying alms, or *zakat*. Most Muslims aspire to undertake the pilgrimage, and for many it transforms their sense of religious identity and their sense of self (Hammoudi 2006). Given the great expense of travel to the Arabian Peninsula, Muslims at the extremities of the Islamic world would often have to save for many years to afford passage and thus fulfill one of the religion's central obligations (Tagliacozzo 2013). When the opening of the Suez Canal and the advent of the steamship made pilgrimage increasingly possible, the absence of any institutional alternative to conventional interest-based finance left prospective pilgrims with three choices, none of which were particularly appealing. One could deposit one's savings in a conventional bank, entrust them to a local confidant such as a religious leader, or squirrel them away at their places of residence. In Malaysia stories abound of rural inhabitants burying gold in their garden plots or stashing their wealth "under the pillow" to save for the pilgrimage while avoiding the interest economy.[1] Conventional banking presented aspiring pilgrims with a no-win situation. Depositing savings in an interest-based bank would entail incurring interest and, consequently, one would paradoxically commit a grave sin while preparing to participate in one of the holiest rituals in Islam. The problematization of interest reveals the cultural norms implicit in finance. Interest has long been the object of ethical reflection not only in the Muslim world but in other religious traditions as well (Buckley 2000; Nelson 1949). While Christianity has gradually adapted to interest as a necessary instrument of finance, debates in contemporary Islamic finance demonstrate that interest need not be taken for granted as a constitutive feature of financial practice (Geisst 2013).

In an effort to resolve the predicament of creating an institutional mechanism to facilitate saving for the pilgrimage without incurring interest, the Malaysian government supported the creation of the country's first Islamic financial institution. This corporation was the brainchild of the economist Ungku Aziz, father of the long-serving governor of the Central Bank, Zeti Aziz, and cousin of the trailblazing postcolonial scholar Syed Hussein Alatas.[2] Aziz outlined the first scheme that enabled saving for the pilgrimage without incurring interest in a paper titled "Economic Improvement Plan for Prospective Pilgrims." This document laid the foundation for the establishment in 1963 of the Muslim Pilgrims Savings Corporation (Çizakça 2011, 207–213). This was the precursor to Tabung

FIGURE 4. The headquarters of Tabung Haji, which manages shariah-compliant investments assembled from the savings of prospective travelers intending to undertake the hajj pilgrimage to Saudi Arabia. Photo by author.

Haji, established in 1969, which remains the central Malaysian institution responsible for managing savings for the hajj (see figure 4). A massive corporation with an impressive hourglass-shaped office tower that forms a prominent landmark on Kuala Lumpur's skyline, by the early 2010s Tabung Haji had more than five million depositors, over three hundred branch offices across Malaysia, and deposits of $9 billion (Ishak 2011).

During the 1980s the common presumption that economic development was a strictly secular project underwent a thorough reexamination in Malaysia. In part this reflected the influence of the 1979 revolution in Iran, which saw Islamic religious authorities for the first time assume power in a modern state (Fischer 1980). This event coincided with and, some have argued, spurred a wider resurgence of Islam around the world (Esposito 1998, 309–310). In Malaysia, the growing popularity of the Islamist opposition political party Partai Al-Islam Se-Malaysia, and particularly its condemnation of the ruling United Malays National Organization (UMNO) for, in their eyes, catering to Chinese, Indian, and foreign business interests pushed UMNO to a deeper embrace of Islam (Ong 1990; Peletz 2002, 10–11). Perhaps most significantly, Mahathir Mohamad, who became prime minister in 1981, initiated a measured rejection of some of the tendencies often associated with modernization. He sought to counter the presumption that the manner in which economic development had unfolded in the West was a universal model for developing countries to follow. Mahathir launched his Look East Policy and invoked Japan as an alternative model of development, embracing so-called Asian values (Ong 1999, 73). Responding to Islamist critiques often couched in moral terms, he suggested that Malaysia did not need to abandon its cultural inheritance while aggressively pursuing economic growth (Ong 1999, 197). This led to an interpretation of Islam that represented the religion as broadly complicit with modernity and capitalist development.

Mahathir's rejection of "western capitalist blueprints" for modernization (Ong 1999, 73) entailed in part the creation of a viable financial system grounded in Islamic prescriptions for economic action. Unlike Sudan, Iran, and Pakistan, which all sought the wholesale transformation of their banking systems into full-fledged Islamic systems in the early 1980s, Malaysia "initiated Islamic banking in parallel with conventional banking on a trial basis" (Venardos 2006, 146). In 1981 the state formed the National Steering Committee on Islamic Banks, consisting of twenty experts who were tasked with outlining the development of an Islamic banking sector (Abdalla Khiyar 2005, 204). The committee's recommendations laid the basis for the Islamic Banking Act of 1983 and the establishment of the nation's first Islamic bank, Bank Islam Malaysia Berhad in the same year (Laldin 2008, 9–10).

From its inception, the National Steering Committee realized that a financial system based on Islamic principles would require a comprehensive financial network consisting not only of banks but also an Islamic money market, Islamic capital markets, and an Islamic insurance system. Experts in Malaysia and beyond point to the comprehensive nature of this system as a unique advantage of Islamic finance in Malaysia. Following the establishment of Bank Islam, the state embarked on the creation of an Islamic insurance system "based on the concept of *takaful*, which means taking care of each other" (Iqbal and Molyneux 2005, 57). Toward this end, in 1984 the parliament passed the Takaful Act, which facilitated the establishment of Syarikat Takaful Malaysia a year later. This was the first takaful operator to provide equity-based mudaraba contracts for shariah-compliant insurance. Takaful is analogous to cooperative forms of protecting against risk, such as mutual insurance, in which policy holders agree to insure each other against damage or loss, using a company to act on their behalf as trustee of the premium contributions of each participant. The premiums, which are invested in shariah-compliant investments, form the fund from which both claims and any surplus is paid out to policyholders based on prearranged profit-sharing ratios.

The Nationalization of Islamic Finance

Islamic finance expanded alongside Malaysia's explosive economic development through the 1980s and early 1990s. Malaysia's central bank, Bank Negara Malaysia, has played the central role in the development and growth of Islamic finance. Bank Negara granted Bank Islam the first Islamic banking license in the country under the 1983 Islamic Banking Act. This was the world's first national law specifically dedicated to the regulation of Islamic banks. Bank Negara provided Bank Islam a decade to establish its operations before subjecting it to competition from other firms. As one former CEO of an Islamic bank told me, "At that time [in the 1980s] there was one Islamic bank in Malaysia . . . which effectively had a monopoly." He continued, "They were given ten years to establish themselves. . . . Then Bank Negara noticed that Bank Islam was making progress and decided it would license one more Islamic bank, Bank Muamalat, and also encourage conventional banks to open Islamic windows." To further facilitate the growth of Islamic finance, the Malaysian government sought to build a network of Islamic banking institutions rather than rely on a single Islamic bank. The "dual banking system" that Malaysia established "allowed Islamic banking and conventional banking to co-exist side by side" (Venardos 2006, 146). To encourage conventional banks to participate in the Islamic system, in 1993 the central bank introduced the Interest-Free Banking Scheme (Skim Perbankan Tanpa Faedah, SPTF) (Iqbal and Molyneux 2005, 46).

Importantly, this state-sponsored program used the word *faedah* rather than riba. "Faedah" can be translated as either "interest" or "benefit" and, although derived from the Arabic word *fawadah*, it carries less of a religious connotation, unlike the word riba, which appears in the Qur'an and is thus marked with a religious valence. By framing Islamic banking in terms of faedah, which is seldom used in religious discourse in Malaysia (for example, it is never used in mosque sermons during Friday prayers, one Islamic bank employee told me), the SPTF obscured explicit references to Islam. Employing faedah rather than riba was thus perhaps intended to make Islamic banking appear less explicitly religious and more palatable to non-Muslims, given that two out of every five citizens are not Muslim and a number of major banks were founded by and continue to be under the influence of non-Muslim Malaysians of Chinese descent. One former official of Malaysia's Central Bank told me that the bank sought to make interest-free banking appeal to all potential consumers irrespective of their religious orientation and also as something that might be offered in banks owned by non-Muslims or with large numbers of non-Muslim employees.

The SPTF program offered tax breaks for conventional banks to open Islamic "windows," which could offer Islamic financial products through a separate division that would be located under the same institutional rubric as the parent bank. Conventional banks could use their existing infrastructure to offer Islamic products under the same umbrella. The Islamic window scheme offered the most cost-effective and efficient way to "disseminate Islamic banking on a nation-wide basis, with as many players as possible, so as to be able to reach all Malaysians" (Iqbal and Molyneux 2005, 146), facilitating the rapid growth of Islamic financial firms, instruments, and products throughout the late 1990s and early 2000s.

The expansion of the number of Islamic banks and conventional banks with Islamic windows in Malaysia required the development of coordinating institutions. Most important, the emerging Islamic banking system required a mechanism to facilitate what bankers term "liquidity" to enable banks to balance their accounts on a daily basis. During the 1980s and early 1990s, one of the central problems that Bank Islam faced as the only Islamic financial institution in Malaysia was that it had no recourse to a market if it was short of liquidity. Because there was only a single institution, there was no interbank money market to enable it to balance its books at the conclusion of a business day. An interbank money market is a critical piece of infrastructure in any banking system. Bank Negara established a special government investment certificate (GIC) to provide liquidity to Bank Islam. The GIC had a three-year redemption time instead of the customary redemption time of twelve months and was based on an Islamic contract known as *qard al hasan*, which is a benevolent loan "given to . . . needy people for a fixed period without requiring the payment of interest, profit or reward" (Hasan 2011, 594). Malaysian Islamic scholars ruled that although interest on such a loan would be prohibited (*haram*), it was permissible to give a gift (*hibah*) on such a loan. The Central Bank, ever pragmatic, concocted a device to enable the smooth operations of the country's only Islamic bank.

Hikam, an official with the Central Bank, told me that the bank investing in these products was effectively like the government borrowing from the public, because they were drawing on public funds to enable Islamic banks to operate. Hikam said that in the early years a committee was formed consisting of members from Bank Negara, the Ministry of Finance, Islamic Affairs Division of the prime minister's office, and other religious authorities near the end of the maturity date on the GICs. This committee would determine the value of the hibah to be given to the holder of the papers (see Hasan 2011, 609). The amount of hibah would be determined by comparison with the conventional system.

The hibah convention appears to be a circumvention of the Islamic prohibition on interest, but Hikam said that there was a scholarly rationale for this permission. Islamic scholars have interpreted the Qur'anic prohibition on riba as a divine injunction against any guaranteed profits. This is based on the Islamic legal maxim *al-ghorm bil ghonm,* or "There is no reward without risk." Scholars have interpreted this maxim to mean that profit is only permissible when an entrepreneur incurs risk. Hikam argued that the hibah paid on the GICs was deemed shariah-compliant because the amount of the gift was not predetermined, and therefore the one who provided the capital incurred risk. Whereas an interest rate was predetermined, the shariah board of the Central Bank ruled that hibah was permissible because it was variable.

Hikam said that later the underlying contract for these GICs was changed from qard al hasan to bai al inah, which allows for a prearranged profit rate. However, after 1993, when the number of Islamic banks expanded rapidly, the government decided to establish a more market-oriented technique to facilitate the ability of Islamic financial institutions (IFIs) to settle their accounts. In 1994 an Islamic interbank money market was established to facilitate the provision of short-term capital between Islamic banks to enable them to balance their books on a daily basis (Venardos 2006, 153).

In spite of the Asian financial crisis of 1997–1998, Islamic banking in Malaysia continued to expand rapidly, which exacerbated concerns over the possibility of conflicting shariah interpretations among different banks. Seeking to preempt a crisis of confidence, Malaysia's Central Bank made its National Shariah Advisory Council the sole authority advising the bank on shariah issues in Malaysia in 1997 (Venardos 2006, 147). The council was made up of prominent shariah scholars, jurists, and financial professionals. The council gave the Central Bank a considerable degree of power in the enactment of guidelines for banking institutions offering Islamic financial products, but its legal status as the final authority over Islamic banking was not established until over a decade later. Furthermore, in 1998 the SPTF was renamed the Islamic Banking Scheme (Skim Perbankan Islam) which explicitly denoted its Islamic orientation. The renaming of the program at this specific time is noteworthy, as it coincides with the Asian financial crisis, which, as I describe below, prompted Prime Minister Mahathir to cast blame for Malaysia's fiscal difficulties on Western finance and financiers.

Throughout the 1990s the Malaysian state had continued to build the infrastructure to facilitate the development of a viable national Islamic financial system. After the establishment of the Islamic banking and insurance sectors, the Central Bank sought to create an Islamic securities market. At first this project was undertaken with the Ministry of Finance, which was responsible for securities regulation until the Securities Commission (SC) of Malaysia, equivalent to the Securities and Exchange Commission in the United States, was established in 1993. In 1995, the Shariah Advisory Committee of the SC developed Malaysia's first shariah screening methodology, and by 1999 the Bursa Malaysia[3] launched the Kuala Lumpur Shariah Index (KLSI), based on stocks listed on the Bursa. This coincided with the 1999 launch of the Dow Jones Islamic Market Index by the private financial information firm Dow Jones (Maurer 2005, 105–108). As Bill Maurer has pointed out, shariah screening methodologies for stocks proceed under the assumption that "any business activity *permissible* according to Islamic norms . . . is itself *Islamic*" (Maurer 2005, 105; italics in original). As Izat, an employee of the SC, explained to me, a company can be deemed shariah compliant even if its owners or employees are not Muslim and the products it makes or services it provides have nothing to do with Islam. This suggests the difference, discussed in detail below, between Islamic finance that is compliant with shariah and that which is "shariah based." Shariah-compliant Islamic finance can be determined through a purely formal approach, namely by establishing the absence of any qualities explicitly prohibited by the Qur'an and the hadiths. (The hadiths are the recorded words and deeds of the prophet

Muhammad and are often used as the basis for Islamic law.) In contrast, shariah-based instruments are generally considered to be more genuine, as they have some substantive historical or textual connection to Islamic principles and practices. In broad terms, the opposition between shariah-compliant and shariah-based Islamic finance maps onto the opposition between debt-based and equity-based instruments. While debt-based instruments achieve shariah compliance, they are generally viewed as adaptations from conventional finance and therefore are not considered shariah based. Equity, investment, and profit-sharing instruments, in contrast, are seen to be shariah based, as injunctions toward equity investment are seen to stem from the Qur'an and the hadiths.

The Securities Commission vigorously sought to distinguish its shariah index from the rival Dow Jones product described by Maurer. Izat explained that one key goal of the KLSI was to "foster the Islamic equities market." In the interest of achieving this, the SC, unlike Dow Jones, did not charge fees to finance professionals who wanted to use the SC's shariah screens to create finance portfolios. The premise behind making a roster of shariah-compliant securities readily available without charge was that private companies and individuals would have fewer barriers to creating Islamic mutual funds and other investment instruments based on the information that the SC was providing. Izat said that this was the main difference between the SC's list and the shariah-compliance screens used elsewhere. If fund managers want to design a shariah-compliant fund for a particular country, Dow Jones charges them for its list of companies that have been denoted as shariah compliant. Another advantage that the SC has over private companies such as Dow Jones is that it has regulatory power, so it can require companies to provide information not in their audited financial statements. In contrast, Izat told me that Dow Jones has "to rely on the audited financial statements" to compile its lists, while "we can go deeper and get more detailed information." Again, the efforts of the SC to foster a shariah-compliant equity market illustrates the extent to which the Malaysian state went to create a national Islamic financial system. The next challenge was to create an Islamic financial network that was not limited by national borders but was in fact global in scope.

Making a Global Hub

Following the Asian financial crisis of 1997 and 1998, the Malaysian state began to aggressively position the country as a global center for Islamic financial services. Indeed, the public quarrel between Mahathir Mohamad and the financier George Soros suggests the extent to which the influential Malaysian prime minister had become critical of the conventional financial system, in which old colonial centers such as New York, London, and Paris exerted outsized global influence. Mahathir famously referred to the currency speculators, with Soros foremost among them, as "unnecessary, unproductive and immoral" (*Economist* 1997). In addition to suggesting that financial markets should be subject to moral regulation, Mahathir's criticism of Soros also asserted that it should be in the service of what he called the "real economy," which echoed the language in which experts in Islamic finance distinguish it from its conventional counterpart. In contrast to the "real economy," Islamic finance experts view conventional finance as characterized by the speculative use of elaborate financial instruments, such as derivatives, that are divorced from material production. The real economy is defined as the domain in which physical commodities are produced and tangible services are provided. The Malaysian state's accelerated interest in developing an Islamic alternative to conventional finance must therefore be understood in the context of the geopolitics of finance in the late 1990s and especially Mahathir's criticism of financiers based in former colonial powers.

Furthermore, the infrastructural innovation in the industry during the early 2000s demonstrates how these years entailed a changing prerogative for Islamic finance in Malaysia. With strong state involvement the industry had matured to the point where there was a critical mass of Islamic financial firms and a whole array of other firms offering subsidiary services, from back-office computer systems to employee training. Daud Vicary described the climate in the early 2000s, when he was working for the multinational professional services firm Deloitte:

> It was in 2002 that things really started changing. . . . I returned to Malaysia with Deloitte, and the first business opportunity I had in the financial services sector was to help convert a conventional bank to opening [an Islamic] window and offering some products. . . . From a business perspective I could see the situation in Malaysia was that there was going to be a revenue stream from doing similar sorts of work here. Things were taking off!

Experts such as Vicary saw that there would be growing commercial possibilities ("a revenue stream") from Islamic financial services in Malaysia. As the industry began to accelerate both domestically and transnationally, the state made a number of key interventions, including reducing ambiguity in

Islamic financial services, supporting research on shariah matters, developing innovative instruments, and creating new institutions.

Regulatory reforms introduced around this time were intended to reduce ambiguity in Islamic finance. Notably, the existence of Islamic "windows" within conventional banks had raised questions about how institutions organized along such lines could guarantee the separation of their conventional operations from their Islamic banking business. In 2004 the Central Bank terminated the Islamic windows program and required conventional banks with Islamic operations to establish full-fledged subsidiaries. The reason behind this move, according to my interlocutors, was that having an Islamic window in an otherwise conventional bank raised concerns regarding the religious legitimacy of the institution. Islam appeared to be more of a superficial brand than a distinctive form of economic action grounded in moral principles discrete from those characteristic of conventional finance. The Central Bank required that Islamic banking operations be distinguished within conventional banks by what experts called a "firewall." This entailed the segregation of Islamic funds from conventional funds, with each of these segments containing its own individual handling and clearing account numbers (Venardos 2006, 147–148).

Nonetheless, the fact that some institutions offered both Islamic and conventional financial services in the same branch raised questions as to the effectiveness of the firewall. I was told that it was an open secret in Malaysian Islamic banking that even with the firewall in place, funds were occasionally mixed. This was most commonly the case when Islamic subsidiaries would fall back on their "parent" institutions to settle overnight debts. Although the subsidiaries could have resorted to the Islamic money market, they were often hesitant to do so due to the higher cost of its funds. Public questions regarding the religious authenticity of Islamic banks led to some firms shifting their operations to "100% Islamic," which subsequently was an advertising slogan deployed by those banks to differentiate themselves from less rigorous competitors (see figure 5).

Another important infrastructural intervention was legal reforms intended to reduce uncertainty in Islamic finance by eliminating conflicts over differing interpretations of Islamic law. The Central Bank of Malaysia Act, passed in 2009, contained key provisions regarding the status of the National Shariah Advisory Council (NSAC), which was housed at Bank Negara. These provisions sought to more effectively administer compliance with Islamic prescriptions by granting NSAC the status

FIGURE 5. An advertisement for Bank Rakyat proclaims that it is "100% Islamic banking." Photo by author.

of the sole authoritative body on shariah matters pertaining to Islamic banking, takaful, and Islamic finance. The act granted NSAC the power to prevail over any other ruling passed by a shariah body in Malaysia.[4] In addition, the act stipulated that courts or arbitrators are required to refer to NSAC rulings in any dispute pertaining to Islamic financial business. Finally, it mandated that any rulings of NSAC be binding. This essentially gave NSAC supreme authority in the arbitration of matters connected to Islamic finance. These provisions were spurred by several instances in which the shariah boards of different banks had come to different conclusions regarding the permissibility of the same instruments and products.

One distinctive feature of Malaysian law is that it consists of a "dual legal system" including civil courts operating according to the norms of British common law and Islamic courts making decisions on the basis of Islamic law. However, Islamic courts are limited to jurisdiction over disputes pertaining to family matters, issues around succession and inheritance, and certain criminal cases (Peletz 2002, 66). According to the federal constitution, all commercial disputes are required to be adjudicated in the civil court system, which has led to the incongruous situation in which judges trained in British common law adjudicate shariah questions in Islamic finance in what is "essentially an English [legal] system" (Peletz 2002, 66). This has sparked the criticism of Islamic scholars who are incensed over civil court judges examining whether "the practices of Islamic banking . . . were contrary to the religion of Islam" (Hasan 2011, 45). The case most often cited as an egregious example of civil court judges infringing on Islamic law was that of *Zulkifli vs. Affin Bank*, described in further detail in chapter 5. To address this problem Malaysia took a characteristically pragmatic approach: the chief justice of Malaysia introduced a special court to "handle and manage Islamic finance disputes" (Yaacob 2011). Common law judges in this special "Muamalat court" have specialized training in shariah matters that is supposed to qualify them to adjudicate Islamic banking disputes. Although this approach raises questions about the distinction between religious and secular law, it is the type of pragmatic solution that many recognize as distinctive of Malaysia's efforts to create a comprehensive Islamic financial system.

Another key infrastructural reform in Islamic finance contained in the Central Banking Act of 2009 required civil courts to refer any shariah matters to NSAC prior to making a ruling. It also made the ruling of the council "binding" on the civil courts, a regulatory change lauded by Lukman, a lawyer who worked at one of Kuala Lumpur's largest firms handling Islamic finance cases. He told me it brought greater "clarity" and made Malaysia's Islamic financial system distinctive from other national jurisdictions. Lukman took pride in the smooth functioning of the regulatory infrastructure in Malaysia: "Nowhere else in the world do you have this kind of a clear structure for resolving shariah issues, except in Malaysia. . . . The decisions of the national SAC are binding on the courts and have legal force. . . . So now judges in Malaysia have to refer to the SAC of [the Central Bank] if there is a shariah matter." Lukman said that this resolved many incidents that had occurred in the 1990s and early 2000s in which common law judges in civil courts would adjudicate on shariah questions that emerged in Islamic finance cases. He said that because common law legal practice is adversarial in nature, the lawyers would frequently mislead the judges into making incorrect decisions. However, this became gradually less prevalent after the 2009 reforms, because the courts are required to consult with NSAC on shariah matters. The members of NSAC are senior shariah scholars who are appointed by Malaysia's ruling monarch.

Standards and Expertise

A commonly circulating argument was that Islamic finance had "imitated" its conventional counterpart and what was needed instead was more "innovation" in the industry to more clearly demarcate it. In this sense, the obstacle to becoming a clear alternative to conventional finance was represented as a deficiency of knowledge and expertise. To redress this deficiency, the Malaysian state invested heavily in creating key institutions for the production of such knowledge. Furthermore, it sought to attract experts from around the world to staff these new institutions. Indeed, part of making Kuala Lumpur a global hub for Islamic finance entailed making the country a center for institutional regulation, experimentation, and knowledge development. Toward this end, the state invested heavily in establishing the key research, regulatory, and educational infrastructure necessary for an Islamic financial system.

Perhaps most visible among these institutions is the impressive headquarters of the Islamic Financial Services Board (IFSB). After a successful lobbying initiative by then prime minister Mahathir Mohamad, the Organisation of Islamic Cooperation decided to headquarter the IFSB secretariat in Kuala Lumpur in 2003 (see figure 6). This institution sets international standards and guiding principles for Islamic finance that can then be used by the more than twenty central banks and monetary authorities that are full members of the institution. In its role of devising standards and guiding principles for the Islamic finance industry, the organization is analogous to the Basel Committee on Banking Supervision for conventional banking. Islamic finance experts refer to the IFSB as responsible for "prudential" oversight of the industry, by which they mean it is responsible for developing supervisory standards to ensure the viability of individual Islamic banks and the integrity of the Islamic financial system as a whole. They contrast it with another key supervisory institution in Islamic finance based in Bahrain, the Accounting and Auditing Organization for Islamic Financial Institutions, which focuses on religious and shariah standards for Islamic finance. The IFSB works closely with the Basel Committee, whose members are invited to comment on the standards developed by the IFSB. At the beginning of 2018 the total membership of the IFSB consisted of 185 institutions, including 75 regulatory supervisors such as central banks and securities regulators, 102 financial institutions and professional firms, and 8 international

FIGURE 6. The headquarters of the Islamic Financial Services Board in Sasana Kijang. Photo by author.

intergovernmental institutions, such as the Asian Development Bank and the Islamic Development Bank. These institutions were based in fifty-seven different jurisdictions. Although a portion of the IFSB's employees are from Malaysia, it is a cosmopolitan institution, and during workshops and meetings I encountered employees of the IFSB's secretariat who were native to Pakistan, Turkey, Sudan, Korea, the Arabian Gulf region, Central Asia, and North Africa.

The IFSB is a pivotal entity in the globalization of Islamic finance and a critical piece of infrastructure. Sponsorship of the secretariat is one manifestation of the investment that the Malaysian state has made in seeking to position the country as a central node in the global Islamic financial network. The major function that the institution has taken has been to create "standards" that serve as guiding documents for Islamic financial regulation and operation around the world. In the words of one IFSB employee, these standards identified the "best practices" for the regulation and operations of Islamic finance. Between 2005 and 2017 the IFSB had published a total of nineteen standards on topics as diverse as risk management, capital adequacy, and stress testing. The amount of work that goes into creating these standards is impressive. Following research for and drafting of a standard, which can take over a year, the IFSB team responsible for its drafting holds a variety of workshops and consultative meetings to solicit comments and criticisms from regulators, practitioners, and other experts. This feedback is incorporated into the final document, which is then issued and serves as a template for Islamic financial operations. The IFSB subsequently hosts workshops for regulators from member institutions, primarily central banks and monetary authorities, on how best to implement the standard.

The centrality of debt in conventional finance proved a particular obstacle when translating conventional standards into Islamic analogs. The IFSB conducts research into the form of a particular standard, drawing on the Basel Committee's standards but also considering specific requirements in Islamic finance. Lukman, the lawyer quoted above who had previously worked for the IFSB before going into private practice in Malaysia, told me that the most difficult challenge for IFSB employees was figuring out how to translate standards that take debt for granted as the central tool of finance into an Islamic financial environment in which financing was primarily based on equity. For example, the Basel Committee prior to the 2008 financial crisis recommended a "capital adequacy ratio" of 8 percent. This meant that financial institutions should hold eight cents on deposit for every dollar it lent out. However, calculating such a ratio for Islamic finance was complicated by the fact that its liabilities are often in the form not just of debt but also of equity. Raising his voice animatedly, Lukman said, "OK, I can calculate the 8 percent, but what is it based on? What 8 percent?" I return to this problem in chapter 7, where I discuss how one IFSB team figured out how to calculate the liabilities of banks offering financial products based on equity and profit-sharing contracts.

The building to headquarter the IFSB, Sasana Kijang, exemplifies the Malaysian state's ambition to make the country a global hub for Islamic financial services and a leading regional center for "promoting regional and international collaboration and best practices in central banking and financial services" (Bank Negara Malaysia 2015). Sasana Kijang was also

FIGURE 7. The front of Sasana Kijang, built by Bank Negara Malaysia to incubate and share the knowledge required to make the country a leading regional center in central banking and financial services. Photo by author.

built to host the South East Asian Central Banks Research and Training Centre and Bank Negara's art and money museums. Designed by the renowned Malaysian architect Hijjas Kasturi and completed in 2011, the building claims inspiration from traditional monetary and cultural forms (see figure 7). A bird's-eye view reveals that the building's physical form replicates the shape of a cowrie shell, which was widely used as money in Southeast Asia and beyond prior to and during the early modern period (Reid 1988, 195; Wicks 1992). The building's physical form signals its content: a structure in the shape of historical money was the site where contemporary finance was regulated, represented, and reimagined.

The references to traditional cultures of finance did not stop there. From street level the structure's façade revealed diamond-shaped geometric patterns derived from *songket*, a handwoven fabric produced in the Malay archipelago characterized by intricately woven designs and ostentatiously accented with the substances of finance: threads made of gold and silver (Rodgers 2012, 117–119). The official interpretation of the architecture referred to the enduring relevance of the traditional form: "Like the songket, the central banking community is interlinked through their similar objectives and bonded through collaboration, strategic alliances and knowledge sharing" (Bank Negara Malaysia 2015). Sasana Kijang was further marked by frameless glass walls, open atriums, and long sightlines that made figures and objects visible over extended interior spaces.

The building stood in stark contrast to the fortresslike headquarters of the Central Bank a short walk away. Built of dreary concrete in the 1970s with the gray visage, narrow windows, and dull lines of an army bunker, the bank's headquarters appeared as a building inscrutable, seeking to hide even from itself and girdled by an imposing security fence (see figure 8). At the ostentatious Sasana Kijang, in contrast, even the elevators were constructed of translucent teal glass, making it appear as if passengers were levitating through the building's diaphanous spaces. The contrast between the open sightlines of Sasana Kijang and the Central Bank's headquarters of decidedly earlier vintage could not have been more evocative of Douglas Holmes's reflections on the translucent design of the European Central Bank building in Frankfurt, which in his words represented "the free movement of ideas and information, countering the (historically correct) suspicion that central banks are resolutely secretive" (Holmes 2014, 55–56). Sasana Kijang likewise appeared intended to convey openness, transparency, and freedom of movement.

The state has also sought to cement Malaysia's position as a key Islamic finance center through the production and dissemination of Islamic financial expertise. The Central Bank has spent over $200 million to create key research and educational infrastructure intended to address what practitioners termed a "knowledge gap" in Islamic finance. This has enabled the establishment of two prominent institutions: the International Centre for Education in Islamic Finance (INCEIF) and the International Shari'ah Research Academy for Islamic Finance (ISRA). INCEIF was formed primarily to alleviate a shortage of qualified personnel familiar with the intricacies of Islamic finance and capable of staffing Islamic financial institutions. During its first thirty years, most employees in the industry had previous experience in conventional banking and learned how to conduct Islamic finance on the job. This inspired criticism because many of those who occupied such positions were inclined to replicate forms and instruments from conventional banking. In response to this "knowledge gap," in 2006 the Central Bank founded INCEIF and designated it the "global

FIGURE 8. The dreary headquarters of Malaysia's central bank, Bank Negara Malaysia. Photo by author.

university" for education in Islamic finance. The goal was to create professionals as well versed in shariah as they were in finance. The former deputy governor of the Central Bank, Dato' Muhammad Razif, who held Malaysia's Islamic finance portfolio at the bank until 2011, expressed the hope that institutions such as INCEIF would address this breach: "My suggestion [is] that banks would employ shariah scholars as bankers" (*ISRA Bulletin* 2009a, 2).

INCEIF occupies a well-appointed new campus close to the national university, the prestigious University of Malaya, and offers MA and PhD degrees in Islamic finance as well as a master's in Islamic finance practice degree, designed to equip professionals with the skills necessary to work within Islamic banks and other financial firms. INCEIF has hired some of the world's most prominent academic experts in Islamic finance and over one-third of the faculty was from outside Southeast Asia, including professors from India, Iran, Afghanistan, Algeria, Egypt, India, and Turkey, in addition to Malaysia. As degree programs in Islamic finance have proliferated around the world,[5] INCEIF has quickly become regarded as a leading site for Islamic finance education. One of the distinguishing features of the university's curriculum is that it requires students to complete coursework not only in conventional and Islamic finance but also in Islamic law (shariah) and jurisprudence (fiqh). A standard curriculum includes courses ranging from financial econometrics to *usul al-fiqh* (the origins of Islamic law). The curriculum entailed something like having theological seminarians with expertise in canon law teaching MBA students at a North American business school.

The juxtaposition of this incongruous assemblage of financial and religious expertise speaks of the experimental nature of Islamic finance. A crucial presumption is that diverse domains of knowledge with radically different methods and orientations can be reconciled. Indeed, they must be reconciled if Islamic finance is to simultaneously be a viable means to enable modern economic and commercial activity and uphold Islamic religious principles. The knowledge that INCEIF seeks to produce combines the deeply interpretive methods of Islamic law and the highly quantitative approach of corporate finance.

Students at INCEIF, like their professors, hail from around the world; one joked to me that it was a "mini United Nations." Indeed, while I was studying there in 2010 and in 2014, I met students from Asia, Africa, Europe, the Middle East, North America, and Australia. This included countries with small Muslim populations, such as Canada, Russia, Korea, and China. The goal of the university is to develop the human resources and thus a critical mass of professionals, skilled in both shariah and finance, to staff Islamic financial institutions around the world. Another effect of this initiative is to extend the influence of what experts call the "Malaysian model" by making the distinctive approach particular to Islamic finance in the country into a global norm. Since Islamic finance is still a project that is in formation, planners recognized that a key part of becoming a global hub for Islamic finance entailed hosting the institutions that would create Islamic financial knowledge. Educating students from across the Muslim world and beyond is one means by which the engineers and planners behind Malaysia's Islamic finance project seek to make the version of Islamic finance developed in Malaysia a global standard.

Another obstacle to the growth of Islamic finance has been a lack of basic knowledge in the field and the fact that it faces challenges that are unique. The resolution to these challenges requires innovative thinking. Practitioners seek to adapt financial contracts that were characteristic of the Arabian Peninsula during the seventh century CE to contemporary contexts, seeking to reconcile principles from the Qur'an and the hadiths with the demands of modern capitalism. Furthermore, contemporary Islamic finance is emerging in the context of its powerful conventional counterpart, which has had a five-hundred-year head start in developing its core contracts, instruments, and practices.

In response to the lack of consensus over precisely which religious principles should govern Islamic finance, the Malaysian Central Bank established ISRA in 2008. ISRA was initiated to conduct and promote applied research on shariah questions in Islamic finance and "bridge the gap" between shariah scholars, Islamic economists, regulators, and Islamic finance practitioners. It is the sister institution of INCEIF and occupies the same well-appointed campus a short taxi ride from central Kuala Lumpur. The campus, which was formerly a training center for Central Bank employees, comes complete with well-manicured sports facilities, including a tennis court and swimming pool, although they appeared to be seldom used. In addition to creating new knowledge, it is also a repository of knowledge for shariah decisions (*fatwa*) on Islamic finance and examines debates over the role and interpretation of shariah in the Islamic financial industry both in Malaysia and abroad. A major issue in Islamic finance is differences of opinion between shariah scholars in the Middle East, South Asia, and Southeast Asia regarding the permissibility of certain contracts. ISRA facilitates interaction among shariah scholars in the diverse regions of the Islamic world by translating Arabic documents into English and vice versa, thus reducing language barriers to the circulation of knowledge in fields pertaining to Islamic finance. It also seeks to enhance communication among shariah scholars by holding two major meetings each year. One is considered regional and consists of scholars from Southeast Asia, including Malaysia, Indonesia, Brunei, Thailand, and the Philippines. The other is global and is attended by scholars from across the Muslim world. When I participated in ISRA's Eighth International Shariah Scholars Forum in October 2013, attendees included scholars from Saudi Arabia, Kuwait, Bahrain, the United Arab Emirates, Egypt, Morocco, Algeria, Sudan, Nigeria, Guinea, Malaysia, and the United States.

In addition to establishing institutions designed to produce and circulate Islamic finance knowledge, the Malaysian state has sought to draw upon the expertise incubated in the country to design institutions that can enable the industry to function more effectively. One innovative effort that has established Malaysia as a hub in the global network of Islamic finance was the establishment of a financial exchange, Bursa Suq Al-Sila', in August 2009. Bank Negara and the Securities Commission collaborated with Bursa Malaysia, Malaysia's private stock exchange, to create this exchange. Combining the Arabic words *suq* (market) and *sila'* (commodity) and the Malaysian translation of the French word *bourse*, meaning exchange, Bursa Suq Al-Sila' is a commodity-trading platform established to facilitate liquidity management in the Islamic banking system. As noted above, one of the initial problems facing Islamic finance was how to coordinate the movement of money (liquidity) between large banks to enable them to balance their accounts on a daily basis. The exchange functions similarly to a money market in conventional finance by enabling banks to reconcile their accounts. However, whereas in the conventional system banks lend money to one another on the basis of the so-called overnight rate (known as the prime rate in the United States or London Interbank Offered Rate, LIBOR, in the United Kingdom), such lending is prohibited in Islam due to the Qur'anic prohibition on interest. The Bursa Suq Al-Sila' enables Islamic financial institutions in need of capital to avoid interest-bearing debt by using a sale contract rather than a loan. Initially the exchange used Malaysia's most important agricultural commodity, crude palm oil, as the underlying asset in the sale. Under a shariah-compliant contract known as a commodity *murabaha*, a bank in need of capital to balance its accounts at the end of a business day purchases palm oil and then sells it on a deferred payment basis to another bank at slight loss. The purchasing bank then immediately sells back the palm oil on the spot market for its actual value, making an incremental profit (Dusuki 2010). The two sales, the deferred payment, and the difference in payment provide a shariah-compliant alternative to interest-based lending.

By the mid-2010s Bursa Suq Al-Sila' had become an indispensable part of the global Islamic finance infrastructure, and there were sixty financial institutions that used the exchange to manage liquidity and facilitate financing arrangements. Twenty of these firms are from outside Malaysia, including four from Saudi Arabia, two from Jordan, one from the United Arab Emirates, three from Kuwait, and one each from Hong Kong, Singapore, Brunei, and Germany. The trading platform is open six days a

week from 7:00 a.m. to 11:00 p.m. Malaysian time and caters mainly to
institutions based in Southeast Asia and the Middle East. Ashraf, an executive with Bursa Suq Al-Sila', told me that the exchange faced difficulty
with attracting participants from Great Britain due to the considerable
time difference. However, this may have also been due to the fact that the
exchange's main competitor, the London Metal Exchange, was located in
the UK capital. Ashraf said that when the idea for the exchange was first
broached, there was concern that the "debt-based" nature of the commodity murabaha would be criticized. Those planning the institution sought to
deploy an equity-based device as the underlying contract for transactions
on the exchange. However, he said that this proved impossible due to the
volatility and unpredictability of equity-based contracts. He said market
participants needed "certainty" regarding the value of their contracts; otherwise risk management would become "too complicated." The creators of
the exchange decided to use a commodity murabaha contract (also known
as *tawarruq*) because it had been deemed permissible by shariah scholars in
both Malaysia and the Middle East.

Ashraf told me that when the shariah committee for Bursa Suq Al-Sila'
approved the structure of the commodity murabaha contract used by the
exchange, it stipulated that the commodity traded to create the financing
must be "real and actually existing." The exchange frequently hosts trips
by shariah scholars from its member institutions to view the independently
operated palm oil mills that buy and sell their commodity on the exchange.
The scholars can verify that there is an actual commodity traded on the exchange, witness the physical production facilities, and view the tanks where
the oil is stored. Ashraf said proudly, "We can actually point to the tank
where the palm oil their firm traded is stored." To ensure that the mills
are accurately reporting the trade of a "real commodity," the exchange re-
serves the right to audit a mill at any time. Furthermore, the firms using
the exchange are entitled to audit the suppliers up to two times per year.
When Bursa Suq Al-Sila' audits one of the suppliers, it not only looks at the
records of palm oil held for the day in question but also checks the mill's
historical records to ensure that the palm oil they have sold to the market
actually existed in the quantities stated on the day of the trade.

Ashraf told me that the fee ratio to complete a trade on the exchange
is fifteen units per one million units (the units could be Malaysian ringgit,
US dollars, British pounds, Saudi riyal, or any of dozens of other currencies). Nine units of the fee go to the mill that supplied the palm oil and six
go to Bursa Suq Al-Sila'. In 2009 Bursa Suq Al-Sila' was only turning over

on average RM200 million per day in sales.[6] Therefore it only generated about RM3,000 in fees per day, but by the end of 2013 Bursa Suq Al-Sila' was doing RM3.8 billion per day in business. Ashraf estimated that the rate of growth suggested that the exchange would be generating between 6 and 10 million ringgit per day. The growth of the volume of exchanges taking place on Bursa Suq Al-Sila' testifies to its popularity.

Ashraf told me that some Islamic scholars had expressed concern over some of the provisions used in Bursa Suq Al-Sila'. The main shariah issue has to do with the fact that the sales of the commodity (palm oil) are "prearranged." However, the shariah committee of Bursa Suq Al-Sila' concluded that, in the current market, a prearranged contract is necessary because otherwise firms could not manage their risk. The contract was validated on the basis of the fiqh principle of *darurat* (necessity). In this case, the pragmatic concerns of a functioning financial system took precedence over religious imperatives. Another shariah issue was a requirement that the commodity being traded must have a substantive relationship with the object being financed. Ashraf said that in Kuwait shariah scholars ruled that crude palm oil could not be used to finance residential real estate development because its connection to home construction appeared arbitrary and random. The Middle Eastern scholars sought some sort of indexical relationship between the commodity used to facilitate financing and the objects being financed. They quite logically concluded that palm oil was simply of no utility in building houses. In response, the management of Bursa Suq Al-Sila' decided to add hardwood and softwood lumber to the commodity trading profile. In exchanges involving Kuwaiti firms and real estate investment, the financing trade is based on an exchange not of palm oil but of lumber. In addition to lumber, the exchange also used plastic resin and refined, bleached, and deodorized palm olein as commodities that could be traded on the exchange and used as the basis for shariah-compliant contracts.

Prior to the establishment of Bursa Suq Al-Sila', the function of liquidity management in Islamic financial institutions had mostly been handled through murabaha[7] trades using brokers on over-the-counter markets among Islamic finance experts in Malaysia. Foremost among these was the London Metal Exchange (LME), where brokers traded metals such as aluminum, copper, and zinc to facilitate financing. Neither gold nor silver could be used in Islamic finance, because they are considered in the hadiths to be equivalent to money and any exchange of money for money is prohibited.[8] Accounts of the impropriety of UK-based brokers using the

LME to facilitate shariah-compliant transactions abounded. Foremost among these was a widely circulating story that unscrupulous brokers had sold the same piece of "unusable Russian scrap aluminum" thousands of times to facilitate shariah-compliant transactions. This was taken to violate the spirit of shariah, if not the letter, because the commodity used to finance the transaction had no utility and therefore was of no value. Since the aluminum scrap material was useless, the transactions were viewed as suspect: it simply could not be argued that there was ever any intent to use the scrap material, and therefore it functioned only as a vehicle to facilitate financing. In contrast to the dubious practices of the LME, those involved in Bursa Suq Al-Sila' publicized the fact that it used commodities with real utility as the basis for shariah-compliant transactions.

The growth and success of Bursa Suq Al-Sila' emboldened the Islamic finance industry and represented a countercolonial response to the spatial regime of conventional global finance. Indeed it raised the question of why an Islamic finance transaction between firms in Muslim countries, a bank in Malaysia and a company in Saudi Arabia, for example, would be facilitated in the secular city of London. Ashraf recalled the triumphal feeling that shariah scholars felt after the establishment of Bursa Suq Al-Sila'. In the concluding panel of the Kuala Lumpur Islamic Finance Forum that Ashraf and I had both attended in September 2013, the prominent scholar Sheikh Nizam Yacuby exclaimed, "Now that we have Bursa Suq Al-Sila' we can kill the LME brokers!" Ashraf said that this endorsement of Bursa Suq Al-Sila' in violent terms astonished him: "We were surprised to hear that from a scholar on an international stage like that, promoting us." However, the endorsement of Bursa Suq Al-Sila' over LME by a prominent shariah scholar should perhaps not be so surprising. The sheikh was undoubtedly aware that the use of an exchange in London to facilitate shariah-compliant transactions replicated a colonial relationship in which the pivotal infrastructure of the global economy was located in Europe. The establishment of Bursa Suq Al-Sila' represented a recentering of the global network of Islamic finance, in which an institution pivotal to the operation of Islamic finance located in Malaysia displaced one located in its old colonial metropole.

These efforts to create the infrastructure for an Islamic financial system reveal how the Malaysian state is seeking to develop a new network as an alternative to the one characterized by conventional finance and premised upon the arrangements of earlier colonial networks (Escobar 1995; Wolf 1982). Proponents of Islamic finance envision a new arrangement of global finance in which Europe and North America will play a subordinate role to critical nodes located in the Middle East and South, Southeast, and East Asia. This Islamic financial network will be centered in cities like Kuala Lumpur, Dubai, and Manama instead of New York, London, and Hong Kong. Key to this remapping is the role that religion plays in enabling the formation of these networks. Efforts to make Malaysia a key node in the network of an Islamic alternative to the conventional financial infrastructure is commensurable with the country's aspirations to become a leader in the Islamic world (Mutalib 2008, 32).

CHAPTER TWO

Expertise in Action

This book is grounded in conversations with, observations of, and interactions with members of four categories of experts most intimately involved in contemporary Islamic finance in Malaysia: practitioners who work in Islamic financial firms, Islamic economists who are usually based at universities, regulators who staff supervisory and monitoring institutions, and shariah scholars who are schooled in branches of the classical Islamic educational disciplines, especially fiqh. By describing these four categories of experts, I seek to illuminate the "culture of expertise" that comprises contemporary Islamic finance (Holmes and Marcus 2005, 237). A key focus of my approach is on how the authenticity of Islamic finance is contested among the various members of this culture of expertise.

In focusing on these experts I further draw on the work of Joshua Barker and Johan Lindquist, who have recently enjoined anthropologists to focus on "figures of modernity": social types who, in their words "comment upon a particular historical moment in the complex articulation of large-scale processes" (Barker and Lindquist 2009, 37). Indeed, interactions with these four types of figures illuminated contemporary debates over Islamic finance and revealed the experimental nature of its practices. I also interacted with a number of other experts involved in Islamic finance in Malaysia, including academics who are not specialists in Islamic finance, activists, businesspeople, students, lawyers, and government officers. In some cases these groups were not mutually exclusive, such as students who had also formerly worked in the Islamic finance industry.

These categories are not only analytical devices that identify specific positions, interests, and practices within the expert networks of Islamic finance; they are also native categories that are often invoked by experts themselves. In conversation and in written documents, Islamic finance

experts would often refer to themselves and each other using these labels. For example, an introduction to the Proceedings of the ISRA–
IRTI–Durham University Strategic Round Table Discussion[1] notes that
the "significant stakeholders of the Islamic banking and finance industry"
are "Shariah scholars, Muslim economists, industry practitioners as well
as regulators" (ISRA 2013). This chapter describes the individuals that
made up these types with the goal of explaining how they are positioned
in the industry as a whole. I show how their intellectual formation and
specific concerns with regard to Islamic finance leads members of each
group to different conclusions regarding the authenticity of Islamic finance
and what makes it an alternative to its conventional cousin.

Islamic finance experts in Malaysia were diverse, especially in terms of
gender and national origin, and were generally well off, especially by Malaysian standards. The prominent role that women played in Malaysian
Islamic finance (especially notable in comparison to the paucity of women
working in prominent roles in Arabian Gulf–based Islamic financial institutions) confirms the relatively high status of women and gender par-
ity that has long characterized Southeast Asia (Atkinson and Errington
1990; Brenner 1995; Peletz 1996; Reid 1988). Women were highly visible
in Islamic finance in Malaysia and were strongly represented among all
four categories of experts. Indeed, during the time I was conducting fieldwork for this project, a woman, Raja Teh Maimunah, was appointed CEO
of Hong Leong Islamic Bank. In addition there were three female members of the National Shariah Advisory Council, the highest authority for
Islamic finance in the country: Engku Rabiah Adawiah Engku Ali, Rusni
binti Hassan, and Shamsiah Mohamad. While I was conducting fieldwork
in Malaysia, two of the leading state economic actors, the chief executives of both the Central Bank of Malaysia and the country's Securities
Commission, were women (Zeti Akhtar Aziz and Zarinah Anwar, respec-
tively). Indeed, Dr. Zeti Akhtar Aziz, who between 2000 and 2016 was
the widely respected and profoundly influential governor of Malaysia's
Central Bank, was one of the most respected state officials in the country.[2]
Malaysia has also sought to attract some of the world's foremost talent in
Islamic finance, male and female, from around the Islamic world, especially
among the ranks of shariah scholars and Islamic economists.

The most visible marker of difference among the four key groups of
experts active in Islamic finance is dress. As anthropologists have shown,
clothing serves as a key means of marking contemporary Islamic identities, conveying religious piety, and conferring religious authority and

authenticity (Jones 2010; Moors and Tarlo 2013). For the most part, both male and female practitioners wear dress that would be virtually indistinguishable from those working in conventional finance. Practitioners working for Islamic financial firms regularly appear at public events with sharply tailored suits and immaculately knotted ties. Male regulators wear business attire as well. Senior managers are more disposed toward wearing ties, while those at the middle and lower levels of the Islamic banking department at the Central Bank generally go without them. Employees at lower levels typically wear a collared shirt with slacks. Female regulators, like most urban Malaysian women, typically wear the *baju kurung*, a knee-length blouse worn over a long skirt. This is almost always accompanied by a headscarf (*tudung*), although senior officials such as Zeti Aziz and Zarinah Anwar almost never wore them while acting in a professional capacity.

When I met with the assistant governor of Bank Negara responsible for Islamic finance, he wore a fashionable double-breasted black business suit. As we sat in the bank's cafeteria, his jacket opened up enough to reveal that his name was monogrammed in gold underneath the interior breast pocket. Regulators at the IFSB were similarly attired. Islamic economists whose primary occupation involves university education are slightly less well appointed, appearing not terribly dissimilar from the typical business school professor at a North American or European university. They often wore a business suit or sport coat and slacks with a collared shirt, which was typically unbuttoned at the top. I rarely encountered an Islamic economist wearing a tie, unless it was at a formal event at an institution like Bank Negara or the Securities Commission or a landmark event, such as the Kuala Lumpur Islamic Finance Forum, held at an upscale hotel.

Clothing that was easily marked as religious played a key role in conveying Islamic authority among Islamic finance experts. For the most part shariah scholars differentiated themselves from the other figures of Islamic finance through dress, making the specificity of their knowledge and their claims to embody it readily apparent. For example, scholars such as Akram Laldin, who sits on Bank Negara's shariah advisory committee, mixed conventional business attire with non-Western dress. He always wore a suit jacket and slacks but no necktie and a buttoned shirt with a mandarin collar. Older shariah scholars who started their careers during the first phase of Islamic finance in Malaysia would often pair a cap known as a *songkok* and associated with Islamic piety in Malaysia with a business suit, again without a necktie. Female shariah scholars also wore the baju kurung or "enclosed dress," the common Malaysian female dress consisting of a headscarf concealing everything but the face (Ong 1990, 269). The younger generation of shariah scholars in Malaysia, often employed in the shariah departments of Islamic banks, typically wore a suit and tie and no songkok. Their clothing evoked the standard uniform of business and capitalism. Indeed, many of them appeared indistinguishable from the other bankers, accountants, lawyers, and executives with whom they regularly interacted. In fact, since shariah advisory has become a lucrative business, many scholars have indeed gone into business themselves. For example, the dean of shariah scholars in Malaysia, Daud Bakar, the chairman of Bank Negara's shariah advisory committee, is the founder and CEO of Kuala Lumpur–based Amanie Advisors, which provides shariah services to the Islamic finance industry and in 2017 had offices in Dubai, Leeds, Cairo, and Astana.

The clothing worn by Malaysian shariah scholars differed markedly from to the style of dress of shariah scholars from other parts of the Muslim world. Shariah scholars from countries that have a legacy of state-driven secular nationalism, such as Syria and Egypt, generally wore conventional business attire with a necktie. Shariah scholars from the Arabian Gulf region, including Bahrain, Saudi Arabia, and the United Arab Emirates, such as Mohammed Ali El-Gari and Sheikh Nizam Yacuby, wore a white robe called a *thobe*, head cover (*ghutra*), and cord (*agal*) to hold the head covering in place. Although such dress was common among businessmen in the countries of the Gulf Cooperation Council, Islamic finance professionals from the Gulf often wore conventional business attire when attending meetings and other events in Malaysia. In contrast, shariah scholars did not change their clothing style. At the International Shariah Scholars Forum I attended, I noticed that Ibrahim as-Darir, a leading Sudanese shariah scholar, was particularly striking in his bright white turban and luminous white thobe. The scholars from West Africa, including Nigeria and Senegal, were divided. Some wore traditional West African dress with a cap, and others wore business suits.

Dress served as a key marker by which experts conveyed their position in the world of Islamic finance. Those who relied on religious expertise typically conveyed it through clothing that explicitly referenced their Islamic authority. In contrast, those who worked more on the commercial side tended to adopt the standard uniform of contemporary capitalism and finance: the dark business suit. Having given these visible differences in the outward appearance of members of each of the four main groups of experts in Islamic finance, I now move to consider some of the differences in the knowledge formation of these groups and describe how they are differently positioned within the Islamic finance industry.

Putting Islamic Finance into Practice

Practitioners do the day-to-day work of Islamic finance and staff Islamic financial institutions. I include in this group employees at various levels of the corporate hierarchy of actually existing Islamic financial institutions, from CEOs of banks to clerical workers. This category also includes entrepreneurs who had established Islamic wealth management funds and lawyers who facilitated Islamic financial transactions. Most practitioners working for Islamic financial institutions hold degrees in conventional finance, accounting, economics, law, or related fields. Contrary to Bank Negara deputy governor Razif's hopes, none of the practitioners I encountered had degrees in any specialized field of the classical Islamic sciences. For those actually engaged in the day-to-day business of Islamic finance, the dominant knowledge framework has been conventional finance and economics—a problem recognized by industry leaders in Malaysia. The notion that Islam and finance should be on equal footing and that practitioners should have a strong foundation in each domain is a recent development and is reflected in the faculty and curriculum of INCEIF. In 2017 the university had four full-time professors who specialized in Islamic sciences, mainly shariah law and the methodology of fiqh. Furthermore, students in the Chartered Islamic Finance Professional program, intended solely for those who plan to work as practitioners in the Islamic finance industry, took courses in Islamic economics, the shariah aspects of business and finance, shariah rules in financial transactions, and shariah issues in modern Islamic finance.

These efforts aside, most Islamic finance professionals typically view Islamic finance as a derivative of conventional finance rather than a distinct field of knowledge and practice. In this sense, they conceptualize the theories, methods, and axioms of the conventional financial system as a set of universally applicable principles on top of which Islamic finance sits. For example, when I interviewed Rahman, the CEO of a major Islamic bank in Malaysia, he reiterated that he was in "full support of the free market" and suggested that he saw the principles identified by conventional economics as universal principles, which applied just as much to Islamic finance as they did to its conventional counterpart.

This message was also apparent in the reactions of two of his staff members who sat in on our conversation. They both reacted viscerally at two different points in the interview when I referred to Islamic finance as an "alternative" to conventional finance. The first time I did so, one of the staff members became visibly uncomfortable and quickly interjected, pointedly enjoining, "Business is business!" Later during the interview I inadvertently repeated my earlier assertion, and another staff member, Iqbal, who had joined the meeting midway through, jumped in:

> There is misalignment between the business division of the industry versus the more religious idea of Islamic finance from some of those scholars. . . . There is one side that looks at it from a very religious, faith-based perspective, politicizing the industry unnecessarily. Whereas I think Bank Negara and players like us—of course there are certain rules and regulations we have to abide by—but in the end it's business, right? We have to give a return to shareholders!

The concept of shareholder value was seen as an underlying principle of modern capitalism, independent of religious knowledge or practice. This concluding invocation echoed Karen Ho's observation about how shareholder value became the overriding concern of Wall Street executives during the 1980s and 1990s as they sought to rationalize their operations and maximize the book value of their firms (Ho 2009). By claiming that "business is business" and that they were morally obliged to maximize returns for shareholders, Islamic finance professionals suggested that shareholder value was a universal principle to which Islamic finance was just as beholden as conventional finance.

While such claims could be interpreted as cynical, they reveal the constrained position in which practitioners find themselves. On the one hand, they must fulfill the expectations of those who expect the appellation "Islamic" to yield a morally superior means of facilitating commerce that serves as an antidote to economic problems such as inequality and instability. On the other hand, they must survive amid intense competition with both Islamic and conventional financial institutions and the expectations of shareholders and investors. From their perspective, the survival and growth of their firms requires conforming to the contemporary logics of capitalism.

I found that while Islamic finance practitioners were committed to Islam and observed its practices, they were exceedingly cautious in making any claims to substantial divergence between Islamic finance and conventional finance. Rather, they operated according to a formal logic that viewed creating an Islamic financial device as purely a matter of testing an instrument against literal prohibitions in the texts. The logic here was the fiqh principle that any action is permissible, according to Islam, unless there is a specific prohibition against it in the Qur'an or the hadiths. This sentiment was often echoed by those who defined Islamic finance in formal terms.

Making an Islamic Economics

Whereas the formalist approach to Islamic finance embraced by practitioners held that any action is permissible unless explicitly forbidden in the Qur'an and the hadiths, Islamic economists typically looked more to the substance of the activities that constituted Islamic finance and economic action. Rather than merely checking Islamic financial instruments for shariah compliance, they sought to identify the substantive values that marked Islamic economic action as distinctive. By extracting economic principles from the central texts of Islam, the Qur'an, and the hadiths, they sought to synthesize a distinctive version of Islamic finance from the ground up.

The substantive approach in Islamic economics was evident at the eighth International Conference on Islamic Economics and Finance held in Doha, Qatar, in December 2011. In a plenary session on the second day of the conference, Asad Zaman, a professor of economics at the International Islamic University in Islamabad, Pakistan, delivered a blistering attack. In front of an immense conference hall, with close to a thousand people in attendance, he pronounced, "The methodology of modern economics is fundamentally flawed. . . . All the basic theories are wrong!" With degrees in economics from Stanford and MIT, Zaman spoke eloquently amid the emergent opulence of the brand-new Qatar National Conference Center. The light from dozens of five-foot-tall teardrop-shaped lamps, each adorned with 12,700 Swarovski crystals, slowly rotated through a rainbow spectrum—scarlet, orange, gold, emerald, sapphire, indigo, violet—painting the room in an ever-changing glow that ranged from soothing blue to anxiety-inducing green. Zaman's passionate oration seemed to stir the audience from the mild mid-morning fatigue that had set in among many of the jet-lagged attendees as the infusion of attention-enabling caffeine from the last coffee break was rapidly dissolving in our bloodstreams.

He was dressed in an elegant beige *shalwar kameez*, chocolate-colored turban, and olive vest, and his long white beard and spectacles lent him an air of practiced dignity and moral authority. In escalating tones Zaman began to list what he saw as the fundamental fallacies of modern economics, his voice rising as he leveled each indictment: "Consumer theory is WRONG! Consumers do not maximize utilities! . . . If you try to use consumer theory to make predictions, you will be incorrect. . . . Firm theory is WRONG! Firms do not maximize profits! . . . Price theory is WRONG! Prices are not determined by supply-demand equilibrium." Amid the extravagance of the outsized hall, Zaman invoked the recent financial crises that had shaken countries from Britain to Botswana as evidence of the shortcomings of economics: "Since World War II there have been more than ninety monetary crises. We have no understanding of how to prevent these monetary crises!" He argued that economic theory had demonstrated itself to be wholly inadequate to the task of stable economic growth. With no shortage of hyperbole, he then connected the failure of the discipline of economics to economic development: "There have been sixty years of World Bank efforts at implementing different types of development policies, and there is not one example of success!"

Shortly thereafter Zaman shifted away from the crescendo of prosecutorial invective and began to speak in more measured tones, arguing that the failure of conventional economics could be attributed to its flawed anthropology. As a solution he urged conference participants to relinquish efforts to reconcile Islam with conventional economics and finance, because "ignorance cannot be combined with wisdom—all attempts to do so have failed!" As an alternative, he implored us to start over "from the bottom up." In his view, the routine methods of Islamic finance, which basically amounted to adapting conventional financial instruments by checking them for shariah compliance, were bound to fail. Only through synthesizing methods directly from the sources of Islam could this be remedied and new human beings be formed. The radical step was necessary because, he exclaimed, only the Qur'an "provide[s] complete guidance to solve our current economic problems. . . . The key to the Islamic approach is the transformation of human beings. Muhammad made Muslims moral people, and the Qur'an teaches generosity and kindness and compassion." Zaman exuberantly segued into his final argument: "These values, not the accumulation of wealth, will change the world!" His exasperation was palpable, and by the time he reached this climactic pronouncement, it appeared that he had moved many of the attendees, who had just minutes earlier been in a state of semitorpor, to the edges of their seats.

The difference between conventional and Islamic economics became clear following his diatribe when the moderator solicited questions from the audience. The third response came from a gentleman with a precisely clipped British accent wearing an elegantly cut business suit. He rose near the front of the massive room and in pointed terms delivered a polite but incisive rejoinder to Zaman. He reversed the terms of Zaman's argument, portraying economics as universal and Islam as particular. In calm and confident tones he offered a measured defense of some of the central tenets of neoclassical economics: "For every example of non-maximizing you come up with, I can bring for you a hundred examples of maximization! . . . Even Amartya Sen, when he went back to Harvard, said, 'The offer was so big, I could not resist.' . . . You simply cannot eliminate maximization from human life." He concluded, "The ideas in economics are so logical we cannot refuse them!" This disagreement illustrated how many of those who operate within the discursive regime of neoclassical economics see its anthropological presumptions as universal. This knowledge formation defines the human as motivated by imperative toward maximization and rational self-interest. In contrast, Islamic economists began with a different configuration of human nature, representing the human as both a spiritual and a collective being, motivated by existential and social concerns as much as profit maximization. A central critique that Islamic economics makes of conventional economics is that the latter takes for granted the separation of the economic from other domains of human life.

Islamic economists are practicing Muslims with graduate degrees in conventional economics who seek to combine the discipline of economics with their religious piety. Many of these individuals were educated at universities in Europe or North America and had spent large portions of their career seeking to reconcile secular economics with Islamic doctrine. In general, they were more comfortable with the abstract theories and mathematical models of economics than with the nuances of interpretation that form the methodological habitus of shariah scholars. They tend to have an orientation marked by the existence of definitive truths and in which they see the world in black-and-white terms. In contrast, shariah scholars tend to emphasize gray areas, indeterminacy, and the incompleteness of human knowledge. As a discipline, Islamic economics was institutionalized only in the 1970s. Indeed, several authors have identified the first version of the International Conference on Islamic Economics (a later iteration of which Dr. Zaman had spoken), held in Mecca from February 21 to 26, 1976, as the moment at which Islamic economics emerged as a discrete domain of knowledge and practice (Nagaoka 2012, 119; Wilson 2004, 200). This discipline poses an approach to understanding production, consumption, and exchange based on the values inherent in Islam rather than the principles of conventional economics. Islamic economics has an anxious relationship with conventional economics on the one hand and with Islamic finance on the other.

Islamic economics posits a human being with a universal set of needs and interests as its object and argues that Islam offers the best solution to achieving human fulfillment. In a widely referenced pamphlet titled "What Is Islamic Economics?" one of the discipline's leading exponents, Umar Chapra, writes, "The primary function of Islamic economics, like that of any other body of knowledge, should be the realization of human well-being through the actualization of the *maqasid*." The maqasid refers to the goals or intentions of shariah and is discussed in detail below in chapter 6. Chapra defines it as a "branch of knowledge which helps realize human well-being through an allocation and distribution of scarce resources that is in conformity with Islamic teachings without unduly curbing individual freedom or creating continued macroeconomic and ecological imbalances" (Chapra 1996, 33). Islamic economics is a critique of much conventional economics in that it questions the assumption that human action is solely motivated by rational self-interest and an imperative toward maximization. The discipline seeks to integrate moral and spiritual values into an economic science that it sees as overwhelmingly focused on material relations:

> All human effort, irrespective of whether it is for "material," "social," "educational," or "scientific" goals, is spiritual in character as long as it conforms to the value system of Islam. . . . Ideal behavior within the framework of this paradigm does not thus mean self-denial; it only means pursuing one's self-interest within the constraint of social interest by passing all claims on scarce resources through the filter of moral values. (Chapra 1996, 26)

Although Islamic economics acknowledges self-interest as a motive for action, it adds the caveat that moral values and social interest should frame such action.[3] Many Islamic economists are critical of the liberal notion that the economy exists autonomously, and they define as Islamic any human exertion that conforms to Islamic principles for action.

In addition to their antagonism toward conventional economics, Islamic economists are among the most vocal critics of Islamic finance. This is in part due to the fact that they challenge some of the humanist claims of Islamic finance practitioners. Practitioners often take many of the presumptions of conventional economics, such as the imperative toward maximization and rational self-interest as the motivating factors for human action, for granted. For example, Dr. Mustafa, an influential Islamic economist working in Malaysia, told me that if there were not significant changes to Islamic finance it would become "a bastard of the conventional system." He thought Islamic finance risked becoming nothing but the illegitimate offspring of conventional finance and economics rather than an autonomous discipline in its own right. In a subsequent conversation Dr. Mustafa told me, "The world will have to move toward an Islamic vision of the economy, because it is based on ensuring collective interests, whereas conventional finance is based nearly exclusively on self-interest. . . . We're going to kill each other if we keep up with the self-interest based system!" In a sense, Islamic economists are the moral conscience of Islamic finance. Given that they usually work for academic institutions and are not directly dependent on the success of Islamic financial institutions, they usually do not face the calculative constraints faced by the other key figures. Indeed, the two groups considered next, regulators and shariah scholars, often find themselves positioned between the pragmatism of industry professionals and the idealism of Islamic economists. On the one hand, they work to ensure the stability and growth of the industry, but on the other, they must ensure that it conforms to its Islamic proclamations.

The Fine Balance of Regulation

Like most Islamic economists and practitioners, the vast majority of regulators working in Islamic finance have backgrounds in conventional finance and banking. Their academic credentials usually entail undergraduate and graduate degrees in fields such as conventional economics, finance, or accounting. Most regulators started out working in the supervision of conventional financial institutions and moved over to Islamic finance later in their careers, although in the 2010s this was beginning to change with the proliferation of university degree programs in Islamic finance. In the course of my fieldwork in Malaysia I observed, interacted with, and interviewed three major categories of regulators: those working for Bank Negara Malaysia, who supervised Islamic banking and insurance; those working for the country's Securities Commission, which governed the Islamic capital market; and those working for the Islamic Financial Services Board, the international standards-setting body headquartered in Kuala Lumpur.

A distinguishing feature of Islamic finance in Malaysia, in comparison to other parts of the world, has been the active role that the state and particularly its central bank, Bank Negara, has played in fostering the coordinated development of the industry. Both Malaysian and non-Malaysian experts in Islamic finance claimed that Malaysia had the "most well-regulated" Islamic finance industry in the world. One Islamic finance professional noted this difference, explaining that in countries of the Gulf Cooperation Council (GCC) there is a "free market view" in which the prevailing ethic has been "anything goes," whereas in Malaysia the industry is "highly regulated." He explained that in the GCC central banks are less rigorous about certifying both the fiscal integrity and religious comportment of Islamic financial firms. In contrast, Bank Negara has developed a comprehensive regulatory environment consisting of taxation, legal, accounting, and shariah infrastructures for Islamic finance. An oft-cited example of the highly regulated nature of Islamic finance in Malaysia was the fact that Bank Negara had established a clear hierarchy of shariah interpretation as it pertained to Islamic finance. Arif, a lawyer with extensive experience in Islamic finance at one of Malaysia's largest law firms, took pride in the fact that Bloomberg News reported that it is more difficult to get an Islamic finance instrument approved in Malaysia than in the GCC.[4] He said that another major difference was that in the GCC there were no national shariah boards: in Gulf countries each Islamic financial firm has an individual shariah committee, alongside the shariah committees for the Organisation of Islamic Cooperation's Fiqh Academy and the Accounting and Auditing Organization for Islamic Financial Institutions (AAOIFI)—but there is no equivalent to the Malaysian national advisory board that could set uniform shariah standards or maintain consistency in shariah interpretation and the sanction given new products.[5]

Nik, who worked for the Islamic arm of a massive French bank, BNP Paribas Najmah,[6] told me that "Malaysia is the strictest country in the world" when it comes to regulating Islamic finance, and so "the segregation between the conventional and Islamic side is guaranteed." In contrast, he told me that Bahrain and Dubai were different because "the conventional side can offer Islamic-branded products" that were Islamic

in name only, whereas in Malaysia regulators insisted on a "firewall" between accounts and funds. Abdi, a professor of Islamic law at a Malaysian
university, concurred with this assessment. He said that the advantage that
Malaysia holds over the Middle East is that Islamic finance is much better
regulated in Malaysia. He attributed this to the fact that in Malaysia there
is a dialogue between the regulators and industry professionals: when
Bank Negara plans to introduce a new rule or guideline, there is a long
period of comment and consultation in which feedback on the new policy
is actively solicited. He said that this kind of consultation was foreign to
the Middle East, which was more authoritarian in operation: regulators
were used to giving orders and then having others conform to them. Referring to recent efforts by Bank Negara to tighten shariah requirements,
Abdi said that this demonstrated the careful watch that regulators keep
over the industry. He said that this was further evidence of a "strong, well-
run system." He explicitly contrasted it to Gulf and other Middle Eastern
countries, which he said had inconsistent policies toward Islamic finance
and often did not bother regulating it closely. He said that foreign scholars
often praised the regulation and governance of Islamic finance in Malaysia, even if they were critical of some of the instruments that had been
approved.

The coordinated regulation of Islamic finance in Malaysia is in part
due to the fact that Bank Negara has a dedicated unit, the Department
of Islamic Banking and Takaful (Jabatan Perbankan Islam dan Takaful,
JPIT), which is responsible for both the financial and religious oversight
of Islamic banks and insurance firms operating in the country. In general,
regulators are tasked with ensuring the stability of Islamic financial institutions. Although this at first appears to be strictly a question of financial prudence, regulators often find themselves confronted with religious
questions. This is due to the fact that failure to comply with shariah regulations is represented as a distinctive form of risk, to which regulators
and others refer as "shariah risk" or "shariah noncompliance risk." Unlike regulators at central banks in Europe and North America, not only
must regulators at Bank Negara ensure the financial soundness of the Islamic banking industry; they also are inevitably enmeshed in setting religious standards for the industry.

I was told that during the early days of Islamic finance in Malaysia, shariah compliance was essentially left up to financial institutions themselves.
This is evident from examination of the Islamic Bank Act of 1983, which
provided the initial legal foundation for Islamic finance in the country.

The act is perhaps notable for its perfunctory language and mostly deals with the technical and legal issues, such as the conditions for receiving an Islamic banking license and the role of Bank Negara in regulating Islamic banks. For example, "Islamic banking business" is defined very broadly as banking activity that does "not involve any element which is not approved by the Religion of Islam" (Legal Research Board 2011, 6). Only in 2003 was the act amended to require an Islamic bank to utilize a shariah committee to "advise the bank on the operations of its banking business in order to ensure that they do not involve any element which is not approved by the Religion of Islam" (Legal Research Board 2011, 8). However, the specific content of what was encompassed by the phrase "approved by the Religion of Islam" was left undefined.

Following efforts from the early 2000s to make Malaysia a global hub for Islamic finance, regulators at Bank Negara have taken an increasingly active role in the shariah dimensions of Islamic finance. The first Guidelines on the Governance of the Shariah Committee for IFIs were produced in 2004 and were updated in 2010 with the issuance of the more comprehensive Shariah Governance Framework. Furthermore, beginning in 2013 Bank Negara began to issue shariah governance standards for the twelve most widely used contracts in Islamic finance in Malaysia. In general, like the shariah scholars discussed below, regulators are tenuously positioned between Islamic finance practitioners who work in the industry and its critics, most of whom come from the ranks of Islamic economists or are disillusioned former industry professionals. Such regulators are aware of the critiques leveled against Islamic finance, but they are extremely cautious about making changes too quickly. One academic in Malaysia said that this caution was borne of a sense that too much change too quickly could threaten the entire industry with collapse. Nonetheless, they seek to cultivate an ethic of innovation among Islamic finance practitioners.

There is a recurrent sense among regulators that Islamic finance, as it is currently practiced, is imperfect. Experimentation is necessary to "push the industry forward," as Ridwan, a Bank Negara official, explained. In a meeting room high in the staid Bank Negara office complex, with the dull roar of expressway traffic rushing by seven floors below, Ridwan told me that the rationale behind the 2013 Islamic Financial Services Act (IFSA) division of Islamic bank accounts into deposit and investment accounts was to create "more clarity and more innovation." Despite the complaints of many Islamic bankers, he said the banks were already "being innovative in determining substitute products." As thirty years had passed since the initial establishment of Islamic finance in Malaysia, Ridwan felt that the industry had reached a level of permanence such that the early exceptions granted to Islamic banks to facilitate their growth could gradually be phased out. Regulators prodded Islamic financial institutions to develop new instruments and products to replace ones that had been called into question by critics of the industry. On the one hand, regulators were aware of the fact that Islamic finance often differed only in form, not in substance, from conventional finance. On the other hand, they were conscientious of the possibility that rapid reform might inhibit the stability and growth of an emergent sector.

Efforts to reform Islamic finance were met with no small measure of discontent by Islamic finance professionals. In early 2014, as we chatted over a decidedly mediocre simulacrum of a British pub lunch in a nondescript strip mall outside central Kuala Lumpur, Lukman, the lawyer quoted in the previous chapter, was candid and caustic in his criticism of the recently passed IFSA. Rather than spurring the industry toward reform, he thought that the new law did nothing more than aggrandize the regulators themselves. He rhetorically asked, "Do you need penalties for noncompliance? Does it mitigate risk? Does the law benefit the consumer? Or the ego of the regulators?" He saw the new law as a covert ploy by regulators to consolidate their power over the industry and did not accept the argument that IFSA would better position Malaysia globally by addressing criticisms by outsiders. In fact, Lukman suggested that there was a political strategy by those who had laid a trap into which Malaysian regulators had unwittingly stepped. He speculated that the criticisms that had spurred efforts at reform were part of a broader conspiracy by competitors in the Gulf to supplant Malaysia as the global hub of Islamic finance: "We have built the best Islamic finance system in the world and the new law threatens to bring it all down!"

The sentiment expressed by Lukman was quite common. In general, industry professionals exhibited an air of intellectual superiority in comparison to the regulators who supervised them. For example, Rahman, the CEO, told me that Bank Negara was "not very smart" and that the recent regulations they had issued were "confusing." He said that one of the problems at Bank Negara is that it is a big institution and the various units do not effectively communicate with each other: "You have the supervisory side, you have the policy side, you have the Basel team, and you have JPIT. . . . I can tell you that they are not talking to each other. They have to be very clear. JPIT must understand Basel. [The] Central Bank needs to look at itself!" He suggested that Bank Negara paid too much heed to critics of the industry who questioned his bank's shariah compliance. He even admitted he'd had some queries from supervisors questioning him on some of his products. Rahman expressed frustration that religious authorities with jurisdiction limited only to specific states were calling into question his firm's nationwide banking products. He said, "States have jurisdiction over religion. . . . I've had Bank Negara supervisors coming to me and questioning me about claims from certain religious authorities. . . . I said, 'You've got to be kidding, man. I am governed by the IFSA, by the Central Bank Act.' "

Rahman also expressed concern over the growing influence that he perceived Bank Negara exercising over the Islamic finance industry. Like Lukman, he saw the new law as an attempt by the bank to consolidate power over the industry, which was threatening to the stability of the industry: "If I may be very blunt, I am not sure what the Central Bank is doing! . . . The timing, there are a lot of regulations and so forth. They really distract us, our compliance, our business guys are overcapacity looking at this." He continued, explaining that the IFSA "gave too much power to the Central Bank. Where is [sic] the checks and balances on the Central Bank? . . . If I say it out loud in public, I might lose my position. . . . Who is governing the Central Bank?" Perhaps not surprisingly, this Islamic CEO, like his conventional counterparts in the North American financial world, expressed disdain toward state regulation. In his eyes IFSA's empowerment of the Central Bank might lead to more bureaucratic requirements by a regulatory institution that, he felt, had little accountability. He concluded, heatedly, "Who controls the Central Bank?" Caught between the criticisms of Islamic economists and recurring claims by practitioners that too much regulation too quickly could strangle the development of the industry, they sought to balance the commercial, social, and ethical imperatives that experts and laypeople asked Islamic finance to fulfill.

Between Profit and the Prophet

The most complexly positioned group of experts I encountered in Malaysia was undoubtedly shariah scholars who sit on the advisory boards that regularly evaluate the religious permissibility of Islamic financial products. These committees are in many respects among the most distinctive features of Islamic finance. In Malaysia and most other national jurisdictions, every Islamic financial institution—including banks, insurance companies, and regulatory institutions such as the Securities Commission and the Central Bank—is required to have a shariah advisory committee. Religious scholars, most often trained in fiqh, are contracted by Islamic financial institutions to evaluate and authorize every Islamic product designed by the institution. Serving on a board is not full-time employment, as the committees typically meet on a monthly or bimonthly basis. Many scholars typically teach Islamic law at a university in a regular, salaried position and serve on shariah advisory committees on an intermittent, retainer basis.

The authority of shariah advisory committees has been long established in Islamic finance, but in Malaysia it is also legislated in IFSA. The act requires any institution holding an Islamic banking license to "establish a Shariah committee for purposes of advising the licensed person in ensuring its business, affairs and activities comply with Shariah" (Legal Research Board 2013, 30.1). The guidelines for the operation of shariah committees, which must consist of at least five members, are detailed in the "Shariah Governance Framework for Islamic Financial Institutions" report, which was published by Bank Negara on October 26, 2010, and went into effect in January of the following year (Islamic Banking and Takaful Department 2010). The framework codifies three main qualifications for becoming a member of a shariah committee. First, he or she must be a "Muslim individual." Corporations, institutions, or other collective bodies cannot constitute or serve on a shariah committee. Second, "The majority of members" should "at least hold [a] bachelor's degree in Shariah, which includes study in Usul Fiqh (the origin of Islamic law) or Fiqh Muamalat (Islamic transaction/commercial law) from [a] recognised university" (Islamic Banking and Takaful Department 2010, 30). The third criterion is linguistic, to which I return below.

The document provides no definition of what constitutes a "recognised university." Further, some experts argue that the narrow focus on fiqh has obscured a broader interpretation of Islam that would integrate social justice concerns. Sheikh Ibrahim, an activist and critic of some of the practices of Islamic banks in Malaysia, articulated such a critique. Ibrahim did not possess a university degree in Islamic sciences. Rather, he had earned a university degree in tourism management from a technical school. However, he was proud of the fact that he possessed an *ijazah*, which literally translates as "permission" and refers to the authority to teach and preach Islam that one receives from studying with a recognized Islamic scholar

(Makdisi 1989). His father had been a respected scholar and traced his scholarly lineage and religious authority back to the prophet Muhammad.

Ibrahim pointed out that "shariah" (as in "shariah advisory committee") is a much broader term than "fiqh." He argued that fiqh scholars focused too much on the formal questions of the permissibility and impermissibility of contracts, whereas other branches of Islamic sciences looked at the substantive values and ethical principles constitutive of Islam. Ibrahim told me:

> The problem with Islamic banks today is that the scholars have only looked to fiqh and ignored the other branches of shariah: *tawhid* and tasawwuf.[7] Fiqh scholars just look at the rules, but tawhid scholars look at the logic [behind the rules]. Tasawwuf scholars' specialty is *roh* [spirit] and questions of intention and sincerity. A fiqh scholar will look at a chicken and only ask if it was slaughtered according to fiqh rules. But a tasawwuf scholar will look at how the chicken was raised, where the money to buy the chicken came from, and so forth. Fiqh is just rules for the sake of rules, whereas tasawwuf is more holistic.

Ibrahim's criticism of the emphasis on formal rules by Islamic scholars who authorize instruments and devices for the industry echoes critics who assert that, in the practice of Islamic finance, shariah has been narrowly equated with fiqh and has been "rule bound." This means that they address the formal properties of Islamic financial products based on criteria of permissible (halal) and impermissible (haram) rather than taking into consideration broader issues of justice, equality, and other substantive religious principles. Testing for shariah compliance is less an exercise in religious interpretation than a technical process based on this binary logic of permissibility and impermissibility. Ibrahim's critique that scholarly arguments have shown a preoccupation with form is common in Islamic legal education (Nakissa 2014, 225). In making this argument, Ibrahim alleged that the narrow, fiqh-bound focus of shariah advisory in Islamic finance was itself an effect of Western colonialism that sought to distill Islamic law into a codified system of rules (Skovgaard-Petersen 1997). For evidence, he cited the appointment of Muhammad Abduh by Lord Cromer as the sheikh of Cairo's Al-Azhar University (Sedgwick 2010), noting that Abduh "got rid of all the sciences and only focused on religious knowledge." The modernist separation of religion from other disciplines thus led to a focus on formalistic "matters of ritual" to the exclusion of theological values.

The third criterion stipulated by the Shariah Governance Framework for serving on a shariah committee is linguistic, for "the majority members of the Shariah Committee should be able to demonstrate strong proficiency and knowledge in written and verbal Arabic, and have good understanding in Bahasa Malaysia and the English language" (Islamic Banking and Takaful Department 2010, 30). Ahmed, a native of North Africa who had been a professor of Islamic law at a Malaysian university for over twenty years and was a shariah board member at a large private bank, told me that until the 2000s it was rare for Malaysian shariah advisory committee members to demonstrate any ability in Arabic beyond rudimentary understanding. Although many of them had studied in the Middle East, they usually possessed limited knowledge of Arabic. This may in part be because for centuries knowledge of Arabic in Islamic schools in Southeast Asia has focused on linguistic form rather than content. Thus, students in such schools would learn Arabic through rote memorization by repeated recitation of the Qur'an, without comprehension of the actual words articulated (Gade 2004). Ahmed noted that beginning in the late 1990s, a different generation of scholars began to ascend through the ranks of shariah committees. This younger cadre was far more proficient in Arabic. He attributed this increased proficiency to the fact that although earlier generations had also studied at major Middle Eastern universities, typically they would live in dormitories with Malaysians and Indonesians and thus have reduced exposure to Arabic.[8] By the early 2000s this enhanced fluency was evident as younger scholars began to join the shariah committees of Islamic financial institutions.

Shariah scholars occupy perhaps the most complex position in the Islamic financial services industry. They are looked to as stewards of Islam, and their authority rests on their adherence to the religion. Unlike industry practitioners, they cannot resort to shareholder value or customers' interests to justify their decisions and practices. And unlike academics, they are directly accountable not just to the institutions that they serve but also to the Islamic financial services industry, in the sense that their decisions could have severe repercussions for the viability of the industry. There have been several instances where shariah scholars have made public pronouncements judging certain instruments to not be compliant with shariah, which caused a great deal of tumult in the industry and heightened anxiety about shariah scholar pronouncements. This fear is pervasive enough that industry professionals refer to "shariah noncompliance risk" as a type of risk in addition to those that are familiar to the risk calculus of conventional finance.

Building on Ulrich Beck's germinal account of the centrality of risk to contemporary capitalism, anthropologists have shown how risk is central not only to configuring economic subjects but also to fostering and managing human life (Beck 1992; Boholm 2003; Garsten and Hasselström 2003; Lee 2004; Power 2007). Indeed, instilling techniques of risk calculation has been constitutive of efforts to inculcate efficiency and accountability in economic subjects (Maurer 1999; Poon 2009; Zaloom 2004). In Islamic finance the concept of shariah noncompliance risk illustrates how questions of the calculation of financial risk is inextricably bound up with ethical prescriptions drawn from Islam's sacred texts. Indeed, the terms "shariah risk" and "shariah noncompliance risk" represented a new object distinctive to Islamic finance. In conventional finance risk is typically classified into four main categories (credit, liquidity, market, and operational), which all pertain to economic conditions or commercial processes. For example, credit risk refers to the risk that a borrower will default on a debt by failing to make contractually required payments. Market risk refers to the possibility of losses incurred as a result of fluctuations in market prices—for example, the risk of a decline of the market valuations of share prices in a given portfolio. These categories are all subject to calculation, and financial firms have sophisticated mechanisms for "measuring, modeling, managing, predicting, commoditizing, and exploiting" them (Appadurai 2011, 522–523). Risk is something that can be subjected to various statistical models and tests that discern the relative probability of distinct events. In this sense it differs from the related financial concept of uncertainty, which is less amenable to probabilistic forecasting. The commercial decisions made by conventional financial professionals are largely guided by the risk calculations that they make. The creation of the object known as shariah noncompliance risk demonstrates the prominent role shariah scholars fill in Islamic finance.

In Malaysia an oft-cited example of shariah noncompliance risk was the court case that pitted Blom Bank, based in Lebanon, against Investment Dar, based in Kuwait. Saif, a former official with Pakistan's central bank who was based in Kuala Lumpur, invoked the case in a workshop I attended. He explained that Blom Bank claimed in court that its contracts with Investment Dar were not shariah compliant, even though its very own internal shariah committee had authorized them. Blom Bank sought to use the fact of shariah noncompliance as grounds for not distributing the profits it made on the contracts to the Kuwaiti firm (Gaunaurd, Abdelhady, and Issa 2011, 274–275). Saif noted that there was no lack of irony in an Islamic bank declaring that its own contracts were invalid and using it as a justification for not distributing profits to its customer. Saif exclaimed, "Of course, normally [an Islamic] bank would not advertise the fact that it was not shariah compliant!" He also cautioned that it could have long-term implications for Islamic finance in general, because if people did not trust IFIs, then they would "run away." Saif ominously declared that cases such as these could lead to systemic risk and the downfall of the Islamic financial system as a whole.

Shariah scholars are lightning rods in the Islamic financial industry, not just because they are associated with the uncertainty of shariah noncompliance risk but also because of their tenuous position. On the one hand, they exercise quasi-regulatory power in the industry, in the sense that they are responsible for ensuring that products offered by Islamic financial institutions are compliant with shariah. On the other hand, they are tasked with overseeing the very institutions whose shariah affairs they are contracted to regulate. Therefore, they do not enjoy the same independence as regulators or Islamic economists.

Two aspects of the working relationship of shariah scholars have come under particular scrutiny and criticism. Malaysian regulations permit each shariah scholar to advise only one institution in a particular sector of the Islamic financial services industry. A scholar may simultaneously sit on the boards of both an Islamic bank and a takaful company but may not sit on the boards of multiple Islamic banks or takaful firms at the same time. Outside Malaysia, however, there are few regulations regarding the number of boards on which a shariah scholar may sit. This has led to a situation in which a relatively small group of prominent scholars sit on a large number of shariah committees (Bassens, Derudder, and Witlox 2012). One study of the shariah committees of 212 Islamic financial institutions found that the shariah committees were dominated by thirteen especially active scholars who all sat on more than ten boards each (Bassens, Derudder, and Witlox 2011). The most prominent scholars in the study who all sat on more than thirty boards were Sheikh Nizam Yacuby from Bahrain, Abdul Sattar Abu Ghuddah from Syria, Mohammed Ali El-Gari from Saudi Arabia, and the Malaysian Mohammad Daud Bakar. One Islamic financier in Malaysia referred to this group as members of the "big five," also including the American sheikh Yusuf Talal DeLorenzo, who the financier told me converted to Islam over thirty years ago and attended a Deobandi madrassah in Pakistan during the 1980s and 1990s. Bank Negara has actively sought to court this influential group of shariah scholars and often invites them to Islamic finance events in Malaysia. They all attended the International Shariah Scholars Forum that I observed in October 2013.

Relatedly, there was a sense that shariah committee membership was what one research participant called "a closed shop." Senior shariah scholars held a knowledge monopoly in the provision of shariah advice to the industry, which limited the ability of junior scholars to break in. This was in part due to the fact that well-established global scholars held considerable standing in the industry and lent no small measure of shariah credibility to the institutions for which they served as advisors. Scholars who sit on the AAOIFI shariah committee are in especially high demand.

The second major criticism of shariah scholars regards the compensation packages that are paid by Islamic financial firms. In Malaysia the standard monthly retainer paid to shariah advisors is between RM2,500 and 10,0000 per month.[9] One Malaysian researcher I interviewed smirked, sarcastically commenting, "It is a small price to pay to make something halal!" Given that in the countries of the Gulf Cooperation Council there are no restrictions on the number of shariah boards on which a single scholar can sit, shariah expertise has recently become a lucrative career choice, provided one can skillfully market one's expertise. A regulator from the Central Bank of Bahrain told me that some of these scholars had become extremely rich and one of them had even bought a new luxury condominium in Mecca immediately adjacent to the Al-Haram mosque.[10] She said, "They could see the Kaaba[11] from the condo, so he could just pray there. . . . He didn't even have to go down to the mosque." Stories such as this about the generous compensation afforded to shariah committee members circulated widely among Islamic finance experts.

Similar to membership on a corporate board, a shariah committee membership is not a full-time occupation. Noor, a shariah scholar on the committee of a medium-sized Islamic bank in Malaysia, received an amount that was toward the lower end of the compensation spectrum. She told me that Bank Negara required shariah committees to meet a minimum of six times per year with the understanding that further meetings might be required should an urgent matter arise. Furthermore, serving as a shariah committee member is only one segment of the market for what has become known as "shariah advisory services." Far more lucrative than sitting on a shariah committee is advising on the structure of a *sukuk*. Sukuk are financial instruments used by corporations and governments to raise capital for activities such as business expansion and infrastructure development and are often referred to as "Islamic bonds" in media coverage.

These bonds are regularly in denominations of over $100 million. Because fees for providing advisory services on a bond issue such as legal, tax, and other professional services are calculated as a percentage of the overall total value, expenses for shariah advisory on a sukuk can total in the hundreds of thousands of dollars. One academic I met told me that one of his colleagues was paid a commission of RM250,000 for advising on a sukuk deal.[12] He said that the standard fees for shariah advisory on a sukuk issue were usually about one-quarter or one-half of a percent of the total value. He joked that Islamic finance had made the knowledge of shariah scholars newly valuable and created a situation of "sheikhs for rent."

Several participants in my research were nonplussed by the wages earned for shariah advisory, pointing out that these were a pittance compared with the retainers for other forms of professional expertise. Uzair, an Islamic finance professional who invited me to accompany him to several sukuk negotiations, emphasized how little shariah scholars were paid compared to lawyers and accountants. He said that a major scholar like Sheikh Nizam Yacuby might earn $300,000 working on a sukuk deal for a big bank, but this was "a drop in the bucket" compared to the fees generated on the same deal by lawyers and consultants. Uzair said that if a major Islamic bank such as HSBC Amanah does a $1 billion sukuk, they might pay $50 million in fees to lawyers and accountants but only $200,000 in fees for shariah advisory. Uzair explained that his firm, based in Australia, had contracted Sheikh Nizam for its shariah committee, and his fees were less than the cost of a used car. Uzair said that the first-class airfare to travel to the committee meetings cost more than the fees he charged. He had met with Sheikh Nizam at his office in Bahrain, and it was very simple: "It is in a strip mall and he doesn't even have a secretary!" The office was cluttered with numerous fiqh volumes on his desk in various states of inspection. To illustrate his humility, Uzair told me that when prayer time came, Nizam invited him to pray together with him.

Uzair's counterpoint to the outcry over the income of shariah scholars sheds light on how different knowledge practices are valued economically. Observers of the Islamic finance industry often criticized shariah scholars for the compensation they received, but never criticized lawyers, accountants, tax advisors, or other experts for their even larger fees. The notion that religious knowledge should not be compensated on the same scale as other forms of technical expertise takes for granted the modernist presumption of a secular separation between religion and other material domains. In this schema, itself likely a product of Western historical practices dividing the spiritual and the material, religion is presumed to be isomorphic with the immaterial, and the economy is represented as an inferior domain (Rudnyckyj and Osella 2017). Islam, through the notion of *tawhid* (unity), challenges this economy of knowledge by suggesting that religion cannot be so neatly cleaved from other domains.

Nonetheless, in Islamic finance religious knowledge was consistently subjected to the capitalist logic of rationality and efficiency that Max Weber identified in Ben Franklin's injunction that "time is money" (Weber [1920] 2001, 14). This was particularly evident in conversations with Islamic finance practitioners, who often commented on the time that it took members of the shariah committees to review new products and instruments. Zamir, who had worked in an executive capacity at Malaysia's Bank Islam for over ten years before transferring to an Islamic bank in the Middle East, complained about the pace at which shariah boards work. He told me, "You need a shariah board yesterday, but they have their meeting and then they ask one question. Take three weeks and decide they have three more questions. Then in the meeting they don't ask relevant questions."

Islamic bankers working within Islamic financial institutions expressed a similar sentiment. Fadzilah, a Malaysian executive with a major GCC-based Islamic bank active in Kuala Lumpur, was always on the lookout for new investment opportunities for her firm. However, she expressed frustration with the slow pace at which the bank's shariah committee worked and was pointed in her criticisms of scholars on her firm's shariah advisory committee. She said that everything had to be mapped out for them so that they "could make a fatwa." She said, "It takes ages for them to read, so it is easier if you facilitate them by getting everything prepared in advance. . . . One transaction can take ages!" The different pace at which the commercial and shariah sides of Islamic financial institutions operate and the assumptions they make about time illustrate another challenge in the knowledge economy of Islamic finance. On the one hand, it seeks to enlist shariah knowledge to authorize the products and instruments it has developed. On the other hand, it is subject to the temporal logic of capitalism, in which modern technology has made the transmission of knowledge (if not its production) instantaneous through the vast network of interconnection that mobile computers and smartphones have created. Yet shariah scholars operate according to a different logic, in which the authority of knowledge was practiced in the production and interpretation of texts (Masud, Messick, and Powers 1996).

The differences in pace between the knowledge practices of shariah advisory and financial action is but one illustration of the intermediate position of shariah scholars within the broader Islamic finance network. They are interstitial figures who must mediate the demands and interests of Islamic finance practitioners, regulators, Islamic economists, and the public at large. Indeed, they are sometimes subject to criticism from all these groups: from practitioners for not working quickly enough, from regulators for being too obscure and idealistic, and from Islamic economists and the public for being economically compromised due to the sometimes generous compensation they receive from Islamic financial institutions.

This widespread and varied criticism illuminates their interstitial role but is also an indication of their sense of responsibility and accountability: both toward Islam as a religion and also in nurturing the Islamic finance industry. That is to say that shariah scholars must balance the religious ideals of Islam with the awareness that constructing a viable alternative to the infrastructure of conventional finance cannot be accomplished overnight. Indeed, in my interactions with them, shariah scholars seemed to view themselves less as gatekeepers, as a recent account suggests (Bassens, Derudder, and Witlox 2012), than as caretakers of the industry. As caretakers, they expressed an obligation to be pragmatic in their rulings to ensure that religious idealism does not constrain the growth of the industry or threaten to derail it completely.

In public forums shariah scholars often articulated a desire to ensure the ongoing viability of the industry. For example at the 2013 International Shariah Scholars forum, Mohammed El-Gari expressed anxiety about proclamations that Islamic finance had reached its pinnacle. "If we have reached our peak," he said, "the only place to go is down!" He implored the audience, consisting mainly of shariah scholars from across the Muslim world, not to become complacent but to continue trying to "perfect the framework of Islamic finance." El-Gari's statement reflects the awareness among shariah scholars of the tension between the viability and development of Islamic finance and conforming to shariah prescriptions. Scholars feel pressure to act pragmatically, searching for a balance between protecting the future of what has become a trillion-dollar industry and the ethical imperatives of Islam that they are expected to bring into being.

Shariah scholars are presented with a quandary: What is the best means of achieving an Islamic finance that achieves the principles of Islam? And what Islamic principles should be emphasized? A radical option would entail the fabrication of a completely new financial infrastructure synthesized from Islamic sources. Although there are some innovative attempts along these lines emerging in the industry, by and large this is not an approach that the industry has pursued. Instead, Islamic finance professionals whose educational and career backgrounds are mainly in conventional banking, finance, or law have pursued another option: adapt or reengineer conventional financial instruments and structures to achieve shariah compliance. I describe the methodology used in this approach in chapter 5.

In evaluating the structures, instruments, and products that result from this approach, shariah scholars have been less revolutionary than reformist. That is to say, they have been willing to accept Islamic financial instruments that meet the letter of Islamic law but not necessarily its spirit. However, they have often deemed these instruments shariah compliant with the caveat that the industry seek to develop less ambiguous shariah-based instruments in the future. For example, one of the most contentious contracts in Islamic finance globally is the bai al inah contract discussed in the introduction, which mimics a loan contract through two sales and a deferred payment at a markup (see figure 9). Two dominant schools of Islamic jurisprudence (fiqh) have come to different conclusions regarding the permissibility of bai al inah (Rosly 2005, 239–241). The Shafi'i school of thought (*mazhab*), the predominant fiqh school in Southeast Asia, has typically emphasized form over content and avoided legal decisions that ascribe intent to actors, asserting that only Allah can discern individual intentions (Hallaq 2009, 241). In contrast, jurists from the Hanafi school, which is common in South Asia and parts of the Middle East and North Africa, generally emphasize substance over form and hold that intentions can be deduced from actions. In practice, this has led to a situation in which certain financial and banking instruments permitted by scholars in Southeast Asia have been explicitly prohibited by scholars in South Asia and the Middle East. These differences have also led to somewhat surprising interventions, such as cases in which bankers have weighed in on matters of religious scholarship. For example, Badlisyah Abdul Ghani, who until 2015 was the CEO of CIMB Islamic (Malaysia's second-largest Islamic bank) and subsequently was appointed deputy CEO of Tabung Haji, was particularly vocal, stating that while other fiqh traditions emphasize form over content, "only the Hanafi School of Law advocates for 'the substance over form' outlook, putting emphasis on the intention of both parties" (Abdul Ghani 2009, 14).[13]

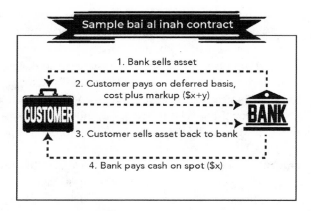

FIGURE 9. A sample bai al inah contract structure. Credit: Jos Sances.

In Malaysia this contract was permitted because Shafi'i scholars argued that only Allah has access to human intentions, and therefore no judgments can be made regarding the substance of a contract or how the funds facilitated were being used in practice. They judged the contract based only on its formal properties, finding it permissible because it involved two separate sales, no money lending, and, most important, no agreed interest payment. In sum, it met all the criteria for permissibility according to the formal criteria of fiqh. In contrast, in the Middle East, shariah scholars argued that bai al inah was impermissible because, although it fulfilled these formal requirements, the *objective* of the contract was to replicate a loan. Although it met the standard of formal compliance, an examination of its substance revealed that it was a legal stratagem (*hiyal*).

The rationale for the implementation of bai al inah illustrates the ethic of experimentation in Malaysian Islamic finance. Although Malaysian scholars had approved the bai al inah, there was an understanding that this approval was provisional until something superior was devised. The interim nature of the use of the bai al inah contract is evident in the rationale provided by Bank Negara's shariah advisory committee for its approval. In a compendium titled *Shariah Resolutions in Islamic Finance*, the shariah advisory committee writes that the bai al inah "concept is used in the Malaysian Islamic banking and Islamic capital market system to fulfill the various needs of market players, *mainly during the initial development stage of the Islamic financial system*" (Bank Negara Malaysia 2010, 109;

emphasis added). In large part, the popularity of the bai al inah contract in Malaysia was due to the fact that it could easily replicate the features of a conventional loan with a markup on a deferred sale of an asset, essentially duplicating market interest rates. Bank Negara's stated rationale for permitting it demonstrates both the pragmatism of shariah scholars and the experimental, contingent nature of Islamic finance in Malaysia. Experts are cognizant of the emergent nature of Islamic financial knowledge in that certain products that are used in the present will not be used in the future. Indeed, as I detail in chapter 7, in December 2012 a Bank Negara circular dramatically altered the way in which bai al inah could be executed—a change that led to a decline in the popularity of the contract among Islamic financial institutions in Malaysia.

Several participants in my research told me that shariah scholars became more stringent with the shariah approval process following the global financial crisis of 2008. One regulator at the IFSB attributed this greater stringency to a sense among scholars that the crisis was evidence of a fundamental flaw in conventional finance: they thought that the crisis was, at root, the inevitable outcome of a debt-based financial system with lending at interest as a constitutive feature. Scholars had become increasingly adamant that Islamic finance should clearly demarcate itself, or else the cataclysm that struck the conventional financial architecture would similarly afflict the Islamic system.

Most of my interlocutors in Malaysia viewed the 2008 financial crisis through the prism of the Islamic prohibition on debt. There was a widespread perception that Islamic financial firms had performed better in the years following 2008, with many fewer bankruptcies and no large-scale state intervention needed (such as the Troubled Asset Relief Program, or TARP, in the United States). Indeed, a recurrent theme of experts was the greater stability of Islamic finance during the crisis. For example, at a 2010 forum titled "The Contribution of Islamic Finance Post-Global Financial Crisis" jointly hosted by the Oxford Center for Islamic Studies and Malaysia's Securities Commission, Ahmad Hizzad Baharuddin, the head of Bank Negara's Islamic Banking and Takaful Department, stated, "After the recent financial crisis, Islamic banks seem to be emerging stronger than the conventional banks." Attributing the crisis to the pervasiveness of subprime loans, the securitization of those loans, and an overheated real estate market in the United States, he continued, "Islamic banks were sheltered from the subprime mortgages and collateralized debt obligations fallout due to the shariah restrictions. . . . Islamic finance has minimized its involvement in overzealous financial innovation, excessive risk taking, and indiscriminate lending, due to the fact that shariah requires greater engagement with real sector and more direct involvement with economic development." In invoking the "real sector" Baharuddin echoed the common contention that Islamic finance is more focused on the mobilization of what Islamic finance experts often proclaim is the "real economy": tangible goods and services as opposed to the highly abstract instruments, such as derivatives, that are common in conventional finance and are often several steps removed from labor and material production. Furthermore, referring to the lack of any restrictions on the sale of debt that is characteristic of conventional finance, he added that the Islamic finance industry was protected because of "the inherent inability of Islamic banks to create the origination and [sale mechanisms that have] been plaguing the conventional banking commercial industry" (Securities Commission Malaysia 2010, 88). Here he alluded to the fact that Islamic banks were sheltered from the subprime mortgages and collateralized debt obligations that plagued conventional securities markets and were judged by many to have precipitated the 2008 financial crisis.[14]

Whereas regulators and Islamic finance professionals tended to attribute the success of Islamic finance to better underlying economic fundamentals, shariah scholars and some Islamic economists saw it as a result of adherence to the Qur'anic prohibition on interest. The depth and severity of the 2008 crisis lent increasing credibility to this line of reasoning. One official with the IFSB told me that after the crisis, shariah scholars became more serious about their role as religious regulators: "They read documents much more closely and [those from the Middle East] insist that everything concerning a new product be presented to them in Arabic." Another Islamic finance expert told me with a slight smile that scholars "saw the financial crisis as proof" that the Qur'anic injunction against interest-bearing debt was a divine truth.

The crisis also prompted shariah scholars to take a more active role in exerting their collective authority over the industry. Scholars from across the Muslim world and beyond sought to develop a more unified collective voice following the crisis and increasingly demanded that Islamic finance fulfill its social mission. The politics of Islamic financial knowledge were made visible in a series of "strategic roundtables" that were co-organized by three of the most well-respected and influential institutions for the production of Islamic financial knowledge: the Kuala

Lumpur–based International Shari'ah Research Academy for Islamic Finance, the Islamic Research and Training Institute in Jeddah, and Islamic Finance Program of the United Kingdom's Durham University. The first roundtable was held in 2011 in Durham, and they were held annually until 2015, rotating between the United Kingdom, Malaysia, and Saudi Arabia. These roundtables brought together shariah scholars, Islamic economists, and industry practitioners to discuss key issues in contemporary Islamic finance, with the goal of coming to a consensus among some of the world's leading experts in the field. Each roundtable culminated in a "declaration" that sought to articulate a unified position regarding the core principles of the industry.

Influenced in large measure by the work of Islamic economists such as Abbas Mirakhor, the central focus of discussion at these roundtables has been the role of risk sharing in Islamic finance. Following the second roundtable, held in Kuala Lumpur, the participants issued the "Kuala Lumpur Declaration," which criticized conventional finance and enjoined governments from Muslim countries to exert greater support for Islamic finance. The declaration asserts the ability of Islamic finance to offer an alternative to its conventional counterpart: "The participants acknowledged that the financial crisis . . . highlighted the fact that the most salient feature of the dominant conventional financial system is the transfer of risks away from financial institutions onto customers, governments and the public at large. Islamic finance is in a unique position to offer an alternative to the present interest-based debt financing regime that has brought the whole world to the edge of collapse" (quoted in Hasan 2016, 33). The document affirms risk sharing as a constitutive feature of Islamic financial contracts: "Shariah emphasizes risk sharing as a salient characteristic of Islamic financial transactions. This is not only exemplified in equity-based contracts, like *musharaka*[15] and mudaraba, but even in exchange contracts, such as sales and leasing, whereby risk is shared by virtue of possession" (quoted in Hasan 2016, 33). With reference to both the origins and effects of the financial crises that started in 2008, the document goes on to critique inordinate debt, stating that although Islam permits debt, "it is acknowledged that excessive debt has detrimental effects on society" (quoted in Hasan 2016, 33). The document then concludes with a call on officials to facilitate Islamic finance, stating that "governments should endeavour to move away from interest-based systems towards enhancing risk-sharing systems by levelling the playing field between equity and debt" (quoted in Hasan 2016, 33).

The "Jeddah Declaration" following the third roundtable, held in 2013 in Saudi Arabia at the headquarters of the Islamic Development Bank, continued to emphasize the centrality of risk sharing in Islamic finance. Unlike the Kuala Lumpur Declaration, the Jeddah Declaration included the names of the forty-two shariah scholars, Islamic economists, and industry professionals, including shariah luminaries such as Mohamed Ali Elgari and Abdul Sattar Abu Ghuddah, who signed the document. The group condemned the debt-based nature of conventional finance in bold terms, stating, "The participants acknowledged that the recent global financial and sovereign debt crises were the result of over-dependence on interest-based debt-financing instruments, which reflect the concept of risk transfer that is central to the conventional financial system paradigm" (ISRA 2013).

The document then reiterated the emphasis on risk sharing that had formed such a prominent part of the first declaration, stating, "Risk sharing is applicable across all products and instruments in the Islamic financial sector as it is inherent in the various *mu'amalah*[16] contracts that underpin them. Indeed, the acceptance of risk is the justification of the profits earned by participants" (ISRA 2013). This declaration also referred to the social nature of Islamic finance, albeit this time referring not to the adverse effects on society created by debt but rather the social benefits of risk sharing. It proclaimed that "Islam promotes redistributive risk-sharing instruments through which the economically more able segment of the society shares the risks facing the less economically able segment of the population" (ISRA 2013). The document then enjoined regulators within the Islamic finance network to both "promote equity-based financing" by creating "a level playing field for equity vis-à-vis debt" and to "monitor and control the extent and use of debt and of products that can have detrimental effects" (ISRA 2013). Islamic finance experts viewed these strategic roundtables and the declarations that they produced as pivotal events in the recent history of Islamic finance because they sought to resolve the impasse that had emerged between the high-minded ideals and the actual practices of Islamic finance. One Islamic economist told me optimistically that the Kuala Lumpur and Jeddah declarations "pronounced that the essence of Islamic finance was risk sharing." He saw it as an indication that shariah scholars had committed to embrace risk sharing, one of the constitutive principles that he saw as forming the substance of Islamic economic practice.

The roundtables sought to achieve a fundamental transformation in Islamic finance. Previously, the knowledge deployed in Islamic finance was disaggregated. Religious legitimacy was conferred through the iso-lated and disparate rulings of shariah advisory committees, each of which had considerable leeway to act independently. These rulings were often pragmatic in nature, taking into account the specific context in which a particular shariah issue had to be evaluated. As Bill Maurer noted in the mid-2000s, shariah scholars in practice acted as "bricoleurs, drawing from any jurisprudential source they deem appropriate for a particular prob-lem" (Maurer 2005, 105). Shariah advisors had a great degree of flexibility and could make decisions based on whatever textual sources seemed to fit a given issue at a given time.

However, following the global financial crisis and the widespread soul searching that this cataclysm engendered among Islamic finance experts, calls for standardization and harmonization accelerated. The strategic roundtables were one of several efforts to bring practitioners and observ-ers together in an effort to achieve some degree of coherence in Islamic finance. Indeed the declarations themselves mark an effort to develop a unified knowledge foundation for Islamic finance. The elements of this formation included

- defining risk sharing as the fundamental feature of Islamic finance
- explicitly demarcating Islamic finance from conventional finance based on interest-bearing debt
- emphasizing the equity-based nature of Islamic finance
- proclaiming Islamic finance as both an economic and a social undertaking.

In addition, the declarations sought to compel shariah scholars to em-brace the definition of Islamic finance as a risk-sharing enterprise, a posi-tion that had long been championed by Islamic economists.

At the same time as scholars themselves began the effort to implement a coherent vision of Islamic finance, the regulation of shariah scholars be-came more stringent. A watershed in this change was provisions contained in the Islamic Financial Services Act, which was passed at the behest of Bank Negara by Malaysia's parliament in 2013. One of the central goals of the new act was to ensure stricter shariah compliance by Islamic financial institutions, which previously had been only loosely enforced. According to a number of observers with whom I spoke, among the most significant changes precipitated by the new act were provisions that enabled Bank Negara to impose severe penalties for shariah noncompliance. Toward this end, the act states that any person who contravenes shariah standards "commits an offence and shall, on conviction, be liable to imprisonment for a term not exceeding eight years or to a fine not exceeding twenty-five million ringgit[17] or to both" (Legal Research Board 2013, 29.6). Prior to the act shariah compliance in Islamic financial institutions was generally subject to fairly lax enforcement, but the new provisions gave Bank Negara far-reaching powers of enforcement.

Not surprisingly, however, Malaysian shariah scholars and others working in shariah advisory bristled at the new penalties for shariah noncompliance. One scholar told me that the new penalties for shariah noncompliance consisting of prison time and heavy fines were "ridiculous" and "too extreme." He said that the sanctions were unnecessary because Bank Negara already had effective means at its disposal to ensure compliance. For example, if the central bank conducted an audit of an Islamic financial firm and its activities were found out of compliance with shariah, the CEO could be terminated. This would effectively end the CEO's career because he or she would never get another job. He also said that such threats were unnecessary for shariah scholars because they were all aware that they would be accountable for their worldly deeds in the *akhirat* (afterlife). Another shariah committee member likewise displayed resentment regarding the new penalties for shariah noncompliance, bitterly stating, "They are making us into criminals."

When I raised these points with a member of Bank Negara's Department for Islamic Banking and Takaful (JPIT), he dismissed the anxiety that the penalties had created. He said that the goal was to give shariah compliance "more visibility" and to "make banks take it seriously." The heavy penalties in IFSA to ensure shariah compliance were intended to give compliance more "prominence" and make it "more authoritative." Furthermore, he said that there was a misunderstanding among shariah scholars because the penalties were not directed at the scholars but rather at the executive leadership of IFIs. The jail term and fine would be levied against the members of the board of directors of the bank but not against the members of the shariah committee.

The vulnerability of shariah scholars was made especially evident to me when I interviewed the CEO of one of Malaysia's largest Islamic banks. He said that the shariah committee is "the least of my worries" when his team devises a new Islamic product or instrument. If he did not like the verdict a shariah advisor gave him, he said he would "just replace him with a new advisor." If they are "not ready to put their neck on the line," he continued, "I just get rid of them!" Some of this bravado might simply be attributed to executive bluster, but it also underscores the tenuous position that shariah scholars occupy and the limits of their ability to exert authority over the industry.

In sum, the four groups of Islamic finance experts described in this chapter are complexly positioned with regard to one another. Regulators are uncomfortably caught between Islamic finance practitioners and Islamic economists. Practitioners, like their non-Islamic brethren, often decry regulators for intervening too much. On the other side, Islamic economists often call for regulators to deploy a more willful gaze to guarantee the distinctiveness of Islamic from conventional finance. Nonetheless, all three of these groups are grounded in the secular knowledge that is taught in most universities, in both the North Atlantic and the Muslim world. Even Islamic economists often take the truths of economics for granted, insofar as they seek to show that Islam is congruent with these truths. The only group that challenged the hegemony of secular approaches were shariah scholars, who deployed methods of legal reasoning that had been used in Islamic juridical traditions for centuries. Nonetheless, they too were enmeshed in a series of constraints and uncomfortably positioned between religious and commercial imperatives. The fissures between these groups were further revealed in their respective approaches to Islamic finance. It is to the debates over defining Islamic finance that I turn in the next chapter.

CHAPTER THREE

Counterdebt

B ill Maurer has argued that Islamic finance "should be viewed not simply as the implementation of Qur'anic prohibitions against riba[1] but as the debate over riba itself" (Maurer 2006, 27). I extend Maurer's argument by showing how the broader question of what constitutes Islamic practice is debated in contemporary Islamic finance. Islamic finance experts are asking a series of questions that range beyond a debate over usury: What denotes authentic Islamic practice in economic affairs? Is Islamic practice a formal operation, or does it indicate substantive content? And, ultimately, what makes Islamic finance Islamic? Answers to these questions of course differed depending on who answered them and his or her particular orientation. For some, Islamic finance is Islamic by virtue of its adherence to certain moral principles. For others it is compliance with the injunctions contained in Islam's key texts (the Qur'an and the hadiths). Still others see Islamic finance as the effect of the performative acts of shariah scholars who proclaim financial instruments or products to be Islamic. For some the defining feature of Islamic finance is achieving social justice through the alleviation of poverty. Finally, there are those who see it as simply the financial system in which Muslims are obligated to participate by virtue of their religious identity.

This chapter addresses two of the most commonly deployed definitions of Islamic finance. In many respects questions of the religious authenticity of Islamic finance and the extent to which it offered a genuine alternative to conventional finance hinged on whether it was defined in terms of formal operations or substantive criteria. In other words, the answer could be distilled down to the question of whether one sought to identify its Islamicity through formal operations or through the specific content of its economic devices and practices. Industry professionals and many shariah scholars most often defined Islamic finance in formal terms, seeking to identify whether a device or practice conformed to scriptural prohibitions. However, Islamic economists saw these prohibitions as surface manifestations of an implicit set of substantive economic principles. Thus they sought to extract an authentic Islamic economic theory from these texts and contrast it with conventional economics.

In the everyday practices of Islamic financial institutions, the prevailing rubric for Islamic finance was purely formal. The formalist approach identified Islamic finance as an economic system free from three specific prohibitions in Islamic texts: injunctions against riba, *gharar* (uncertainty or ambiguity), and *maysir* (gambling, often extended to cover speculation as well). Indeed, these criteria are widely used in defining Islamic finance in everything from newspaper articles to textbooks. I also heard these criteria recited in public addresses about Islamic finance, in interviews, and in personal conversations. They were offered in published material, including everything from the 2001 *Capital Market Master Plan* developed by the Securities Commission of Malaysia (intended as a blueprint for the development of Malaysia's financial sector) to brochures published by Islamic financial institutions. For example, in 2013 I picked up a brochure for the Al-Awfar Savings Account offered by Malaysia's first Islamic bank, Bank Islam. After giving the meaning of *al-awfar* as "prosperous investment," it subsequently stated that a prize drawing for those who opened such an account was permissible according to Islam because there were "no elements of riba (usury), gharar (uncertainty) and maysir (gambling)."

The prohibitions against riba and maysir are based on explicit Qur'anic injunctions. The verse most often cited as religious justification for prohibiting riba states:

> Those who live on usury will not rise (on Doomsday) but like a man possessed of the devil and demented. This is because they say that trading is like usury. But trade has been sanctioned and usury forbidden by God. Those who are warned by their Lord and desist will keep (what they have taken of interest) already, and the matter will rest with God. But those who revert to it again are the residents of Hell where they will abide forever. (Qur'an 2:275)

This uncompromising tone toward those who collect riba suggests the gravity of the sin and the moral pressure experienced by many Muslims when confronted with the possibility of riba. As one former conventional banker in Malaysia (who had by his own account "converted" to Islamic banking) told me with a wry smile, "The prophet Muhammad stated that collecting interest is a sin worse than committing adultery thirty-six times." This calculation was mentioned to me by other Islamic finance experts in defining the existential predicament confronting those who sought to engage in commerce and simultaneously live according to the prescriptions set forth in key Islamic texts. They left little ambiguity as to the moral stakes of participating in riba.

The question of riba was complicated by the rulings of prominent Islamic scholars who seemed to permit the collection of interest on a small scale. For example, in 1989 the former grand mufti of Egypt, Muhammad Sayyid Tantawi, issued a ruling that declared that in some cases the collection of interest could be permissible (Alim 2013, 61). However, this interpretation has been dismissed as flawed by the vast majority of Islamic scholars. By the 2010s there was broad consensus that any amount paid on a loan above the principal is prohibited by the vehement Qur'anic injunctions against such practices.[2]

In addition to stern prohibitions against interest, the Qur'an contains equally rigid language discouraging gambling (*maysir*), which is on two occasions compared to alcohol in its destructiveness. One particularly evocative passage enjoins,

> O believers, this wine and gambling, these idols, and these arrows you use for divination, are all acts of Satan; so keep away from them. You may haply prosper. Satan only wishes to create among you enmity and hatred through wine and gambling, and to divert you from the remembrance of God and prayer. Will you therefore not desist? (Qur'an 5:90–91)

Islamic finance experts have interpreted the admonition against gambling as a broader injunction against speculative commercial action of any kind. The primary aim of this interpretation has been to eschew derivatives, which are financial contracts that conventional banks use to hedge risk (Riles 2011, 2). There is a vociferous debate among Islamic finance experts regarding the religious permissibility of derivatives. Those critical of derivatives couched their opposition in terms of the fact that this type of speculative investment played a key role in precipitating the 2008 financial crisis. Derivatives symbolized "shifting" risk rather than sharing it. Those in support of derivatives argued that they were necessary to "hedge risk" in modern economies against the possibility of fluctuating foreign exchange rates or volatility in the price of commodities.

The restriction on transactions with gharar is based not on Qur'anic injunctions but on hadiths in which the prophet Muhammad is reputed to have enjoined against the sale of "birds in the air and fish in the sea," the contents of the "wombs of female animals," and other objects for which there is "lack of control and lack of knowledge regarding the quantity and quality of the object" (Zahraa and Mahmor 2002, 385). Although the objects may exist in tangible form, the uncertainty of ownership and the lack of quantitative and qualitative knowledge of the objects makes their exchange impermissible according to Islamic legal reasoning based on these hadiths. Therefore, a fisherman is prohibited from trading tomorrow's catch because to do so would violate restrictions on transactions involving gharar. Any number of scenarios might inhibit his ability to actually sell the prospective catch: he may be unlucky and catch nothing, his boat could spring a leak and need to be repaired, or a storm could come up and make venturing out to sea impossible. Although he may possess the skill and the tools to catch fish, there are too many unknown variables, making sale of his catch prior to actually obtaining it too uncertain.

Nonetheless, while fishermen are prohibited from selling tomorrow's catch due to excessive uncertainty, farmers are permitted to sell future harvests under a contract known as a *bai al salam* (forward sale) (Udovitch 1970, 79). I asked Dr. Sharif, who taught the course in Islamic law that I took in 2010, why a fisherman could not sell his catch in advance but a farmer could sell her crops. Dr. Sharif explained that, according to shariah, selling fish was subject to excessive gharar, and a bai al salam could only be executed under strict conditions. In the case of the fisherman, the future catch was absolutely subject to contingent factors, but so long as the farmer held a known quantity of land and seed and the ability to produce the crops and all the stipulations of the contract were mutually agreed upon, the risk of unforeseen events (such as a flood, a drought, or a plague of locusts) was permissible.

Risk and Society

Another method of defining Islamic finance is based on constructing an Islamic economic theory through analysis and interpretation of passages and statements in the Qur'an. Those who embrace this approach seek to identify the substantive principles that make economic action moral. They argue that Islamic finance is based on "risk sharing," as in the strategic roundtable declarations mentioned in the previous chapter, in contrast to conventional finance, which they view as based on "risk transfer." Again, the 2008 financial crisis serves as a paradigmatic example of how risk is transferred in conventional finance. They point to the fact that during the crisis taxpayers ultimately bailed out financial institutions that undertook excessively risky strategies. Furthermore, before the crisis, the same institutions had enjoyed an increasingly low-tax, deregulated environment. Big banks and other firms had effectively individualized their profits but collectivized their losses, sharing only the downside (not the upside) of risk by transferring it to the taxpaying public (Appadurai 2016, 117). In contrast, those who define Islamic finance in terms of partnership and risk sharing contend that both the upside and downside of risk must be shared to create a stable, just, and ultimately more functional financial system.

Although proponents of this definition and approach to Islamic finance bristled when in conversation I referred to this approach as "interpretive," I did so because it seeks to uncover the meanings behind various Qur'anic injunctions regarding economic practice. Whereas the formalist approaches outlined above were interested in a literal reading of Islamic texts, those who deployed an interpretive approach focused mostly on the Qur'anic prohibition of interest as a surface manifestation of deeper, substantive principles that they believed constituted Islamic economic action: specifically, that Islam endorses risk sharing as opposed to "risk transfer."

One of the foremost proponents of this position is the prominent Islamic economist Abbas Mirakhor, who was born in Iran, obtained a PhD in economics at Kansas State University, and then worked in a senior capacity at the International Monetary Fund (IMF) in Washington, DC, for several decades. After retiring from the IMF, he was named to the first chaired professorship at the International Center for Education in Islamic Finance. As I describe in detail below, officials at Bank Negara held Mirakhor in high esteem, and his vision of Islamic finance has been especially influential on regulators and other policy makers in Malaysia.

The manner in which Mirakhor insists on the criterion of risk sharing is illuminating. Although his formal academic training is in conventional economics, not in the Islamic sciences such as fiqh or tafsir, in his writings and talks he conducts a profoundly imaginative and experimental interpretation of the Qur'an. In a keynote address delivered at the Foundations of Islamic Finance Conference in 2011 he argues that Islam endorses risk sharing as opposed to risk transfer, asking not "What does the Qur'an say about interest?" but rather "Why is interest explicitly prohibited in the Qur'an?" In this sense, Mirakhor is not interested in the debate over interest as such but instead seeks what he terms the "epistemological" reason for its prohibition. Mirakhor (writing with his coauthor Wang Yong Bao) begins with the oft-invoked Qur'anic verse 2:275 (cited above) and points to the fundamental opposition between exchange (*bay'*) and interest (riba) in the Qur'an. He then interprets the "non-permissibility of the contract of al-Riba" as "surely due to the fact that this contract transfers all, or at least a major portion, of risk to the borrower" (Mirakhor and Bao 2013, 33).[3]

When I asked him in conversation about the opposition between exchange and interest, he explained that in trade, both parties take risk, which is shared between them. In contrast, he explained, a loan entails one party extending credit to another and receiving collateral, either from the borrower or from a third party. He referenced the mortgage securities crisis in the United States before the housing crash of 2008. In collateralized loans the creditor is "hedged," meaning he or she has transferred all the risk on his or her capital to other parties. If the debtor is able to pay, the creditor reaps the principle and interest on the original loan. When I objected that lenders also take risks, such as the possibility of default, he acknowledged that although this was theoretically true, in practice major creditors always hedge their risk, either through collateral or other means. He explained that in the event of a default creditors could dispose of the collateralized asset and ensure that their capital and interest is protected. And when firms are threatened by widespread, systemic defaults, they can resort to the "too big to fail" argument and rely on taxpayer-funded bailouts to ensure their survival. For reformers like Mirakhor, the risk transfer practices inherent in loans make interest immoral according to Islam. He and Bao argue, "It appears that the reason for the prohibition of Al-Riba contracts is the fact that opportunities for risk sharing do not exist in this contract" (Mirakhor and Bao 2013, 35). Since riba is a "contract of risk transfer" and it is specifically prohibited, They conclude, "It is clear that by declaring the contract of Al-Riba nonpermissible [*sic*], the Qur'an intends for humans to shift their focus to risk-sharing contracts of exchange" (Mirakhor and Bao 2013, 35).

The argument that risk sharing is the basis for the Qur'anic injunction against interest is based on deduction. The Qur'an does not use the term "risk" or explicitly state the underlying rationale for the prohibition of interest.[4] Whereas the formalist definition of Islamic finance sought to read Islamic texts literally, the interpretive approach sought to excavate underlying meanings of the prohibitions. To support his argument, Mirakhor and

Bao turn to what is sanctioned in the Qur'an and makes a hermeneutic determination regarding the endorsement of exchange from the passage where interest is prohibited. He writes, "All Islamic contractual forms, except spot exchange, involve time. . . . All transactions involving time are subject to uncertainty and uncertainty involves risk" (Mirakhor and Bao 2013, 34). Under conditions of uncertainty the buyer and the seller share "price risk" because prices could go up or down after the sale. Furthermore, they continue, "There are other risks that the buyer takes including the risks of nondelivery and substandard quality. The seller faces additional risks including the risk that the price of raw material, and cost of transportation and delivery, may be higher in the future. These risks may also be lower. Again, these risks have been shared through the contract" (Mirakhor and Bao 2013, 34). According to Mirakhor the market is a vast mechanism through which the aggregated risks of each member of society can be pooled and shared. Whereas liberals see the market as producing the truth of price, or what Foucault called a "site of veridiction" (Foucault 2008, 44), Islamic economists such as Mirakhor see it as a means of sharing risk and therefore producing equality.

Furthermore, Mirakhor argues that even spot contracts entail risk sharing both for the possibility of price changes after the completion of the transaction and for the problem of specialization (the division of labor given its classical elaboration in Adam Smith's analysis of the steps required to produce a pin in a factory).[5] Mirakhor and Bao write, "From the time of the classical economists, it has been recognized that specialization through comparative advantage provides the basis for gains from trade. But in specializing, a producer takes the risk of becoming dependent on other producers specialized in production of what he needs. Again, through exchange the two sides to a transaction share the risk of specialization" (Mirakhor and Bao 2013, 35). Here they appear to embrace the liberal argument, also expounded by Smith, that the market is a means through which social bonds of mutual interdependence can be formed (Muehlebach 2012, 29). Mirakhor and Bao conclude that "it can be inferred that by mandating" sales, Allah "ordained risk sharing in all exchange activities" (Mirakhor and Bao 2013, 34). Especially relevant here is the fact that Mirakhor identifies risk sharing in the sale-based contracts that are often criticized by reformers who decry these contracts due to the fact that they are used to replicate conventional financial devices and, as I describe below, much prefer equity and investment-based contracts.

Mirakhor's interpretation, that the economic ethics of Islam are premised on risk sharing, has been notably influential among leading figures facilitating the development of Islamic finance in Malaysia. Foremost among these is Zeti Akhtar Aziz. Aziz was an influential patron of Islamic finance in Malaysia, and indeed globally. Promoting Islamic finance was a family legacy for her: her father was the economist Ungku Aziz, who (as described above) laid the groundwork for Malaysia's first Islamic financial institution, Tabung Haji. Aziz echoed Mirakhor's definition of Islamic finance as "risk sharing" in an address that she delivered in Jeddah, Saudi Arabia, during a ceremony in honor of a prize she was awarded from the Islamic Development Bank on November 27, 2013. In the address, which explicitly invoked the 2008 financial crisis, she made the case for the deployment of "Islamic finance in modern market economies, taking into account the knowledge that we have today about the vulnerabilities of finance, its causes and its wider economic ramifications" (Aziz 2013, 1). Focusing on the problem of "excessive leverage" that had precipitated the crisis, she commented that risk sharing in Islamic finance puts limits on leverage. Of course, she noted that although it is specifically endorsed in Islam, risk sharing is not foreign to the operations of conventional finance. Drawing on arguments often articulated by Mirakhor, she stated:

> While risk-transfer activities currently dominate the conventional financial systems, risk sharing in the form of equity has long been a cornerstone of capital markets with vibrant stock exchanges. Techniques used by venture capital financiers also have similarities to risk-sharing contracts in Islamic finance. The development towards a more equity-based financial system where risk sharing takes place reduces the over-reliance on debt funding, thus avoiding excessive debt and speculation and thus financial system fragility. In Islamic finance, this is further reinforced by Shariah principles that strongly discourage excessive debt given its detrimental effects on society. (Aziz 2013, 2)

Aziz argued that excessive debt (characterized by risk transfer) is detrimental to social cohesion. The subject of risk sharing is conceived of in more collective terms: an agent willing to take the interests of others into account, work collaboratively in teams, and put the collective good against his or her own individual interests, at least at times.

Counterdebt

A central question posed by experts such as Dr. Mirakhor and former governor Aziz is whether contemporary financial and economic action must rely on debt as a central mechanism. Debates over debt in Islamic finance resonate with current anthropological discussions about the pervasiveness of debt as a ubiquitous form of contemporary social and economic interaction (Peebles 2010; Roitman 2003; Rudnyckyj 2017b; Schuster 2014). While a number of anthropologists have focused on the role of debt in perpetuating inequality (Bear 2015; Kar 2013; Karim 2011; Stout 2016), a key objective of David Graeber's widely read book *Debt: The First 5,000 Years* is to challenge the received wisdom about the moral obligations incurred in a debt relationship. Graeber seeks to rethink the presumption that debtors have a moral duty to repay the funds they have been extended and points out that even those making loans do not expect them to be consistently repaid without fail (Graeber 2011, 4). Graeber views the moral logic of debt as a means of ideological domination in capitalism through which elites exert influence over those subject to their political and economic power. Invoking the US mortgage crisis as an example, he points out that those who financed debt are "bailed out with taxpayer money" while "ordinary citizens" are held liable for the debts they incur (Graeber 2011, 381).

To counter this moral logic of debt, Graeber, like Islamic finance experts, turns to religion: the ethical principles of Judeo-Christian monotheism. Drawing inspiration from Mosaic injunctions in the book of Leviticus and the proposals of contemporary groups such as Jubilee 2000,[6] Graeber proposes a "Biblical-style Jubilee" for "international debt and consumer debt" as a "challenge to the principle of debt itself" (Graeber 2011, 390–391). He contends that those afflicted by debt, such as victims of the mortgage meltdown in the United States or poor African nations subjected to the constraints of IMF lending, should be absolved of their debts through an institutionalized program of redemption in which the indebted are forgiven.

Two questions might be asked about Graeber's solution to the dilemma of debt. First, to what extent does the jubilee challenge the principle of debt? It would seem that the logic of debt is only transformed, insofar as the moral obligation to repay is no longer taken for granted. Rather than challenging a debt-centered economy, the jubilee solution simply institutionalizes forgiveness while taking the other attributes of the cycle for granted. Finance capitalism, the economic edifice in which debt is the fundamental pillar for the mobilization of capital, is little altered. In Graeber's account, individuals and companies would still borrow to finance their present and future needs, and banks, a particular target of Graeber's scorn, would continue to lend at interest. The only difference would be that the obligation to repay would not be strictly observed, as borrowers could decide to wait for the jubilee to absolve their arrears.

Second, it might be asked, what are the political implications of a debt jubilee? Indeed the jubilee presupposes a sovereign power endowed with the authority of the pardon. The act of "wiping the slate clean" is presumed on the agency of a sovereign who can designate what Carl Schmitt, and later Giorgio Agamben, identified as the "state of exception" (Agamben 1998; Schmitt [1922] 2005). The jubilee presumes a state, a king, or other sovereign authority with the power to enforce the cancellation of debts, thereby ensuring no retribution by lenders on borrowers. Therefore, the jubilee as the solution to the problem of debt effectively reinforces sovereign power. The endorsement of sovereign power would perhaps not be so notable were it not seemingly at such stark odds with Graeber's self-proclaimed anarchist political commitments (Graeber 2004).

Islamic finance offers a different alternative to the impasse of the jubilee and its conformity with both the logic of debt and the sovereignty that both enables it and holds the authority to designate its exception. Debt is a recurrent preoccupation and object of reflection among many Islamic finance professionals. They see debt at the core of contemporary capitalism and often attribute economic instability and social problems to the ubiquity of debt and the problems created by overindebtedness. An overriding opinion of Islamic finance experts in Malaysia was that the financial crisis of 2008 was precipitated by a surfeit of debt.

Debt instruments are a central object of reflection in contemporary Islamic finance, and the problematization of debt was quite common among experts in this knowledge formation. For example, Rahim, who directed projects on Islamic finance at a research center in Kuala Lumpur, told me that the problem with debt was that "more money is always spent repaying a debt than is created through the debt in the first place." He compared this to the "desertification of a landscape" where there is "less water falling as rain than evaporates into the air." He said that an interest-based economy creates the same conditions as a desert landscape, "because in an interest economy the investment in the real economy is always less than the amount of money that comes out in interest." Rahim gave several examples drawn from recent news, such as the fact that Greece was paying exorbitant interest rates on government bonds. He continued, "Banks that rely on collateralized loans are not entrepreneurs, but are usurers!" He then likened economic systems based on interest-bearing debt to

communism and warned that the same fate that befell the former Soviet
Union and its allies would strike economies where interest was condoned,
because they did not emphasize production but profit without labor.
"Communism collapsed because it severed the link between reward and
performance. It fell behind capitalism, because there was no incentive
to work. Whether you did a good job or not you still got paid. Capitalism prevailed because it provided incentives for people to work harder to
make more money. . . . But interest goes against that principle because the
banks just get money for nothing."[7] Criticism of debt on both economic
and moral grounds was common among Islamic finance experts, most notably among Islamic economists, but I also heard these sentiments voiced
by shariah scholars and professionals working in Islamic banks.

   In response to what they see as the economic and moral failure of debt,
Islamic finance experts offer a more drastic solution than Graeber's proposal for a jubilee. Instead of waiting for a debt crisis to then initiate a
campaign of forgiveness, they propose an alternative means of finance—
one in which the preeminent financial tool is equity rather than debt.[8]
Rather than Graeber's attempt to include debt forgiveness into an economy that continues to be premised on debt, they seek to create an economy where the central tool for the mobilization of capital itself is different. These experts seek to develop contracts premised on partnership and
equity ownership rather than autonomous debt-bearing individuals. The
mudaraba, discussed in the introduction, is an equity-based contract that
is frequently invoked as a paradigmatic contract in Islamic finance. In
a mudaraba, an entrepreneur (*mudarib*) and an investor (*rabb al maal*)
enter into a partnership (see figure 10). The mudarib typically possesses
expertise and entrepreneurial acumen but no capital. Profits generated
by the business venture are split between the parties according to a predetermined ratio. However, the investor who provides the capital bears
all financial losses, while the mudarib or investment manager is only responsible for the opportunity costs associated with managing the venture.

   The preference among those seeking to reform Islamic finance for partnership contracts (such as mudaraba) in contrast to what they see as debt-
based contracts illustrates how reformers are challenging some of the fundamental devices of modern economics. Extending Mirakhor's effort to
put risk sharing at the center of Islamic finance, proponents hold that economic actors, by forming what is effectively a joint venture, work together
to divide risk equally. In contrast, debt is individualizing. Institutions, such
as banks, transfer risk through such innovations as taking collateral from

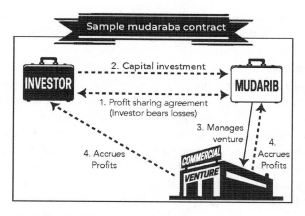

FIGURE 10. A sample mudaraba contract structure. Credit: Jos Sances.

borrowers or securitizing the debt that they create and selling it to others. Proponents of equity-oriented Islamic finance argued that partnership contracts supported collective relationships and mutual equality, whereas debt created hierarchical social relations and actors working in pursuit of individualized interests.

In reacting to the problem of debt by suggesting an equity-based financial system, these experts called for a more radical political solution than the jubilee suggested by Graeber. As noted above, the jubilee ultimately relies on a sovereign with the power to designate the exception. The jubilee is enacted when the sovereign decrees that the normal order of debt accountability has become too onerous and "that all who languished in bondage owing to . . . debts would be released" (Graeber 2011, 82). However, those committed to equity finance attributed their support for it in part to the social subordination inherent in debt. Whereas debt entails an unequal relationship, an economy based on equity would entail partnership, equality, and collaboration.

Finally, it is important to note the differences in the way in which sociality is mobilized in these two critiques of debt. Working in the Maussian tradition, Graeber contends that debt is in a sense intrinsic to society itself, for society is largely constituted through relationships of reciprocal obligation in which individuals are linked to one another through the material exchange of gifts (Mauss [1925] 1990). In Graeber's account, the sociality of debt is evident in what he refers to as "baseline communism" in which everyone contributes what he or she can to the collectivity and withdraws what he or she needs (Graeber 2011). However, in capitalism the jubilee serves to prevent social decay, as it prevents debt from becoming so pervasive that vast swaths of the population are forced to sell themselves to debt peonage.

Reformers in Islamic finance are also making a forceful argument about sociality in their critique of debt. They too view debt as socially corrosive and advocate risk sharing as a central principle of Islamic finance because it encourages the mutual partnership of equals. One Islamic finance expert conveyed this to me by invoking the 2008 financial crisis. He said that under the debt system, people were "left homeless" because when they could not keep up with their mortgages, the banks "just took their homes." He said under an Islamic system, the risks of home ownership would be shared, as described in chapter 5. This would make financial institutions more cautious in their home financing but would also mean that institutions would shoulder some of the burden of the risk taken by home buyers.

Arguments that Islamic finance is premised on risk sharing, as opposed to risk transfer, suggest a form of economic action not premised on the sovereign subject assumed in the neoliberal models that constitute the dominant economic paradigm of our times (Barry, Osborne, and Rose 1996; Foucault 2008; Ong 2006). For example, risk sharing in mudaraba contracts distributes economic hazards between a creditor and a debtor rather than expecting a borrower to assume the entire burden of risk. Those seeking to reform Islamic finance contend that it offers the possibility of creating stronger collective relationships than conventional finance and, in so doing, they create what I have termed "collaborative risk" (Rudnyckyj 2017b). In the end, this produces what is ultimately a more stable system, as there is an acceptance of financial risk rather than a ceaseless attempt to find a counterparty on which to offload risk.

The remainder of this book documents this proposal and the subjects that it elicits. I document how contemporary debt-based Islamic finance works and the methodological presumptions on which it is based. Then I examine the criticisms of the debt-based approach and the proposed alternatives to it. Finally, I describe what an equity-based Islamic financial system would look like in practice, some of the obstacles to implementing one, and explain why powerful Malaysian institutions such as the Central Bank have embraced efforts to shift away from debt and toward equity in Islamic finance.

PART II
Operations

CHAPTER FOUR

Making Bonds Islamic

A fter the turn of the millennium, ambitious efforts to make Malaysia a global hub for Islamic finance were perhaps most evident in efforts to make the country the preeminent site for the issuance of a category of financial devices known as sukuk. Corporations and governments use sukuk to raise capital for economic activities. These devices are often referred to as "Islamic bonds" in popular parlance and media reports. However, sukuk differ from conventional bonds in that sukuk issuers try to avoid interest as the basis of returns. Although there is a wide variety of what experts call sukuk "structures," sukuk are typically created by issuing shares in the ownership of tangible assets. The holders of a sukuk then receive a share of the revenues generated by those assets.

Sukuk are typical examples of "shariah-compliant" devices, which Islamic finance experts contrast with those to which they refer as "shariah based." Shariah-compliant devices are typically structured to meet the formal rules of shariah and, as a category, are associated with techniques to camouflage the use of debt. This chapter demonstrates how conventional devices are often both the starting point and recurrent reference in efforts to design sukuk. More recently, experts have sought to create shariah-based Islamic bonds that are derived from Islamic economic directives and synthesized from devices deployed historically by Islamic financial and political authorities. Devices Islamic finance experts refer to as shariah based are generally premised on equity, risk, and profit sharing rather than replicating debt devices.

As efforts to internationalize Islamic finance accelerated in the 2000s, Islamic finance planners in Malaysia created a series of incentives to attract foreign firms to issue sukuk in the country. These included creating a knowledge infrastructure of experts skilled in the techniques of creating a diverse range of sukuk structures, a legal regime to facilitate the smooth functioning of the sukuk market, and, perhaps most important, a financial infrastructure that created tax incentives for issuing sukuk. Planners made a commitment to ensure what they termed "tax neutrality" for sukuk, meaning that they would not be at a tax disadvantage compared to conventional bonds. This was critical because standard Islamic financial instruments often involve multiple sales, and sales taxes present a potentially paralyzing financial burden for sukuk issuers. Malaysia typically hosts on average about 60 percent of sukuk issuances, and many firms from around the world come to Kuala Lumpur in an effort to, in the words of Islamic finance practitioners, "tap the market."

This chapter documents the centrality of sukuk devices in the everyday practices of Islamic finance. First, I provide a definition of sukuk and the way in which Islamic finance experts have looked to Islamic history to find precedents for these devices in instruments deployed by both the Umayyad and Ottoman states. The latter sections of the chapter document the empirical effects of policies intended to make Malaysia a center for global sukuk issuance by drawing on my experience accompanying Uzair, an Islamic financier from Australia, as he sought to broker a sukuk deal in Kuala Lumpur. In this latter part of the chapter my goals are twofold. First, I document what actually existing, everyday Islamic finance looks like in practice. In many respects, it closely resembles the everyday activities of conventional finance, with the exception of the ever-present specter of a review by Islamic scholars of any prospective financial transaction. Second, I seek to show how the technologies of conventional finance frame business deals in everyday Islamic finance. This is especially evident both in the idiom of "mimicry" that was used by the financier and in how interest rates often explicitly and implicitly frame Islamic financial negotiations and transactions. In so doing, I concur with critics such as El-Gamal and Kuran that shariah-compliant Islamic finance evident in the creation and marketing of sukuk devices is more or less a translation of conventional finance. However, as I show in subsequent chapters, shariah-based Islamic finance, based on equity and investment and avoiding the perils of leverage, may hold the promise of an unequivocal financial alternative.

Historical Precedents

Sukuk have generated some of the greatest enthusiasm in Islamic finance among financial professionals and the business press, both within the Muslim world and outside of it. Definitions of sukuk vary, but in its capital adequacy requirement standard (IFSB 7) the IFSB defines sukuk as "certificates" that represent "proportional undivided ownership right in tangible assets, or a pool of predominantly tangible assets, or a business venture" (IFSB 2009, 3). Rafe Haneef, who until 2016 was the CEO of HSBC Amanah, the global banking giant's Islamic subsidiary in Malaysia, defines sukuk as "transferable certificates representing a share in the ownership of assets or business ventures that entitle the sukuk holders to receive periodic fixed returns and full redemption on maturity of the sukuk" (Haneef 2009, 103).[1] The key in both definitions is the reference to the ownership of assets. Unlike a bond, for which the holder does not possess ownership rights, for sukuk the ownership of the underlying asset is a key component to achieving shariah compliance. In general, sukuk function similarly to bonds in conventional finance insofar as they provide a fixed return to investors who hold them and can be redeemed for full value on maturity. However, sukuk differ insofar as conventional bonds are loans that the certificate holders make to the bond issuer and the "coupon" collected by the holders is effectively an interest payment. In contrast, to comply with the Qur'anic prohibition on interest, sukuk are generally structured so that the return on investment derives from profits generated by the underlying assets. Investors who hold sukuk certificates are entitled to a share of the cash flows derived from the asset.

One common sukuk structure entails transforming a future revenue stream based on the ownership of an asset into a source of capital in the present. The revenue streams securitized through sukuk may include a number of receivables: rents expected for real estate leases, tolls anticipated from highway usage, expected utility payments from electricity generated by power plants, future payments from mobile phone users for cellular bandwidth, and even impending cinema ticket sales to prospective filmgoers. Sukuk are typically issued by either nation-states (commonly called "sovereign issues") or by private corporations. Both entities create these certificates to access capital in the present, either for development and expansion projects or (in the case of some sovereign issues) to meet budgetary shortfalls. By the 2010s most sukuk issues were "oversubscribed," meaning that there was greater demand than supply for these devices. Pension funds and sovereign wealth funds around the Muslim world would snap them up as soon as they were issued. In Malaysia, where there are legal and regulatory requirements regarding the volume of shariah-compliant instruments that state pension and investment funds must hold, sukuk are especially popular. Unlike bonds, which are commonly traded

on exchanges, most sukuk investors purchase and hold bonds in their
broader portfolios, so there is currently no secondary market, although
there is optimism that such an exchange will eventually be formed.

Like histories of money, which often trace the origins of currency to
imperial military campaigns and the need to compensate soldiers (Graeber 2011, 229), histories of sukuk trace their origins back to the military
expansion of early Islamic states. Haneef, whose account of the emergence of sukuk is exemplary in this respect, writes that in "early days of
Islamic civilization," the seventh-century Umayyad state paid soldiers and
civil servants with "commodity coupons." The holder could present a certificate "on its maturity date at the treasury and receive a fixed amount of
[a] commodity, usually grains" (Haneef 2009, 105). Similarly to the way
bonds are traded, these first sukuk were sometimes exchanged for money
prior to their maturity date. The evidence mobilized to identify a precedent for sukuk in early Islam comes largely from the eighth- and ninth-
century writings of the scholar Malik ibn Anas, eponym of the Maliki
school of Islamic jurisprudence. Malik recorded the use and exchange of
sukuk in his magnum opus, a collection of hadith known as the *Muwatta,*
in which he offers this account:

> Yahya related to me . . . that he had heard that receipts (sukuk) were given
> to people in the time Marwan ibn al-Hakam for the produce of the market at
> al-Jar. People bought and sold the receipts (sukuk) among themselves before
> they took delivery of the goods. Zayd Thabit and one of the Companions of the
> Messenger of Allah, may Allah . . . bless him and grant him peace, went to Mar-
> wan ibn al-Hakam and said, "Marwan! Do you make usury halal?" He said, "I
> seek refuge with Allah! What is that?" He said, "These receipts (sukuk) which
> people buy and sell before they take delivery of the goods." Marwan therefore
> sent a guard to follow them and to take them from people's hands and return
> them to their owners. (quoted in Dusuki 2012, 392)

Experts in Islamic finance cite this system, whereby a certificate issued by
an institution (in this case the Umayyad state) stands for the value of an underlying asset (the market products), as providing the elementary building
blocks for contemporary sukuk. Nonetheless, in posing the question "Do
you make usury halal?" Malik's account also illustrates the prohibition on
the sale of food commodities prior to actual possession of them, which according to the hadith is a form of riba. When Zayd Thabit questions the
permissibility of exchanging commodity coupons to Marwan (the fourth

caliph of the Umayyad state), Marwan responds by deploying the sovereign power of the state to enforce religious prescriptions. While the creation of certificates to stand for food commodities is unproblematic, the hadith indicates that exchanging them is questionable. This is due to the fact that they may be sold at a price higher or lower than their face value, contrary to Muslim restrictions on the exchange of such certificates.

Historical precedents for sukuk have also identified Ottoman innovations in the mechanisms of public finance. Murat Çizakça, an eminent economic historian and professor at INCEIF, describes sukuk as a reincarnation of the *esham* system, which was devised in 1775 following a disastrous war against Russia the previous year (Çizakça 2011, 71–75). Desperately short of liquidity to meet a budget shortfall, the Ottoman state sold its citizens *sehm* (shares, the root of the word "esham") in state revenue streams, primarily derived from the various tax monopolies it held. As in contemporary sukuk, the state sought to raise funds by ceding rights to future revenue streams in exchange for capital in the present. Initially the asset used in the esham system was tobacco levies due to the state, but later the system was diversified to include shares in other tax monopolies as well. Although the state continued to manage the collection of duties on these commodities, the yearly profits "were divided into shares and each one of these shares was going to be sold . . . on a lifetime basis" (Çizakça 2011, 72). Those who purchased the shares were granted what amounted to a perpetual annuity in the proceeds from various state revenue streams. If the revenue from these securitized tax monopolies ever fell below a benchmark, the state committed to paying the difference. The sehm further resembled bonds insofar as they could be exchanged by their owners.

Seeking to connect Islamic economic history with contemporary sukuk, Çizakça likens the esham system to the Malaysian Global Sukuk (MGS), a 2002 issue in which state assets were securitized to raise capital for current budgetary needs. Both the historical esham system and the contemporary MGS entailed the sale of an asset held by the state (either a tax monopoly or real estate) and the distribution of the revenue from that asset to certificate holders. In the latter, a special purpose vehicle (SPV), called Malaysian Global Sukuk Incorporated, was established in Malaysia's offshore finance center, the island of Labuan off the north coast of Borneo. The Labuan International Finance Center, where the sukuk was domiciled, was established in 1990 as a special economic zone offering reduced tax exposure and lighter regulatory oversight. Labuan was established to compete with other offshore financial centers, such as the

Cayman Islands, the Isle of Man, and the British Virgin Islands (Maurer and Martin 2012). The Malaysian Central Bank and the Securities Commission sought to capitalize on its strategic advantage, which was that, in contrast to offshore financial locations in the Atlantic Ocean, Labuan was located in the same time zone as major emerging markets in East Asia, including China, Hong Kong, and Singapore. Labuan initially struggled to compete with long-established offshore locales, but the growth of Islamic finance, and especially efforts to make Malaysia a global hub for Islamic finance, breathed new life into Labuan as an offshore location with a focus on handling Islamic financial transactions. The Malaysian state has aggressively promoted it as a site for sukuk issuance, due to its favorable tax and regulatory incentives.

The issuance of the MGS, valued at $600 million, was a landmark event in the historical development of sukuk and in some respects is hallowed as the sukuk industry's coming of age. It was the first global sovereign sukuk, meaning that it represented the initial issue of a sukuk by a nation-state. The structure of the sukuk called for the sale of the beneficial title (*usufruct*) of assets held by the Malaysian state to the SPV. These assets included Selayang Hospital and Tengku Ampuan Rahimah Hospital (state-owned hospitals operated by the Ministry of Health) and state-owned housing and office complexes that were held by the Ministry of Finance, the Ministry of International Trade and Industry, and the Inland Revenue Board (Adam and Thomas 2004, 86). The government then leased the real estate back from the SPV, which collected the rents and passed them on to the investors as dividends. After five years, upon the conclusion of the lease term, the state repurchased the property from the SPV, which used these payments to pay off the investors, who effectively redeemed their ownership shares of the assets on maturity (Rosly 2005, 473–475). The underlying Islamic contract used in this issue was an *ijara*, which entails the "transfer of ownership of usufruct for compensation" (Dusuki 2012, 234). An ijara is essentially a lease or rental contact that is commonly used in Islamic financial transactions. Unlike a sale (*bay*), in which ownership of the corpus is transferred, in an ijara only the use is transferred (Dusuki 2012, 232–234). Maurer reports that ijara contracts are the underlying basis for some shariah-compliant mortgages in the United States (Maurer 2006, 44–49). In addition to lease-based ijara, there are several other market devices that can be used to "structure" sukuk. These include sale-based contracts (such as murabaha, salam, and *istisna'*) and equity-based contracts (such as *mudaraba* and *musharaka*). As part of its effort to standardize Islamic finance and solidify Kuala Lumpur's position as a hub for Islamic finance, between 2011 and 2015 Bank Negara was in the process of seeking to create uniform versions of the most commonly employed contracts in Islamic finance by drafting "standards" and seeking comment on them from various experts in the industry. The bank identified twelve key contracts that it viewed as pivotal to Islamic finance and hoped to standardize (see table 1).

The similarities between the esham system and modern-day sukuk experiments are likely the coincidental effects of shared constraints. As Çizakça writes, the MGS is "an unintentional synthesis and a modernized version of the Ottoman esham and cash waqfs" (Çizakça 2011, 178).[2] Çizakça discounts the possibility that the engineers of modern-day sukuk researched Ottoman history in devising them. Rather, their overriding objective in formulating sukuk was to comply with religious prescriptions, and it was likely this common goal that led contemporary sukuk engineers and Ottoman authorities to come up with a similar solution to the obstacle posed by the Islamic prohibition against interest. Experts seeking to resolve a problem presented by the same doctrinal constraints came to the same conclusions. Sukuk are examples of one popular experiment in Islamic finance and are the contingent effect of efforts to synthesize instruments compliant with Islamic prescriptions.

Nonetheless, some critics of Islamic finance are often highly disparaging of sukuk. For example, the Rice University economist Mahmoud El-Gamal reports that news articles regarding sukuk ironically often characterized them as "interest free" but then report the "profit rate" that such securities pay, noting that in some cases Islamic financial institutions simply substitute the word "profit" for the word "interest" (El-Gamal 2006, 3). Furthermore, he notes the practical similarities between sukuk and conventional bonds, observing that issuers of ijara sukuk, such as the MGS, "obtain the same credit ratings they would obtain for conventional bonds, and . . . pay the same interest they would pay based on that credit rating" (El-Gamal 2006, 6). Indeed, the MGS sukuk described above was "priced at LIBOR + 95bps," which means sukuk holders would earn a return equivalent to LIBOR plus 0.95 percent (Dusuki 2012, 421). LIBOR is a daily reference rate based on the interest rates at which banks extend loans to other banks. The fact that returns from Islamic financial instruments are often indexed to conventional interest rates, such as LIBOR, is a sore point often articulated by critics and reformers of the industry. The fact that Islamic instruments are, in the words of experts,

TABLE I. **The twelve Islamic finance contracts Bank Negara Malaysia sought to standardize after 2011. Officials viewed these market devices as essential infrastructure for Islamic finance as the country sought to become a central hub.**

Category	Type	Name	Definition	Short Description
Equity	Partnership	Musharaka	A profit-sharing contract in which two or more parties agree to pool their assets and labor for the purpose of making a profit. Losses are borne by both parties at an agreed ratio.	Joint venture
Equity	Partnership	Mudaraba	A profit-sharing contract in which one party provides capital and the other provides labor. Losses are borne by the capital provider, while the laborer loses his or her efforts.	Trustee partnership
Debt	Exchange	Murabaha	A contract in which one party sells a commodity to another party at a marked-up price on a deferred payment basis. The increase is not considered interest but rather profit.	Marked-up sale
Debt	Exchange	Istisna'	A contract in which a manufacturer agrees to produce an object for future delivery to a second party at a fixed price.	Manufacturing sale
Debt	Exchange	Tawarruq	A contract in which one party purchases a commodity from another party on a deferred payment basis and then sells the commodity to a third party with an immediate payment.	Commodity murabaha, cash financing
Debt	Exchange	Bai al inah	A contract in which one party sells an asset to a second party on a deferred payment basis and then buys it back from the second party at a lower price in cash.	Sale and buyback
	Charity	Wadiah	A contract in which a party leaves belongings or cash with another for safekeeping.	Safekeeping
	Charity	Hibah	A contract in which one party voluntarily transfers ownership to another without the expectation of compensation.	Gift
	Lease	Ijara	A contract in which the use of an asset is transferred but not the ownership of the corpus of the asset.	Rental agreement
	Security	Kafalah	A guarantee of the repayment of a debt or other liability to a creditor.	Guarantee
	Promissory	Wa'd	A commitment made by one person to another to undertake an action beneficial to a second party.	Promise
	Agency	Wakalah	A contract in which one party delegates another party to act on its behalf.	Agency

"benchmarked" to interest rates, exposes the fiction that debt-based instruments avoid interest altogether, showing that they are in fact framed by interest-based finance and conceived of in ways that mirror interest-based methods.

Of Mimicry and Money

The practices of establishing shariah compliance became evident to me in late 2013 when, over the course of two weeks, I accompanied Uzair on a series of negotiations with bankers and other finance professionals as he sought to raise funds in Kuala Lumpur for a sukuk that would be based on housing mortgages for clients in Australia. Uzair was the CEO of Tasbih Financial, a company headquartered in Sydney that offered financial services to Muslims who wanted to comply with religious injunctions on economic action. He had started the firm after graduating with a degree in finance from the business school of a large Australian university. He approached Islamic finance as a technical problem and was not particularly interested in theological disputes or moral conundrums. He sought to find pragmatic solutions to problems that he saw facing Muslims in his community. One of the biggest challenges faced by Muslims in the West is purchasing a home without resorting to interest-bearing debt. He told me that even clients of his firm who could easily obtain a conventional mortgage would avoid doing so simply because they did not want to engage in what he called the "riba economy." He had come to Malaysia hoping to create a home financing product that would not violate Qur'anic prohibitions on the collection of interest. Uzair's efforts to convince Islamic financial firms operating in Kuala Lumpur to issue and invest in a sukuk, consisting of a vast pool of Australian home mortgages that would be bundled and securitized, illustrated the pivotal role that Malaysia plays in global Islamic finance. Practitioners from around the world view it as the place to conduct Islamic financial transactions.

Uzair and I had met at an event hosted by ISRA and, after learning about my interests in the everyday practices of Islamic finance, he invited me to attend some of the negotiations he had scheduled in Kuala Lumpur. Since he was on his own, he thought that having me along might lend some credibility to his undertaking: he introduced me as an "advisor" to his firm. As we sat in the back of a taxi on the way to a meeting at a major global Islamic bank with sizable operations in Malaysia, he

lamented the fact that the chief obstacle he faced in launching his sukuk
was that no Australian bank wanted to get involved in Islamic finance.
Uzair had accumulated a vast database of thousands of Australian Muslims who wanted shariah-compliant mortgages, but there were no domestic institutions capable of offering such arrangements. He had compiled all requisite legal documentation for the sukuk and had extensive
demand for the mortgages, but he told me that several bankers had told
him that public sentiment after the events of September 11, 2001, had
caused Australian banks to be leery of any association with Islam. The
management of one large bank he had approached was interested but
had faced vehement objections when presenting the idea to the board
of directors. He recalled one agitated director asking, "We don't do Jew-
ish finance or Christian finance, so why should we do Islamic finance?"
The secular position—the notion that commerce and religion should be
kept separate under the presumption that this was the best way to ensure
religious tolerance and equality—served as a means to foreclose participation in Islamic finance. In the eyes of people such as the skittish director, offering a product that was specifically labeled "Islamic" would
make it appear as if the bank was predisposed toward Islam in contrast to
other religions.

Uzair realized that finding an Australian bank to take the lead on his
sukuk was made more difficult in the context of the resurgence of age-
old misconceptions and fears regarding Islam, rekindled over a decade of
conflicts that were often cast as a struggle between the West and Islam.
Although no one had stated these fears explicitly, Uzair concluded that
he would never be able to find the backing for Islamic home mortgages
in Australia, and he would thus remain unable to fulfill the needs of Muslims in his community. After explaining the problem he faced, he said
optimistically, "I believe the Australian solution is here, in Malaysia!" He
was convinced that he could find willing participants in Malaysia, either at
foreign banks with operations in the country or among domestic financial
institutions. Several factors led him to see Malaysia as the solution to the
difficulties he faced at home. Among these was the fact that many influential Islamic financial services firms had operations in Kuala Lumpur.
Other considerations included the well-developed legal infrastructure
and the favorable tax concessions available in Malaysia as an incentive to
make it a site for sukuk origination. Finally, he told me that it was a great
place to market the sukuk: large institutional investors (such as pension
funds) were seeking safe Islamic investments and were eligible for govern-

ment incentives to make such investments due to state support for Islamic finance.

When we arrived at the meeting with Asian Participation Bank (APB) in central Kuala Lumpur, not far from the landmark Petronas Towers, we were ushered into a small circular conference room. This bank is based in the Middle East but has substantial operations in Malaysia. Two employees of the bank, Fauziah and Arif, both Malaysian nationals, shortly joined us in the room. Fauziah, the senior member of the pair, had a brusque but approachable demeanor and feverishly took notes throughout the meeting. She spoke quickly and had a no-nonsense attitude. Arif was more reserved and asked precise technical questions about the details of the transactions that Uzair proposed.

Uzair began by calmly describing the terms of his sukuk proposal with impressive mastery of the intricacies of the deal. He sought to find a "lead issuer" for a $500 million sukuk based on Australian home mortgages.[3] He explained to Fauziah and Arif that the average mortgage in Australia is worth roughly $200,000. His client database contained a waiting list of over six thousand Australian Muslims who wanted a "shariah-compliant" mortgage, so he was confident that there was a market of up to $1.2 billion in potential mortgages that such a sukuk could support. The two Islamic bankers were mildly disappointed when he mentioned that his proposal would generate returns of only about 3 percent per year. However, they perked up slightly when he noted that the advantage of the deal was that there was very little risk due to low default rates on home mortgages in Australia: around 2 percent. While the proceeds would be relatively modest, they would be reliable, and the risk in the deal could be easily "managed." Essentially, Uzair was proposing that APB take the lead role in the deal by fronting the initial $100 million, and then they would work together to convince other banks to put up the remaining $400 million. Tasbih Financial would then handle the retail end of the deal by conducting the necessary paperwork with each prospective homeowner to facilitate the home purchases.

Uzair suggested that the absence of Islamic market devices created social dislocation and other problems in the Muslim community in Australia. Although he was relatively young, only in his midforties, he carried the burden of his community back in Sydney. He suggested that they were relying on him to resolve their financial impasse, a responsibility that he took seriously. At several points Uzair implored APB to get involved based on a sense of obligation to members of the ummah who lived outside the Muslim world. He framed his proposed sukuk as not merely a business transaction motivated by profit but as a means to "help the community," a phrase that he invoked several times during the conversation. He told Fauziah and Arif that Muslims in Australia had pleaded with him to "help get us out of our riba mortgages." He explained that the inability to obtain shariah-compliant home financing in Australia had created discord in Muslim families. One story he recounted concerned the elderly parents of some Muslim immigrants to Australia who joined their adult children several years after the latter had immigrated but refused to live with them because they "didn't want to die in a riba house." In these cases the parents would rent a flat separate from their children to avoid compromising religious principles and jeopardizing their chance for salvation. As Fauziah and Arif nodded their heads sympathetically, he told the story of a couple who had divorced because of disagreements over purchasing a home using a conventional mortgage. The husband felt they had no other choice, but the wife was morally opposed to paying interest. When they could not reconcile these different orientations, they ultimately decided to separate.

As the two parties negotiated, there was as much consideration of the shariah issues attendant in the proposal as there was of the business dimensions. As discussed in the next chapter, there are a multitude of shariah questions regarding home financing in global Islamic finance, as the definition of a shariah-compliant mortgage is highly contested. Indeed, Fauziah and Arif seemed as intent on evaluating the religious credentials of Uzair's proposal as they were on its capacity to generate profit. Uzair seemed conscious of this and framed the negotiation in such a way as to alleviate their concerns. Each mortgage agreement securitized through the sukuk would be based on the diminishing musharaka contract. Uzair explained that the model he sought to use had been developed by Guidance Financial Group, an Islamic financial services company that is the largest provider of shariah-compliant mortgages in the United States, having financed over $2 billion in such mortgages.[4] Several times he noted the highly respected status of Guidance's shariah committee, which was made up of some of the most well-known names in international shariah advisory services. He underlined the fact that a prominent shariah scholar who was both a native and resident of the same country as APB's headquarters had approved the Guidance structure that he planned to use in the Tasbih product. Although this particular scholar was extremely well known, Fauziah and Arif appeared unimpressed by Uzair's name-dropping. Fauziah responded by saying that any deal they engaged in had to be approved by the shariah boards of both APB's Malaysian subsidiary and the headquarters in the Middle East. Thus there were two in-house shariah boards that would have to evaluate any proposed deal.

Fauziah and Arif repeatedly sought to evaluate whether the proposed Tasbih sukuk was worth presenting to their shariah advisory board. After hearing a general outline of the deal, Fauziah asked: "Is the rent linked to the real economy or to a benchmark?" Her question was intended to find out whether the profit due to the financial institution was based on market interest rates, such as the LIBOR rate, or was indexed to property market rental rates, which is viewed as a more authentic version of Islamic finance (see chapter 5). Uzair's response was somewhat evasive, saying that the margin "would be arrived at through negotiation." This response alluded to a core principle of a valid shariah contract. According to most shariah scholars a legitimate sale requires three elements: parties to the contract (a buyer and a seller), a subject matter, and offer and acceptance (*sighah*) (Lahsasna 2014, 85–90). According to many scholars, negotiation through offer and acceptance is the "primary condition of any contract" because "it reflects the consent of the parties" (Lahsasna 2014, 85). Uzair sidestepped the issue of whether the rate was based on a benchmark such as LIBOR by claiming its religious legitimacy on the basis of sighah. Tasbih would offer the mortgages at a specific rate and home buyers were free to either accept or reject that rate. Uzair elaborated on the market nature of the negotiations by explaining, "If I drive someone to the airport, we negotiate over the price and then do it. There is no shariah question once everyone agrees out of their own free will." By analogy, then, he suggested that the origin of the rate did not matter, as long as both parties in the transaction found the terms acceptable. Nonetheless, Fauziah scarcely concealed a concerned frown that revealed that she was not entirely placated by Uzair's justifications.

The three of them continued to discuss the details of the proposal, but Fauziah returned several times to the problem of the basis for the figure of 3 percent as the return on each mortgage contract, at one point asking pointedly, "So, are you calculating backwards?" Again, this question was framed by the problem of religious authenticity. It alluded to the relatively common practice whereby Islamic financial institutions figure out the rate needed to earn market interest rates on an investment by reverse calculation. In other words, a firm would decide in advance that a deal was only worthwhile if it yielded a "profit" of 3 percent. They would then figure out what the markup should be in terms of money over time. Although the word "interest" never appeared in the documentation of the deal, the prevailing market interest rate was effectively the benchmark against which the profit rate was set. Uzair quickly responded, "No, no! We never use a percentage to set the rent. We always use a dollar figure." Again Fauziah appeared unconvinced. Uzair claimed that the profit rate was set through negotiation and not linked to the prevailing interest rate, but he did not provide any evidence to dispel the impression that the profit rate charged in the mortgages was indexed to market interest rates and not arrived at through reference to the "real" economy.

Several times during the meeting Uzair revealed further how the sukuk he was proposing replicated existing conventional financial structures rather than synthesizing a wholly new instrument from abstract Islamic principles. In this sense it illustrated the mechanisms of shariah compliance in Islamic finance. The fact that the Tasbih sukuk was derived from conventional finance was evident in the language he used to describe and explain it, including in other negotiations I attended with him. The replicative nature of the instrument that Uzair was proposing was reflected in his recurrent reference to the fact that on several occasions he remarked that the Tasbih sukuk "mimicked" a conventional bond. For example, when he described the Guidance mortgage-backed sukuk on which the Tasbih contract was based, he said that the instrument "mimics the conventional but is shariah compliant." Later, when describing how in a diminishing musharaka the rent paid to the financial institution decreases with each payment while the principal paid by the mortgage holder increases, he said it was "like a conventional mortgage because it mimics a conventional amortization schedule."

Conventional financial instruments served as a sort of baseline, and their Islamic counterparts were interpreted by contrast against the conventional baseline. To take another example, again describing the amortization schedule for a diminishing musharaka, Uzair said that "mortgage payments decrease based on a reduced balance . . . but this is how conventional [finance] works also." Later when he offhandedly responded to a question about how profit was calculated on a mortgage document, he said, "That's how the Guidance model gets away with it," suggesting that Islamic finance was premised on finding loopholes and workarounds, satisfying the letter of Islamic law without necessarily conforming to its spirit. Indeed Uzair did little to conceal that he saw achieving shariah compliance as a matter of bending shariah principles as far as possible without breaking them. It was as if he took conventional finance for granted and saw shariah as a set of formal rules with which he had to comply, rather than offering autonomous principles for economic action.

The Religiosity of Risk

After the meeting at APB, Uzair and I sat in a trendy coffee shop beneath Kuala Lumpur's iconic Petronas Towers while he explained why the problem of shariah compliance figured so prominently in the discussion of the deal. Uzair said that the shariah advisory board for APB had a reputation for being rigid in its shariah interpretations, so Fauziah and Arif had to be cautious about getting involved with any transaction that had little chance of success. Uzair said that shariah approval was an especially fraught issue in Islamic finance due to "shariah noncompliance risk": the risk an Islamic bank faces if a product they label Islamic is subsequently challenged and found not to be shariah compliant. Uzair's expression turned grave, and he said that this is a major consideration for Islamic banks. "Just one transaction could create huge problems in terms of public perception and among the shareholders of the bank."

Shariah noncompliance risk presents a unique problem for Islamic finance professionals because it does not lend itself to probabilistic forecasting and statistical modeling in the same fashion as the other types of risk with which they are familiar. As one banking professional, Ariff, told me, shariah noncompliance risk presented a unique challenge to Islamic finance, because unlike other forms of risk, "it cannot be measured." Whereas banks had models to calculate market or credit risk, he said, "no one can quantify shariah risk." Some shariah scholars had a reputation for unpredictable rulings, and bankers feared the possibility that a ruling or statement by a scholar could have disastrous consequences for their institutions or even the industry as a whole. Indeed, there had been several notable instances in which statements by shariah scholars had precipitated controversy and instability in the Islamic finance industry.

The most often-cited instance of the threat posed by shariah noncompliance risk occurred in 2008 when the shariah board of AAOIFI, headed by the Pakistani jurist Taqi Usmani, ruled that 85 percent of the sukuk under issue around the world were not compliant with shariah (Maurer 2010, 34). The main problem highlighted by AAOIFI was that most sukuk were asset based rather than asset backed (Usmani 2008). AAOIFI objected to the fact that there was no legal transfer of ownership of the underlying assets to the sukuk investors. As with many conventional bonds, investors did not have recourse to liquidate the underlying asset in the event of a default on payments. According to industry professionals this ruling created a great deal of consternation and hand-wringing in Islamic finance, from Malaysia to London. One professor at INCEIF noted that in the years following the announcement there was a "50 percent drop in sukuk issuance" globally, although he offered the caveat that this decline also coincided with the 2008 financial crisis, so it may not have been wholly due to the inflammatory AAOIFI ruling.

Nonetheless, the anxiety that the ruling precipitated among industry professionals was palpable. In 2010 I interviewed a partner at one of Kuala Lumpur's leading law firms that handled Islamic finance deals. In animated terms, he told me that the potential to be labeled noncompliant was what made Islamic finance "unpredictable" and unable to compete with its conventional counterpart. In exasperated tones he asked, "How do you manage that kind of risk? . . . Who will pay for the losses?" He underscored the difficulty in properly valuing and hedging against such risk, rhetorically asking, "How do you arrange a capital charge for shariah noncompliance risk?" Shariah noncompliance risk stemming from the prospect of unfavorable shariah rulings was one of the chief obstacles in designing an alternative financial system in which shariah scholars, who in some cases might have interests that diverge substantially from those of the bankers, exercise a considerable degree of authority and could invalidate a whole category of assets based on a new or reconsidered interpretation.

After explaining shariah compliance risk, Uzair turned to some of the politics of shariah advisory and the important role of high-profile scholars in lending credibility to institutions and reducing the risk inherent in the interpretive practices of evaluating shariah instruments. One way in which firms seek to minimize shariah noncompliance risk is through the use of a core group of well-regarded shariah scholars. He said that his firm had a "tier one shariah board," meaning that its shariah supervisory board was composed of scholars who also are members of the AAOIFI shariah committee. This committee consists of twenty scholars who are among the most renowned and influential shariah scholars in Islamic finance. A relatively small firm like Tasbih Financial needs recognized scholars on its shariah board to facilitate transactions with other firms. When Tasbih is in negotiations to close a deal, the shariah boards of the Islamic financial institutions with whom it is working will more readily approve the products given the presence of recognizable, high-profile scholars on the Tasbih side who have already approved the deal. Uzair said that if a firm creates a shariah board consisting of scholars who are not well known, then the transactions in which they engage will be subject to increased scrutiny. In these cases, he noted it could take "six months or more" to complete the shariah review process, because the shariah board for the partner institution will exercise greater caution. In part, this explains why a number of shariah scholars exercise outsized influence on shariah advisory services. A small group of about three dozen influential shariah scholars sit on multiple shariah advisory boards around the world, forming what has been referred to as a "global shariah elite" (Bassens, Derudder, and Witlox 2012). Like leading lawyers, doctors, and financiers, prominent shariah scholars constitute a professional elite for whom there is a global demand and high compensation. Furthermore, their opinions and actions carry a great deal of weight in the global industry.

The Hegemony of Interest

Several days after our meeting with APB, Uzair invited me to accompany him to another meeting he had arranged in hopes of finding a potential lead issuer for the Tasbih sukuk. He only had a few days remaining in Malaysia before he was to travel to an Islamic finance conference in Saudi Arabia, where he hoped to network and drum up interest in the sukuk. However, he had yet to obtain a visa from the Saudi embassy. As we waited for our appointed meeting time in the minimalist lobby at a gleaming new central Kuala Lumpur office tower, Uzair chuckled about his travel frustrations in a surprisingly breezy manner. He explained that the delay was due to the fact that after the hajj season the Saudi government was "tight with visas" because it sought to "cleanse the country" of foreign pilgrims who remained in the country in hopes of finding work following the end of the hajj season. Uzair's travel itinerary from Australia to Malaysia and then on to Saudi Arabia demonstrated how Islamic finance is configuring an alternative financial space that links global Islamic cities in Southeast Asia and the Middle East.

Our meeting was with the Islamic subsidiary of CreditBank, a Western-based bank that had opened its Islamic arm in Malaysia only two years previously. The tenor of the conversation differed markedly from the earlier meeting. Whereas the APB representatives worried openly about the shariah credentials of the Tasbih sukuk, for the two CreditBank employees concerns regarding the religious permissibility were of little importance compared to questions about the profit potential of the deal. Uzair later explained that the reason that religious questions, and specifically the issue of shariah compliance, framed the conversation with the APB representatives was that it was a fully Islamic bank, based in the Middle East, with no conventional operations. In contrast, CreditBank was a bank headquartered in a North Atlantic country that had only recently begun to expand its Islamic operations. The contrast in the concerns of the representatives of the two institutions revealed the internal dynamics of Islamic finance and especially the degree to which religious concerns inflect the day-to-day operations of Islamic banks.

Our meeting with CreditBank was held less than a mile away from APB's Malaysian headquarters, but whereas APB's offices were in an older, concrete building that dated from an earlier real estate boom in Kuala Lumpur, CreditBank's headquarters were located in one of the city's most fashionable new steel and glass office towers. Unlike in APB's offices, there was a strict separation between workspaces and meeting spaces, which meant that our meeting offered absolutely no insight into the labor routines of CreditBank. Whereas the APB offices appeared well used, with papers, files, reports, and other materials scattered haphazardly on desks amid a warren of cubicles decorated according to the personal style of their occupants, the CreditBank offices were completely uncluttered, appearing antiseptic and empty. After we arrived, there was some confusion, as the contact with whom Uzair had originally planned the meeting was absent and we were shuffled between increasingly imposing meeting rooms for the better part of an hour. Eventually we were seated in what appeared to be the most formal meeting room, spartanly decorated in the latest Scandinavian style of blond wood and frosted glass, at an expansive table that could easily have accommodated at least a dozen participants. The main appeal of the room was an impressive view of downtown Kuala Lumpur that stretched all the way to its northern extremities and suburbs.

Eventually we were joined by Firman, who explained that he was responsible for "Islamic structuring" at CreditBank. However, he was hesitant to begin discussion of Uzair's proposal until we were joined by his colleague, Chai Leng, who was tied up with other business but who, we were assured, would join us momentarily. As we waited, Firman explained that while CreditBank had operated in Malaysia for some time, it had only received an Islamic banking license from Malaysia's Central Bank three years previously, so its Islamic operations were still in their infancy. In fact, he continued, they had only done a handful of Islamic deals in their first few years of existence. Furthermore, he explained, of the roughly seventy employees working in their Kuala Lumpur offices, only four were "on the Islamic side." Thus, he explained, there was a great degree of overlap and "collaboration" between the Islamic and conventional operations of the bank. Firman defined the respective roles in his division, explaining that on most of CreditBank's Islamic finance deals, Chai Leng "provides the economic structure," while Saiful, the chief executive for CreditBank's Islamic subsidiary and Firman's boss, "helps to make it Islamic." Again, the way in which Islamic finance was construed suggested a concern with fulfilling formal properties: a device was tested for shariah compliance and tweaked as needed to ensure religious permissibility.

Nonetheless, Firman explained that such checks were necessary because of Malaysia's reputation in terms of rigid state management of Islamic finance. He explained that "the segregation between the conventional and Islamic side is guaranteed." He said that the two sides of CreditBank had a "shared platform" but "the products are always segregated." Firman contrasted Malaysia's rigor with the regulations governing CreditBank's operations in Bahrain and Dubai, places where, he said, "the conventional side could offer Islamic-branded products" that were Islamic "in name only." In contrast, the Malaysian Central Bank and the country's Securities Commission required a strict segregation of funds, accounts, and capital. In Malaysia, companies that did not ensure a "firewall" between accounts faced the prospect of heavy fines and even the possibility of the revocation of their Islamic banking license.

The close links between the conventional and Islamic operations at CreditBank were further revealed after Chai Leng arrived. It quickly became apparent that he was the executive member of the team. Firman was largely a spectator, while Chai Leng took the lead role in scrutinizing the particulars of the sukuk deal proposed by Uzair. As the head of a division called Debt Capital Markets, he ran the bond operations for the bank and had a particular expertise in residential mortgage-backed securities, the very credit devices that precipitated the 2008 financial crisis in the United States. As the meeting unfolded, it became clear that he was not a Muslim. After the preliminary contours of the proposal were presented, Chai Leng began to confront him with increasingly incisive questions.

Unlike the APB meeting, in which most of the conversation concerned efforts to evaluate the shariah credibility of Uzair's proposal, the CreditBank representatives made no pretense about the fact that ascertaining the potential profitability of the deal was their preeminent concern. Discussion of interest and interest rates dominated the conversation. In our previous meeting at APB, Fauziah and Ariff were greatly concerned with the source of the profit that the bank would earn and whether it was indexed to prevailing interest rates, but Chai Leng and Firman demonstrated a complete lack of concern regarding these issues, instead focusing on the relationship between market interest rates and the profits that the bank might expect from the deal. Chai Leng had clearly done some research before the meeting and had a firm grip on the scale of returns conducive to an attractive and profitable deal. This became apparent when he expressed disappointment about the prospective profits that Uzair's proposal offered. Chai Leng's dissatisfaction with the deal was mainly due to the fact that the "spread" between an Australian sovereign bond,[5] which was currently about 3 percent, and the Tasbih sukuk, which was in the neighborhood of 4.5 percent, was not very attractive.

Uzair, with the measured countenance of an experienced salesman, tried to smooth things over by explaining that they could probably push the price of the sukuk closer to 5.5 percent because "people in Australia are ready to pay a premium" for a shariah-compliant product. Chai Leng expressed surprise at hearing that some consumers would pay more than market interest rates just to get a mortgage that complied with religious prescriptions. With raised eyebrows conveying a measure of disbelief, he sarcastically intoned, "I need to go to Australia!" His apparent incredulity that Australian Muslims would pay above market interest rates for their mortgages prompted Firman to make his first foray into the conversation since his colleague had appeared, chiming in, "Muslims in the US, UK, and Australia are different than Muslims in Malaysia. They are willing to pay more for products if they want to make sure that they are halal." Perhaps due to the small scale of Islamic financial activity at the bank compared to its conventional portfolio, Firman felt compelled to make a case not for this particular deal but for the sake of the bank's very involvement in Islamic finance.

It quickly became apparent that Chai Leng was wholly unconcerned with the religious questions in Islamic finance, aside from a solitary declaration that "Islamic [bond] structures must be globally accepted to be marketable." Furthermore, his colleague's intervention aside, Chai Leng remained skeptical about the fact that consumers might pay more for a mortgage solely based on religious piety. Indeed, the reluctance of consumers to pay a so-called shariah premium was regularly articulated. Just the previous day I had heard the same sentiment expressed by the CEO of a Malaysia-based competitor of CreditBank's in a workshop at INCEIF. The CEO was addressing the challenges Islamic finance faced in non-Muslim countries and invoked a conversation he had had with a sibling who lived in the United Kingdom. The sibling had sought a shariah-compliant mortgage but ultimately decided to use a conventional device. The CEO said that in Britain, Islamic mortgage rates are "2 to 3 percent higher than conventional rates." He continued, "I was discussing the situation with my brother, who lives in London. He's the son of an imam and a true Muslim, but when he found out how much more an Islamic mortgage would cost compared to a conventional one, he said 'Islam obliges us to make many sacrifices, but it doesn't require us to be worse off!'" The tension between complying with religious injunctions and economic decision making was a recurrent object of reflection among Islamic finance professionals.

The sukuk negotiation accelerated when Chai Leng began to press Uzair on specific details of the proposal. He refused to beat around the bush, asking, "What kind of profits will *you* make?" Uzair sought to avoid the question, but Chai Leng kept pressing, quickly calculating that Tasbih would make roughly 1 percent on the deal. He then asked Uzair how much "seed capital" he already had to put into the project. Uzair said that "several high-net-worth individuals" had "committed to help out." Chai Leng found this justification unconvincing, which Uzair quickly realized, supplementing it with the claim that he had "a commitment from the Islamic Development Bank to buy in." Chai Leng was somewhat satisfied but brought the meeting to a conclusion by telling Uzair that he was doing "conduit financing." In other words, he said that Tasbih was doing nothing more than playing the role of a middleman, liaising between capital-holding banks and mortgage-hungry consumers. Chai Leng suggested that Uzair's firm was not taking enough risk to warrant their profit from the deal, which amounted to about 1 percent of the $500 million total. "At the end of the day," he continued, Uzair "would have to demonstrate that Tasbih has some skin in the game" if he wanted CreditBank to get involved. With this, he brought the meeting to a close, and we left the office. Uzair appeared mildly disappointed with how the meeting had unfolded but maintained the optimistic countenance of a salesman.

The discussions regarding the Tasbih sukuk illustrated the debates over shariah compliance and the varying degrees to which different banks were concerned with fulfilling religious obligations. CreditBank also had a shariah board for both its international and Malaysian operations. However, the tone of the meeting suggested that employees at CreditBank were much less wary of obtaining approval from their board, whereas the potential opinions of the shariah committee were an ever-present specter at APB. Furthermore, the CreditBank meeting illustrated that although technically Islamic finance is supposed to be interest free, it is often framed by calculations based on prevailing interest rates. Although the Tasbih sukuk was based on a diminishing musharaka contract, in which the amount of a creditor's profits are linked to market rental rates rather than interest rates, during the meeting at CreditBank the discussion repeatedly revolved around interest rates: either the Reserve Bank of Australia's cash rate, the rate of Australian treasury securities, or market interest rates. Both Chai Leng and Uzair frequently used the idiom of "spreads," which referred to the difference between the prime rate and the rate that the sukuk would pay. Tasbih was working within the logic of shariah compliance rather than the more challenging paradigm of shariah-based Islamic finance. This begged the question of how Islamic finance might be reformed to be shariah based. The CreditBank meeting illustrated that for the most part, sukuk deals and the discourse surrounding them are constrained by the fact that it is difficult to imagine securitizing home mortgages without reference to interest rates. Both the individual mortgages in which home buyers must enroll and the securities issued based on bundling multiple mortgages together are perhaps unavoidably indexed to interest rates.

The type of shariah-compliant Islamic finance evident in Uzair's sukuk deal does not challenge the hegemony of interest-based debt as an organizing principle for financial action and financial relationships. Although sukuk are often lauded as the most successful instrument used in Islamic finance, they do not present an alternative to the preoccupation with formal differences that characterizes most Islamic finance today. Sukuk offered similar guarantees as conventional bonds and, as the Tasbih sukuk discussions revealed, remained constrained by the logic of debt and the hegemony of interest.

One Islamic economist who was deeply critical of Islamic finance as currently practiced, Dr. Mustafa, was also an outspoken critic of sukuk. He taught at a Malaysian university and wrote extensively about experiments to improve Islamic finance. Although he was very busy and in high demand, he seemed to take an interest in my project and was curious about why an anthropologist was interested in Islamic finance. I chatted with him regularly over the course of several years of fieldwork in Malaysia, and I was surprised one day when he launched into a vehement diatribe against sukuk. Although Malaysia has been one of the pioneers in sukuk, Mustafa argued that they were an example of how Islamic finance had been infiltrated by the logic of debt and had not adequately embraced the equity-based orientation that he viewed as the central distinguishing feature of Islamic finance compared to its conventional counterpart.

Mustafa asserted that debt-based instruments such as sukuk that make up most of Islamic finance were merely "adaptations from conventional finance," not innovations that had been synthesized from inherently Islamic principles. Sukuk, he continued, "are all sold to big financial institutions and don't end up benefiting individual citizens who need Islamic finance." He suggested that Islamic finance, like conventional finance, disproportionately benefited the wealthy who held investment portfolios that could be filled up with instruments such as sukuk. In contrast, he believed that authentic Islamic finance was an instrument to reduce poverty and improve the welfare of the less fortunate. Observing the fact that returns on sukuk often mirror prevailing interest rates, he said, "At the end of the day, sukuk are not really Islamic investments because . . . they rely on the LIBOR rate of return, just like conventional bonds." The fact that Islamic finance simply reengineered conventional financial instruments led Dr. Mustafa to conclude that globalization was foreclosing the possibility of alternative systems of thought and elicited "convergence" from competitors. The Islamic system would ultimately mirror the conventional system: "It's like when the parasite starts looking like the host," he explained. For Dr. Mustafa and other reformers, then, the main challenge for Islamic finance is to develop "shariah-based" instruments that, in his words, "don't replicate" conventional structures but instead are grounded in classical Islamic contracts.

This chapter has documented the operations of shariah-compliant Islamic finance in the fabrication and negotiation of sukuk, one of the industry's most celebrated devices. In documenting a series of sales negotiations over a proposed sukuk, I have illustrated how experts balance the competing demands of religious and financial logic. These debates demonstrate that in practice Islamic finance is often framed by its conventional counterpart. In the following chapter I argue that shariah-compliant Islamic finance rests on a methodological orientation distinct from the methods that characterize shariah-based Islamic finance. I show how the formal approach used in shariah-compliant Islamic finance lends itself to relatively easy replication of conventional financial instruments. I then document contemporary experiments in Islamic finance as experts seek to synthesize shariah-based instruments, which are viewed as having more religious credibility and authenticity.

CHAPTER FIVE

Adjacent System or Original Knowledge?

In Malaysia, Islamic finance was at a crossroads by the 2010s. Sukuk had become a popular new financial device that had generated widespread enthusiasm in the national and international business media. Islamic finance had been lauded due to the perception that Islamic financial institutions had weathered the 2008 crisis better than their conventional counterparts. This led to a common conviction that something intrinsic to Islamic finance yielded a more stable system for the provision of capital. Yet at the same time a vociferous debate emerged over the extent to which it offered an authentic alternative to conventional finance. Criticism was in part precipitated by claims among Islamic finance experts that it "mimicked" conventional finance and conformed to the hegemony of interest. Reformers raised questions about the authenticity of Islamic financial practices, which conformed to the letter but not necessarily the spirit of Islamic law. They advocated moving away from shariah compliance as the standard for Islamic financial devices and toward creating ones that they called "shariah based."

This chapter has two goals. First, I document three reasons why the question of religious authenticity was recurrently posed during the period in which I conducted fieldwork. I argue that this was due in large measure to increasingly vocal criticism of Islamic finance. The financial crisis of 2008 presented the possibility that if Islamic finance was not substantially differentiated from conventional finance, it would suffer the same cycles of cataclysm that plagued conventional finance. Malaysian experts were convinced that a more authentic, shariah-based version of Islamic finance would enable greater transnational integration of Malaysia's Islamic financial system, especially in the countries of the GCC. Moving toward a standard of shariah-based Islamic finance was seen as a constitutive element in the broader project of making Malaysia a global hub for Islamic finance.

The second goal of the chapter is to demonstrate that the difference between the practices of shariah-compliant and shariah-based Islamic finance reflect fundamentally different conceptualizations of the relationship between Islamic and secular knowledge. The difference between the ways in which these systems of thought are represented is largely visible in the distinctive methodological orientation of each approach. Those who deploy shariah compliance as the standard according to which specific financial devices and practices can be deemed permissible subscribe to a formalist epistemology. In this approach the method of determining compatibility with Islam entails testing conventional financial tools and instruments against the litmus of shariah. In other words, existing devices are evaluated against a standard interpretation of Islam, and if they do not explicitly contradict Islamic maxims, they are deemed shariah compliant. A guiding principle of the formalist approach is that any action or object *not explicitly identified* as impermissible in the texts is permissible. This method presumes that Islamic and secular knowledge are parallel systems of thought that are both equally valid.

In contrast, shariah-based Islamic finance does not presume two systems of distinct but commensurable knowledge between which devices can be translated. Rather, Islam reveals truths that exist prior to and independent of secular knowledge. Secular knowledge can be deployed to confirm and better understand the truths revealed in the texts, but these truths are independently valid, irrespective of the truths produced through disciplines such as economics. In this sense, the methods deployed in the shariah-based version of Islamic finance are substantive, insofar as they entail starting with key principles drawn from the Qur'an and hadiths, as well as economic practices historically used in Islam, in an effort to synthesize devices distinctive to Islamic finance. While this project is more ambitious and requires a greater investment of thought and labor, it also can lay claim to greater independence, insofar as it does not seek to adapt conventional financial instruments by testing them for shariah compliance according to a binary logic of permissibility/impermissibility, seeking rather to create a new financial infrastructure from the bottom up. Instead of borrowing conventional financial devices and instruments and then evaluating them against the litmus of religious permissibility, it seeks to synthesize new instruments using tools and techniques distinctive to the discursive tradition and history of Islam.

Problems of Authenticity

The authenticity of Islamic finance became a particularly pressing issue for experts in the 2010s due to a number of critical appraisals of Islamic finance in the popular media, on blogs and other online forums, and in scholarly literature. Interlocutors in Malaysia and elsewhere often invoked academic criticism as a rationale for the need to reform the industry. Foremost among these critiques were texts by prominent Western-based economists that were highly critical of Islamic economics and Islamic finance. One of the most vocal critics, Timur Kuran (an economist based at Duke University), argued that Islamic economics is a regressive political project based on a "nostalgic escape into the imagined simplicity, harmony, and prosperity of an ancient social order" (Kuran 2004, 4) and argued that "in proposing that an Islamic economy will promote harmony, growth, and justice simultaneously, Islamic economics enhances the appeal of an Islamic political order" (Kuran 2004, 6). Similarly, Mahmoud El-Gamal argued that Islamic finance entails rent-seeking "shariah arbitrage" (El-Gamal 2006, 11), in which practitioners use "structured finance technologies . . . to separate would-be borrowers or lenders from interest-bearing loans" in the "forms of multiple trades, or special purpose vehicles, and the like" (El-Gamal 2006, 23). In contrast, El-Gamal sought to identify the substantive principles on which an Islamic economic order would be based by applying "the substantive spirit of Islamic Law" (El-Gamal 2006, 25) to identify a more authentic Islamic finance, which he argues should be premised on "efficiency and fair-pricing" (El-Gamal 2006, 1). El-Gamal's focus on market efficiency in his version of Islamic finance echoes some of the bedrock principles of neoclassical economics, a view that is perhaps not terribly surprising given his training in conventional economics. In sum, both Kuran and El-Gamal see contemporary Islamic finance as little more than conventional finance adorned with a thin and mostly transparent Islamic veneer.

Such criticism, questioning the legitimacy of Islamic finance and voiced by mainstream economists based at prominent American universities, precipitated no small degree of soul-searching by Islamic finance experts. However, more threatening according to many of those with whom I interacted was the financial cataclysm that began with the US mortgage crisis in 2008 and ricocheted around the world in the succeeding years. Islamic finance experts often represented the crisis in apocalyptic terms. For example, in January 2014 I sat in the audience of a public forum in which an Islamic scholar who had formerly sat on the shariah advisory committee of a major Islamic bank in Malaysia said ominously that the near "collapse of the Euro and the financial crisis are really the collapse of the ethical norms and shared values of all the major civilizations." The comments illustrated the sense of urgency among some experts that Islamic finance had to quickly remake itself into a real alternative due to the all but certain failure of the conventional financial system.

Rais, an expert in fiqh who worked as a researcher at ISRA, told me the crisis gave Islamic scholars a greater conviction that Islamic finance must adhere to "authentic" Islamic principles regarding economic action. Elaborating, he told me a story that he had heard about a conflict between shariah scholars and bankers regarding derivatives prior to the crisis. Bankers had pressed the scholars to approve some derivatives that had been adapted from conventional instruments. However, many scholars saw these derivatives as problematic and had refused to deem them shariah compliant. According to the story, a World Bank report had called scholars "ignorant," suggesting they did not understand the instruments. But after the crisis, one scholar boasted, "Thank God we are ignorant!" because Islamic banks had "weathered the crisis better than conventional banks." Rais said that many scholars took credit for the better performance of IFIs during and after the crisis, and this made them more steadfast in their opposition to certain types of debt-based instruments and those that were especially risky, such as derivatives. In essence, their refusal to recognize the legitimacy of derivatives stemmed from the fact that they were too far removed from "the real economy" and as such were characteristic of interest-based conventional finance.

Finally, Malaysian experts sought to formulate a more authentic form of Islamic finance because they believed that this would support the broader project of becoming the central node in a transnational Islamic financial network. Saif, a shariah scholar with whom I regularly discussed issues in Islamic finance, provided advisory services for the Islamic arm of a major Malaysian Islamic bank. He was quite direct regarding the benefits in moving away from shariah compliance as the standard for Islamic finance in Malaysia and toward a shariah-based system. He explained to me that investors and financiers in the oil-rich countries of the Arabian Gulf were favorably disposed toward many aspects of Malaysia's Islamic financial system, especially how well regulated it was from a banking perspective in comparison to Islamic finance in the Middle East. However, he noted that they were less sanguine about its compatibility with shariah, as certain devices had been deemed permissible by Malaysian shariah scholars but were forbidden by scholars based in the Gulf. Indeed, a common perception in the Middle East was that, in spite of its scrupulous attention to developing banking regulations and a legal framework for Islamic finance, Malaysia was not as rigorous in its adherence to shariah in Islamic finance as was the GCC. Thus, whereas the secular governance of Islamic finance was perhaps the most stringent in the world, there were perceived shortcomings in its religious governance.

As I detail below, this impression is not entirely warranted but maps onto an already-existing spiritual geography in which Muslims from the Middle East, especially Saudi Arabia and the other Gulf countries, perceive their version of Islam as the epitome of religious authenticity. Although this view was sometimes contested by Malaysians, it colored perceptions of global Islamic finance, especially since Malaysia permitted certain contracts, such as the bai al inah (sale and repurchase) and *bai al dayn* (sale of debt), which were prohibited in the GCC countries. Observers interpreted the provisions to tighten shariah compliance as an effort to cement Malaysia's position as a central node in the global Islamic finance network. Saif explained, "If Malaysia wants to be the hub, they have to tighten their shariah compliance, because there is lots of skepticism in the Middle East." To alleviate this uncertainty, moving away from a standard of shariah compliance and reformulating the Islamic financial system according to shariah-based principles appeared to be the proper course of action. Indeed, not only had the Central Bank precipitated the debate over shariah compliance by fostering critique through sponsorship of research and education in Islamic finance, but it was also encouraging experiments to fabricate a shariah-based system, with equity, investment, and profit sharing at its heart.

In practice the binary between shariah-compliant and shariah-based instruments framed the way in which Islamic finance was an emergent phenomenon—one whose ultimate form was yet unknown. Nonetheless, the specter of history loomed large over calls to create a shariah-based Islamic finance, presenting a number of challenges. In the 1970s and 1980s a number of Islamic financial experiments in the Middle East had been attempted but were largely considered to have ended in failure. This perspective was evident in several public presentations that I attended. For example, at a forum at the ultramodern headquarters of Malaysia's Securities Commission in the Bukit Kiara section of Kuala Lumpur, "The Contribution of Islamic Finance Post-Global Financial Crisis," several commentators alluded to the history of the sector. The forum was jointly organized with the Oxford Centre for Islamic Studies and was attended by a number of leading figures in the global Islamic financial network. Iqbal Khan, the founding CEO of HSBC Amanah and a longtime veteran of the Islamic finance industry, addressed the obstacles to creating what he considered a "real" alternative to conventional finance. He said that in the beginning, Islamic finance leaders envisioned creating a shariah-based system grounded in the principles of equity finance and risk sharing that most experts agreed represented the essence of Islamic economic doctrine. He explained:

> When Islamic finance started three and a half decades ago, the founders' intention was to create a system based on musharaka, equity, [and] risk-sharing. They were all committed to doing that. So if you look at the first thirty or so contracts executed by Darul Mal Islamic group, by Al Baraka Group they were equity-based contracts. But neither the societies in which they were executed nor the management competency within the institutions were at a level where they could manage the risks inherent in principal investments. As a result, some very large and very good projects . . . went sour and these financial institutions ended up losing a lot of money. (Securities Commission Malaysia 2010, 100)

Khan explained that as a result of the obstacles to creating an equity-based industry, Islamic finance professionals decided that Islamic finance should conform to existing financial, regulatory, and legal frameworks. He justified this decision by stating that "the choice [was made] to exist within a conventional banking framework. If we had waited for that society to evolve—the social system—the economic system, the political system, we would still be waiting and there would have been no Islamic finance industry. So the founders took a view that we must start what is called a shariah-compliant industry and [later] move . . . from being shariah-compliant to shariah-based" (Securities Commission Malaysia 2010, 100). Khan's point was that Islamic bankers had to make a pragmatic decision to get the industry started. Rather than start with the ideal Islamic financial system, which was shariah-based and premised on risk sharing, and an ethos of partnership and equity financing, they sought instead to start with one that was "shariah compliant." In other words, one that obeyed the formal rules regarding economic action but not necessarily the substantive principles that undergirded those rules. The rapid growth of Islamic finance in subsequent years was based on its reinvention as shariah compliant rather than shariah based.

Imitation or Innovation?

By the 2010s there was visible and vocal discomfort with the degree to which Islamic finance had replicated conventional finance. For example, the former deputy governor of Bank Negara, Dato' Muhammad Razif, who held Malaysia's Islamic finance portfolio at the bank until his untimely death from pancreatic cancer in 2011, openly expressed an interest in shifting away from shariah compliance as the standard for Islamic finance and toward a shariah-based system instead. He stated, "If you critically review, even in Malaysia, [Islamic finance] has been based on imitation rather than innovation. . . . Our starting point is compliance, it's not shariah-based. The bankers right now are converts, conventional bankers transformed into Islamic bankers. Of course [their] mind sets are conventional" (*ISRA Bulletin* 2009a, 1). The fact that the highest official responsible for Islamic finance at the Central Bank sought to move Islamic finance away from a standard of shariah compliance and to a shariah-based one indicated the prominence of this problem and the extent to which it was visible among the highest-level officials and regulators.

The differences in these two different knowledge formations were evident in a spirited debate over the religious permissibility of using intangible assets in Islamic financial transactions. Intangible assets are nonmonetary assets that do not have a physical form but from which future economic benefits are expected (International Accounting Standards Board 2004). These assets are objects with economic value but without tangible materiality, including, for example, such things as computer software, internet domains, audio and visual material, licensing and publishing agreements, and airtime on a cellular network. In conventional finance, the definition and accounting standards for intangible assets are elaborated in Standard 38, which was issued by the International Accounting Standards Board. This board is the accounting standards-setting body of the International Financial Reporting Standards Foundation, a nonprofit accounting standards-setting organization headquartered in London.

According to shariah scholars, intangible assets pose a potential "shariah issue" in that there is a high possibility for gharar in transactions in which they are present. In Islamic finance intangible assets are subject to debate because of their capacity to be "securitized" as the underlying assets in sukuk. As Bill Maurer has shown, mobile phone technology is rapidly challenging established financial practices and monetary regimes, and such disruption was also visible in Islamic finance (Maurer 2015). One practice that was the subject of extensive debate was the securitization of airtime on cellular phone networks.

In discussions of the religious permissibility of securitizing intangible assets, Islamic finance experts most often invoked the Axiata sukuk. In 2012 Axiata, one of Malaysia's largest telecommunications firms, with subsidiaries across Asia, securitized future airtime that it owned by issuing a sukuk valued at $1.5 billion. The sukuk used airtime vouchers, representing an entitlement to a specified number of airtime minutes on the mobile telecommunications networks of its subsidiaries, as an underlying trust asset. Axiata sold the airtime minutes in a block to a special purpose vehicle (a limited company created to fulfill temporary objectives) that issued the sukuk, each share of which represented an ownership interest in the assets (the airtime). The sukuk guaranteed periodic payments consisting of a fixed amount to the investors. On the maturity date of the sukuk the SPV, acting as trustee, was to exercise its option to require the obligor (Axiata) to purchase the assets at a previously defined exercise price, an amount equal to the dissolution amount payable to the investors together with any accrued but unpaid periodic distribution amounts (*Star Online* 2012).

Essentially, Axiata raised capital by securitizing the cellular bandwidth to which it owned the rights and then repurchased the bandwidth at a markup through periodic payments. Referring to the Axiata sukuk, Abas A. Jalil, chief executive officer of Amanah Capital Group, Ltd., a consultancy in Kuala Lumpur, was quoted as saying, "Airtime isn't physically tangible but its value, amount and quantity can be calculated and fixed, therefore it can be used as a Shariah-compliant asset. . . . This is what we call innovation in Islamic finance" (*Star Online* 2012). Axiata used an asset (airtime) that it would sell for revenue in the future to raise capital in the present. Jalil's explanation of the shariah legitimacy of the Axiata structure invoked Dato' Razif's language of innovation and pointed to the experimental nature of this device.

The increasing use of intangible assets as the basis for sukuk—including cellular airtime, intellectual property, and future tariffs on electricity—raised the question of whether the concept of intangible assets itself was specifically Western or whether an analogous concept could be drawn from Islamic texts and history. The shariah legitimacy of intangible assets became a recurrent question for Islamic finance experts. At a public forum at INCEIF, the CEO of an Islamic bank deployed a formalist approach, defending the use of intangible assets as the basis for securitization based on the absence of gharar. Juristic precedent for the prohibition against gharar is based on the hadith described in an earlier chapter in which the prophet Muhammad enjoined against the sale of birds in the air or fish in the sea. The gist of this hadith is that uncaught fish are not an asset. In justifying the permissibility of the sale of cellular airtime, the CEO referred to this hadith but distinguished future airtime from uncaught fish in that its ownership rights were unambiguous. He stated, "Airtime is in the air. It is like the birds in the air or the fish in the sea. But the difference is that you have legal title over the airtime! . . . The airtime is there, but you [also] need to have right to the spectrum. Ownership of the spectrum gives [one] rights over the airtime, which they can sell." In essence, he argued that while there were no clear property rights to uncaught fish in an ocean, discrete portions of cellular bandwidth are intangible assets over which an individual or institution could potentially claim ownership.

However, this view was not universally shared. In November 2013 I attended a workshop hosted by ISRA that was, in the words of one organizer, to discuss whether "there is a shariah issue with regard to intangible assets in sukuk issues and commodity trading." The workshop sought to discern whether such assets were sanctioned in Islam. Prior to the workshop, a draft paper written by researchers at ISRA was circulated for comments by industry professionals, Islamic scholars, shariah compliance officers, and regulators. Formal responses were given by the CEO of an Islamic bank, a shariah scholar working at a major Malaysian Islamic bank, an accounting professor who served as the chief executive of a university in Kuala Lumpur, and an expert in fiqh from a prominent university in Malaysia. The difference between Islamic finance experts whose objective was shariah compliance and those who sought to make Islamic finance shariah based was evident in the differences of opinion between the CEO on one hand and the fiqh expert and the researchers who had drafted the paper on the other.

The workshop took place in a massive conference hall, with ceilings at least three stories high, on the grounds of Lanai Kijang, an opulent employee-training complex built specifically for that purpose by Bank Negara. Lanai Kijang is located about one kilometer west of the main Central Bank complex, in a verdant and slower-paced section of Kuala Lumpur. The fact that the facility was made available for such discussions demonstrated the Central Bank's commitment to fostering the development of Islamic financial knowledge. Inside the outsized hall, there were about a hundred Islamic finance experts in attendance, most of whom worked in the shariah departments of Islamic financial institutions.

The CEO, who had extensive training in both Islamic law and Western civil law, illustrated a formalist approach at the outset of his comments on the paper. He stated, "Given the lack of research in fiqh on intangible assets, [we] might start with experiences in the other legal systems." In the absence of specific guidance in Islamic doctrine, his initial impetus was to identify how other legal traditions had addressed the question of intangible assets. To do so, he invoked a court case that involved the inheritance of the literary estate of Charles Dickens, *Re Dickens*, which raised the question as to whether legal ownership of intellectual property was inherent in a literary manuscript itself or in the "literary work embodied in the manuscript (the intangible asset in which the copyright subsisted)" (Bosworth and Webster 2006, 26). The CEO noted that the court found that, due to the fact that Charles Dickens's will had not explicitly referred to the copyright in bequeathing a literary manuscript, the copyright was included in the estate as a whole rather than in the tangible asset itself: the manuscript. Therefore, the ownership of the copyright could be considered separate from the ownership of the manuscript. This meant that the owner of the manuscript could not publish the manuscript, because the inheritor of the estate held the right of publication, not the individual who had inherited the physical manuscript. By invoking the question of intellectual property in the *Re Dickens* case, the CEO looked to British common law to see how questions regarding the ownership of intangible assets were resolved. Rather than seeking to isolate principles from Islamic knowledge and history that might formulate a distinctive theory of intangible assets from an Islamic perspective, he relativized Islam as one particular knowledge formation among others.

This formalist method represents shariah as an adjacent form of knowledge insofar as it is rendered alongside other systems but with the possibility of translation between the two systems. The formalism underlying his approach was further evident in the way in which the CEO approached the problem of whether intangible assets might be contrary to Islam. Whereas in the first example, the adjacent system was the system of thought represented by British common law, his subsequent move used secular accounting knowledge as the comparison. This amounted to an almost line-by-line reading of Standard 38 by the International Accounting Standards (IAS) Board, which outlines international accounting procedures for intangible assets. The standard was first issued by the IAS Board in 1998 and was revised in 2004. The CEO noted that the standard made clear that an intangible asset must be something that an agent controls and noted that requirements for control were similar to definitions of property according to Islamic legal thought. Again invoking the hadith addressing fish in the sea, he said, "For fish in the water, we have no control. The moment the fisherman has caught the fish, through custom, the fish is under control. . . . If you don't have control, it is not property." He then brought up the issue of the disposal of an intangible asset and noted that Standard 38 states that deferred payment for an intangible asset would be considered at its "cash price equivalent" (International Accounting Standards Board 2004).

After invoking this principle, the CEO stated, "IAS 38 says rights to collect money are no longer intangible assets. This is in line with the shariah view where the right to collect money cannot be traded." He continued, "The shariah says money and receivables cannot be traded except at par. This is the guiding principle. . . . If you look at IAS 38 it also excludes money from trading. . . . Applying the concept of tradability, IAS is compliant with Islamic principles." He then concluded, "If you look at IAS 38 there is no conflict with shariah. Nonphysical *mal* [Arabic for property] should be protected. If you do an analysis of IAS 38, it is fully shariah compliant." In contrast, he said, fiqh scholars were not as consistent in their rulings on intangible assets. "The fiqhi are not coherent, they are vague." Given that he saw no conflict between shariah and the IAS standard on intangible assets, and given the lack of consensus among fiqh scholars on the question of intangible assets, he concluded that it was fully shariah compliant and recommended that it be used without alteration by Islamic finance professionals.

What is of interest here is the CEO's method of determining shariah compliance, which relies on a binary comparison of adjacent systems to establish compliance. It takes a device fabricated outside the tradition of Islam and then tests it against the maxims of Islamic law. If there is nothing in the device that contravenes shariah rules, it is deemed compliant, and there are no objections to its use or deployment as Islamic. Because it focuses on the formal similarities and differences between objects in two contexts, I refer to it as formalist. However, like many formalist approaches, such as structuralism, this method raises questions regarding the historicity of knowledge. The method does not problematize the status of Western knowledge, nor does it question the relationship between Islamic knowledge and Western knowledge (Prakash 1999). Furthermore, it does not question the ontological priority accorded to Western knowledge, which serves as a kind of unstated barometer through the application of what might be thought of as a shariah test (Chakrabarty 2000). Any knowledge that passes such a test is deemed shariah compliant.

In contrast, researchers from ISRA responding to the CEO illustrated how a shariah-based approach to Islamic finance entailed a different method of deploying shariah. Rather than simply testing for compliance, they sought to synthesize original instruments based on religious principles to create definitions that are grounded in shariah. In this sense, the devices created through this method are not achieved through comparison with Western knowledge. Rather than beginning with the already-existing global standard on intangible assets, researchers asked how an intangible asset might be synthesized from a precedent in historical Islamic exegesis. In a presentation that followed the remarks of the CEO, they first sought to identify how an asset had simply been defined in Islam. To do so, they examined how *mal* had been defined in Islamic jurisprudence. The presenters noted that in the Hanafi school there were two "views on the concept of property." The first view, attributed to scholars such as al-Sarakhsi (d. circa 1096), Ibn Nujaym (d. 1536), and Ibn Abidin (d. 1836), "limits property to something that has a physical feature only," such that "usufructs and rights are not regarded as property." However, the researchers found that the Hanafi school lacked a uniform consensus on whether nonmaterial assets could be considered property. For "some Hanafi jurists property is not limited to tangible things only but also includes the intangible, such as usufruct." They invoked the work of al-Kasani (d. 1191), who wrote in the twelfth century that "mal covers the corporeal [*ayn*] as well as usufruct [*manfa'ah*]," thus suggesting the permissibility of intangible assets.

The presenters then noted that of the four main fiqh schools of Sunni jurisprudence, the Shafi'i, Hanbali, and Maliki schools recognized "that property is not limited to tangible assets alone but also includes intangible assets," a position that was also endorsed by influential bodies of shariah scholars in the Muslim world, such as both AAOIFI and the International Islamic Fiqh Academy (IIFA) of the Organisation of Islamic Coopera- tion, the main arbiter for international matters of Islamic jurisprudence. The presenters went on to identify differences in how various authorities responsible for regulating Islamic finance had viewed the exchange of in- tangible assets. They observed that both AAOIFI and the IIFA "prohibit trading futures, options, and receivables in secondary market." However, the presenters went on to point out that other Islamic authorities based in Malaysia came to the opposite conclusion and found that "trading fu- tures, options, and receivables . . . [was] acceptable." Using a methodology that sought to infer how various Islamic thinkers would have approached intangible assets, the presenters demonstrated that there was no singular interpretation of the permissibility or impermissibility of intangible assets in the discursive tradition of Islam.

The workshop ended with no firm resolution to the question of whether intangible assets were permissible, but it did illuminate the questions that intangible assets raised for Islamic finance as practitioners work to cre- ate devices adequate to the complexity of contemporary capitalism. Those who sought a precedent for intangible assets in historical debates over the status of property in Islam exemplified the substantive approach that seeks to reveal an original Islamic position based on interpretation of founda- tional texts and historical practices. This approach sought to fabricate and consolidate an Islamic position by starting with Islamic texts and the writ- ings of previous Islamic scholars. Whereas the formalist attempt to de- fine shariah compliance tests the artifacts of Western financial knowledge against shariah, the shariah-based approach seeks to build definitions and instruments by finding analogues in Islamic history or by interpreting Is- lamic texts for their underlying meaning. In pursuing this strategy, experts seek to extract the content and the substantive principles that guide per- missible economic action to build a system of knowledge and practice that does not rely on reference to an adjacent system. The contrast between these two methodological approaches reveals the difference between and the autonomy of systems of thought. The formalist method sees secular knowledge as a formation that exists alongside Islam. Between the two systems there is a possibility of translation, insofar as secular knowledge can be tested for shariah compliance or noncompliance. The substantive approach, in contrast, makes recourse to original Islamic concepts and ap- proaches but does not put the two systems alongside one another by pre- suming that one can translate between them.

The substantive approach was further evident in efforts to use the historical Islamic institution of *waqf* as mechanisms for economic growth. Waqfs are charitable foundations established for a social or religious purpose by benefactors (Atia 2012; Isik 2014; Shatzmiller 2001). In most waqfs, private or public property is endowed for a charitable purpose and the revenue that the property generates is allocated for this purpose in perpetuity. Waqfs have long roots in Islamic history. During the early 2010s they were enthusiastically championed as financial instruments by Islamic economists and other academics and attracted the interest of regulators and industry professionals as well. In 2014 I participated in a workshop on the development of waqf properties in Malaysia that was attended by Dato' Muhammad bin Ibrahim, who by that time had succeeded Dato' Razif as deputy governor of Bank Negara and held the Islamic finance portfolio there. In addition there were four CEOs of Islamic banks and a number of senior industry professionals. The workshop opened with two presentations. The first was given by Murat Çizakça, who gave an overview of the history of waqfs in Islam from the time of the prophet Muhammad until the Ottoman period. The second was delivered by Magda Ismail Abdel Mohsin, an Islamic economist who was also a faculty member at INCEIF. She provided an overview of the successful mobilization of waqfs as financial devices in contexts as diverse as Singapore and Sudan.

Both scholars traced waqfs to early Islamic textual sources. Çizakça said that the origins of waqfs could be found in a statement by the prophet Muhammad known as *thawab ba'd al-wafah* (reward after death), in which he is reported to have instructed his followers that "a Muslim can continue earning *thawab* [merit] even after death." Waqfs could serve as a means through which a deceased Muslim could continue to increase their credentials for admission to heaven even after passing from earthly existence. Mohsin said that precedent for waqfs could be found in a Qur'anic passage that reads, "By no means shall ye attain righteousness unless ye give freely of that which ye love; and whatever ye give of a truth God knoweth it well" (Qur'an 3:92). Thus she saw the origins of waqfs in the content of the Qur'an and its admonitions to generosity. She continued this line of reasoning, citing evidence for the importance of charity in the hadiths. For example, "The prophet said, 'When a man dies, his acts come to an end, except three things, recurring charity, knowledge by which people benefit, and pious offspring who pray for him.'"

Invocations of historical precedent for waqfs were common, although the precise examples invoked varied. In a separate conversation some months before the workshop, Othman, an Islamic scholar, told me that he traced the origins of waqfs to a hadith that recounts the experience of Umar bin Khattab, one of the companions of the prophet and the second Islamic caliph. He told me that Umar went to fight the Battle of Khaybar, after which he acquired a great deal of war booty from that wealthy oasis town. Umar asked the prophet Muhammad what he should do with the plundered spoils and was told to "hold the capital and give away the fruits." Othman said that this metaphorical advice prompted Umar to use the booty to establish the first waqf, mobilizing the treasure for the "improvement of the ummah."

At the Bank Negara workshop, Çizakça looked to Western history for validation of the effectiveness of waqfs, explaining that waqfs were the antecedent for the trusts that initially funded many modern European and North American universities. Referring to the economic benefits of mobilizing financial resources in this manner, he noted that universities had spawned "so much innovation," which had served as the engine of economic growth in the countries of the North Atlantic, especially in the United States. Furthermore, he suggested that it was the global North that was derivative of Islam, insofar as it had deployed a financial device initially fabricated in the Islamic world to create institutions from which considerable economic benefit was generated.

Othman was optimistic about the potential of waqfs to foster economic development and in animated terms regaled me with an account of how waqf property had been mobilized to this end. His story concerned a thirty-four-story skyscraper in downtown Kuala Lumpur that had recently been constructed and now housed the offices of Bank Islam (see figure 11). The building was located on a half-hectare parcel of land that had been established as a waqf by Ahmad bin Dadabhoy Dawjee, a businessman who came from Gujarat in India and lived for a long time in the Little India section of Kuala Lumpur. Dadabhoy passed away in January 1987, and for many years the land had gone undeveloped. Othman told me that it had been used for many different purposes, including a parking lot—"Even a disco!"

Nonetheless, as real estate prices escalated in this part of central Kuala Lumpur, which commercial real estate brokers zealously promoted as the "Golden Triangle," development of the waqf parcel became an increasingly enticing prospect. Development ultimately entailed collaboration between a state religious body and two Islamic financial institutions.

FIGURE 11. The headquarters of Bank Islam with a sign in front noting that the building is constructed on waqf property. Photo by author.

The Federal Territory Islamic Religious Council (Majlis Agama Islam Wilayah Persekutuan, MAIWP)[1] was the trustee of the waqf, Tabung Haji provided the capital for the construction of the office tower, and Bank Islam agreed to a twenty-five-year lease of the building to make the project economically viable. According to Othman, the project demonstrated the economic benefits of waqf. He told me that Tabung Haji invested RM151 million in the project, but real estate professionals estimate that the building and land will be valued at RM300 million after Bank Islam's current lease expires. The MAIWP will receive RM56.6 million over the twenty-five-year period in rental payments and, when the lease expires, ownership of the building will revert to MAIWP.

Othman invoked this project as a prime example of how the financial institutions that originated within Islam could be used to facilitate economic growth. This approach, which seeks to facilitate contemporary economic development by mobilizing institutions that are grounded in the history of Islam and are unassailable in their religious credentials, represents the shariah-based approach to Islamic finance. It entailed a partnership arrangement between Tabung Haji and MAIWP and the mobilization of the factors of production for the real economy.

Manufacturing Moral Mortgages

As in conventional finance, perhaps the single most important consumer product in Islamic finance is home financing. Although shelter is a basic human need, home ownership and the credit technologies to enable it have often been taken for granted as a fact of financial life in North Atlantic economies. However, anthropologists have increasingly shown the profoundly political dimensions of home ownership and the financial devices that enable it (Stout 2016; Weiss 2014). As most mortgage mechanisms are debt based, the debate over whether shariah compliance was a sufficient standard for Islamic mortgages or they should instead be shariah based was a recurrent object of reflection among Islamic finance experts. Devices developed in Islamic finance to facilitate home financing also demonstrate a tension between formalist and substantivist methods. While I was in Malaysia, reformers sought to shift away from a widely used shariah-compliant Islamic mortgage product known as a *bai bithaman ajil* (BBA). This is a debt-based contract frequently disparaged by reformers because it closely resembles a conventional interest-based debt contract. In contrast, reformers sought to replace it with a contract called a diminishing musharaka (also referred to as a *musharaka mutanaqisah*), which is equity based. Efforts to develop this product also reveal some of the differences in how Islamic finance is practiced in Malaysia compared to other jurisdictions, especially the version deployed in the United States and described by Bill Maurer (Maurer 2006).

From the 1980s until the 2000s the dominant home financing contract in Malaysia was the BBA, which relied on some of the roundabout mechanisms that were common in Islamic finance and were the object of reform by critics. This device entails a deferred payment sale at a markup to essentially replicate a conventional home mortgage and involves four steps to complete (see figure 12). First, the customer finds a property that he or she would like to own and informs the financial institution. Second, the institution purchases the asset from the current owner. Third, after momentarily taking possession of the asset, the institution sells the property to the customer at an agreed-upon marked-up price, with repayment scheduled on an installment basis. Finally, the customer pays

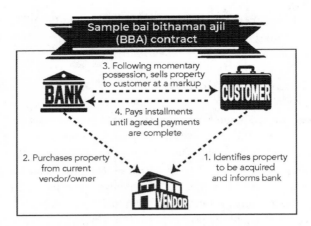

FIGURE 12. A sample bai bithaman ajil contract structure. Credit: Jos Sances.

the required installments on a periodic basis until all agreed-upon payments are complete. These contracts effectively circumvent the Qur'anic
prohibition on charging interest, at least according to shariah scholars in
Malaysia, by having two distinct sales: the institution buys the property
from the current owner and then immediately sells it at a markup to the
customer.

Malaysian scholars found the BBA permissible, as they viewed it as a
variation of a bai al inah contract. As discussed in chapter 2, although shariah scholars in the Middle East had deemed bai al inah not compliant with
shariah because they interpreted it as a roundabout technique to charge
interest, those in Malaysia had come to the opposite conclusion based on
the argument that humans cannot judge the interior intentions of other
humans. This legal loophole meant that, for many of those with whom I
interacted, bai al inah (and by extension BBA) might be shariah compliant
but was not shariah based. Much of the rationale for legitimating bai al inah
was based on the presumption that it would only be used in the incipient
stages of Islamic finance and that once more authentically Islamic structures were concocted, instruments like BBA would be abandoned.

Idris, a former conventional banking employee who had later gone on
to work as a researcher on Islamic finance, told me that BBA violated a
number of shariah principles regarding property. For example, he said
that according to common law, ownership can be separated into legal
ownership (in which one holds legal title to an asset) and beneficial own-

ership (in which one may hold rights to income from the asset but not legal title). In contrast, in Islam this separation of ownership does not exist, because all property "is owned by God." Human beings are viewed only as trustees of the property they hold. While the ISRA scholars working on intangible assets identified two possible perspectives on property, Idris saw only one. He viewed the BBA as contrary to Islamic principles of property rights. "It is a fictitious sale," he reasoned, due to the fact that the financial institution never took "physical possession" of the house. Instead, they only held "momentarily" beneficial ownership before immediately transferring it to the customer.

He said he was first introduced to BBA in the 1980s when he was working for a bank owned by Malaysians of Chinese descent. Bank Islam, Malaysia's first Islamic bank, was using BBA to facilitate shariah-compliant home financing and had to work with conventional banks on mortgage transactions. Idris said that the bank's employees would visit other banks and give crash courses in Islamic finance to their counterparts. "The officers from Bank Islam just came and told us how to do [BBA] financing. We didn't ask any questions; we just took their instrument at face value." The problem, he said, was that BBA essentially replicates a mortgage contract in conventional finance. He implied that Islamic banks were able to pass BBA financing off as Islamic on the basis of "branding": the Arabic moniker and its endorsement by shariah scholars led customers to accept it as Islamic. This version of Islamic finance as a brand, which was increasingly seen as superficial by many experts and others, was easily complicit with the state's broader emphasis on creating a middle class that simultaneously conformed to its vision of Islam and the requirements of contemporary capitalism.

Although the BBA was the most widely used home financing contract in Malaysia, by the 1990s it had become immensely controversial. Indeed, the most commonly cited legal dispute in Islamic finance involved a default on a home mortgage through a BBA facility, when an Islamic bank sued a former employee who was also a customer. The case, *Affin Bank vs. Zulkifli Abdullah*, was finally settled in 2005 but often served as a lodestone for criticism in Islamic banking. In 1997, while an employee of the bank, Zulkifli, signed a BBA contract to purchase a two-story townhouse at a price of RM346,000. In 1999 he resigned from the company, and the financing device was restructured based on a total sale price of RM992,363.40 payable over a period of twenty-five years. This price reflected the sum of the initial sale price and the deferred markup to which the bank was entitled as part of the resale agreement. However, Zulkifli defaulted in 2001 after paying back only RM33,454.19 of the total financing amount. The bank sued Zulkifli in Malaysia's civil court system, and the judge ruled that the defendant had to "pay not only the sum loaned but also the bank's profit margin spanning through the 25-year tenure of the facility" (Patail 2006, 438). The court calculated that the bank was entitled to RM218,767.49 in profit plus the purchase price of the house less the installments already paid (Patail 2006, 440). The defendant was ordered to repay an amount that was nearly twice the initial purchase price of the house!

Reformers pointed to this case as a paradigmatic example of how contracts such as BBA are unjust and contrary to the spirit of Islamic law, which emphasizes fairness. Sharif, a professor with whom I studied Islamic law at INCEIF, invoked the Affin Bank case as an example of the duplicity of Islamic finance as practiced by Islamic financial institutions in Malaysia, suggesting it proved that "Islamic banks were worse than conventional banks." He justified this provocative claim by saying that in a conventional loan the defaulter is only responsible for the accrued interest at the time of disposal of the defaulted property, not the entire profit that the bank is entitled to over the tenure of the deferred payments. This case and the fact that BBA was often explicitly linked to prevailing interest rates in the conventional system led many like Idris and Sharif to criticize the style of Islamic finance with which BBA was associated.

Furthermore, as the state's agenda for Islamic finance changed from largely a domestic one to a transnational, global one, it could no longer depend on a distinctively Malaysian (or Southeast Asian) interpretation of Islamic jurisprudence. Idris told me that Malaysia's desire to become a "global hub" for Islamic finance meant that it had to comply with "international shariah standards" and not merely the opinions of local scholars who resorted to their specific school of Islamic legal reasoning. Malaysia would have to develop and deploy instruments that were viewed as valid in other regions. As noted in chapter 2, different schools of Islamic legal reasoning prevailed in Southeast Asia than in the Middle East, leading to divergences regarding the permissibility of certain Islamic contracts. He said that the recent introduction of foreign Islamic financial institutions from the Arabian Gulf region was one strategy to make Islamic banks in Malaysia competitive and credible elsewhere in the Muslim world, and he viewed the introduction of foreign firms as a "strategy to make us learn."

To enhance the credibility of Malaysian Islamic finance, Idris had worked with others to develop alternative devices that he viewed as "more

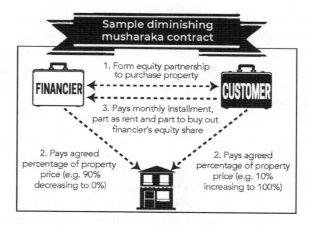

FIGURE 13. A sample diminishing musharaka contract structure. Credit: Jos Sances.

authentically Islamic" than BBA, which was not permitted in most Middle Eastern jurisdictions and elsewhere. He sought to replace it in Malaysia with the diminishing musharaka, which is widely accepted across various jurisprudential schools (see figure 13). Whereas the BBA relies on two sales and a separation of ownership, the diminishing musharaka is a partnership agreement in which the financial institution and the customer "enter into a corporate partnership and form a limited liability company (LLC) together. . . . The LLC owns the property, and the company and the client recalculate their percentage share in the partnership—not in the property—over the term of the contract" (Maurer 2006, 49–50). Whereas the BBA is considered a debt-based contract, because the client effectively assumes the position of a debtor in relationship to the firm, the diminishing musharaka is considered an equity-based, risk-sharing contract because the client and the firm are effectively coinvestors in the property, with the client buying out the bank's share in the property over time.

A persistent problem with any Islamic financial contract is the source of the profit generated, because the prohibition on interest means that no increase is permissible on transactions involving only money without the exchange of a tangible object. The prohibition on interest is clear, but how a financial arrangement is organized to enable a mediating institution to earn a return varies. In the Malaysian BBA, the marked-up sale price mirrors prevailing interest rates, which is the primary reason it was disparaged by professionals such as Idris. In the diminishing musharaka, financial institutions had to figure out some way of realizing a return on the investment. After all, simply coinvesting in a piece of property is not a very effective business strategy, as the financial institution would only realize a profit upon sale and even then only in instances in which property values actually increased. The methods of generating a return from a diminishing musharaka varied across jurisdictions. Maurer reports that in the United States, firms that deploy the diminishing musharaka charge an administrative fee that "is competitive with the interest rates available in the broader home finance market" and "may be linked to an interest rate index" such as LIBOR or the prime rate in the United States (Maurer 2006, 50). Although the company Maurer pseudonymously refers to as Searchlight benchmarks the profit rate it receives to prevailing interest rates in its version of the diminishing musharaka, Maurer found that Muslim consumers in the United States see it as more authentic than competing models "because of its backing by prominent [shariah] scholars" (Maurer 2006, 55). This illustrates the influence wielded by shariah scholars, who can authoritatively deem Islamic instruments compliant or not with little public questioning.

Nonetheless, it is important to underscore that there are different versions of diminishing musharaka. Indeed, the version of diminishing musharaka advocated by Idris differed in a critical respect from the American version described by Maurer. Instead of explicitly linking the company's profit to prevailing interest rates, Idris proposed a diminishing musharaka in which the firm's profit on the monthly installment paid by the client was based on "a rental rate indexed to rental prices on the real market." Financial firms would compile an index of rental prices of comparable properties by location, size, amenities, and other variables and then calculate an appropriate rent based on these variables. The monthly installment paid by the consumer would include both a principal payment to buy out a portion of the company's investment share and a rental payment in return for the use of whatever fraction of the property is owned by the company.[2] Idris argued that the diminishing musharaka he envisioned was superior to the BBA because the profit rate was "determined by supply and demand," rather than an "arbitrary interest rate." This claim reflected the fact that those seeking to reform Islamic finance assert the superiority of certain instruments not only because they are more authentic to Islam, but also because they better conform to the doctrines of liberal economics. When Idris affirms a preference for determining profits based on "supply and demand" as opposed to interest rates, he implicitly endorses the liberal dictum that it is natural that prices be set by the market. This view was further reflected when he argued that his version of diminishing musharaka was based on "fair profit sharing," because the rental rate is indexed to "real market conditions," not a guaranteed interest rate. Idris said that granting Islamic banking licenses to Islamic banks based in the Gulf accelerated the move away from BBA and toward diminishing musharaka in Malaysia. Particularly important was the introduction of Kuwait Finance House as a player in the market, which Idris noted had "introduced the diminishing musharaka" to Malaysia when it started retail operations in the country in 2005.

Importantly, the categorization of contracts in Malaysia differs in key respects from the way in which Maurer found them categorized in the United States. The central distinction drawn by experts working in Malaysia is between debt-based finance and investment (or equity-based) finance. This fundamental opposition undergirded both the way experts represented Islamic finance in Malaysia and how they diagnosed its shortcomings. Reformers and critics saw investment-oriented finance as far superior to the debt-based counterpart, which they viewed as characteristic of conventional finance. For example, Idris argued that the real estate bubbles, defaults, and financial crises at large (as witnessed in 2008) were endemic to debt-based finance models whose defining practice was the collection of interest; he insisted that "the crises in Argentina, Brazil, and Mexico were all debt driven." He saw the diminishing musharaka as a key step toward rectifying the debt-based orientation and the cycle of crisis that he viewed as endemic to conventional finance.

As noted above, reformers and critics in Malaysia divide Islamic finance contracts into two main categories: debt-based contracts involving a sale and repurchase, such as murabaha, bai al inah, BBA, and tawarruq; and equity-based contracts that entail partnerships, such as musharaka and mudaraba (which are viewed as more religiously authentic).[3] Interestingly, in the United States, Maurer found that musharaka and murabaha (a cost-plus contract) were considered "close cousin(s)" and were both viewed as less pure than mudaraba and ijara contracts (Maurer 2006, 52). In the United States, experts do not deploy the opposition between debt-based and equity-based contracts or between shariah-compliant and shariah-based Islamic finance when evaluating the relative authenticity of various contracts.

The opposition between shariah-compliant and shariah-based Islamic finance illuminates how the problem of the religious authenticity of Islamic finance was a recurrent problem for Islamic finance experts in Malaysia.

Indeed, the imperative to reform Islamic finance was largely framed through this opposition as reformers sought to move "to the next stage." However, the opposition between shariah-based and shariah-compliant Islamic finance was not merely a technical problem but an epistemological one. Proponents of shariah compliance as a standard for Islamic finance conceptualized the relationship between Islamic and secular knowledge in a markedly different way from those who sought to devise a shariah-based approach. For the former, Islamic knowledge and secular economics and finance were adjacent systems that could be compared with one another. Islam could be operationalized as shariah, and then secular finance could be tested against it. For those who advocated a shariah-based version, the goal was to formulate a coherent Islamic finance that was grounded in principles internal to Islam itself. This did not entail denying the validity of secular economic knowledge but rather sought to use such knowledge to prove the superiority of shariah-based Islamic finance.

The difference between the ways in which these systems of thought are represented is largely visible in the divergent methods used in each approach. Those who judge shariah compliance as the standard according to which specific financial devices and practices can be deemed permissible subscribe to a formalist epistemology. In brief, in this approach, the method of determining compatibility with Islam entails testing conventional financial tools and instruments against the litmus of religious permissibility. In other words, existing devices are evaluated against an interpretation of Islam and are deemed shariah compliant if they do not explicitly contradict Islamic principles. As the CEO of one Islamic bank emphatically put it, "Anything that is not specifically identified as impermissible in the texts is permissible." This method presumes that Islamic and secular knowledge are parallel systems of thought that are both valid and exist alongside one another.

In contrast, shariah-based Islamic finance does not presume two distinct systems of equivalent knowledge between which units can be translated. Rather, Islam reveals truths that exist prior to and independent of secular reason. Starting with principles drawn from the Qur'an and hadiths, as well as economic practices historically used in Islam, those who embrace a shariah-based approach seek to synthesize devices distinctive to Islamic finance. While this project is more ambitious and labor intensive, it also can lay claim to greater independence and distinctiveness. It does not seek to adapt conventional financial instruments by testing them for shariah compliance but rather seeks to cut a new financial infrastructure out of whole cloth. Rather than adapting bits and pieces of conventional finance that are evaluated for religious permissibility, it seeks to synthesize radically new instruments using tools and techniques particular to the discursive tradition of Islam.

Ultimately the opposition between shariah-compliant and shariah-based Islamic finance illuminates the question of what makes a financial alternative. Proponents of shariah-based Islamic finance suggested that a standard of shariah compliance did not offer the possibility of a legitimate alternative. Rather, it merely replicated existing financial devices and institutions while subjecting them to a sort of filter that removed anything identified as impermissible. However, as one reformer worried, when "the next crisis hits" such a filter would be insufficient to protect a shariah-compliant version of Islamic finance. So, as I describe below, the imperative to create a shariah-based system was driven by the conviction that such a system would present a genuine alternative to conventional finance, one that would ultimately not be as prone to crisis and cataclysm.

CHAPTER SIX

Consuming Form,
Investing in Substance

On a typically muggy day in January 2014 I sat with Sameer at a drab
restaurant in the Little India district of Kuala Lumpur. It was a Sun-
day afternoon, and the streets outside were busy with a diverse mix of
hawkers, shoppers, and other city dwellers enjoying a last bit of unen-
cumbered time before another hectic workweek would begin the following morning. Sameer was a bright young British-educated Islamic finance
professional of Pakistani descent who had previously worked for the Malaysian subsidiary of a major multinational Islamic bank. We had first met
three years previously at a conference on Islamic economics and finance
in Qatar. He was working toward a PhD in Islamic finance at a Malaysian
university, and his curiosity and keen intellect had led me to maintain a
long-distance correspondence with him. We were finishing up a few last
dabs of curry and naan while discussing his research and recent controversies in Islamic finance in Malaysia when he effortlessly articulated the
central question that I later realized preoccupied many of the interlocutors with whom I interacted: "What is the Islam in Islamic finance?" In
animated tones he continued, offering various possibilities as to what the
"Islam" in "Islamic finance" might index: "Is it compliance with texts? Is
it morality? Is it improving the human condition through alleviating poverty? Is it a set of rules?"

Some weeks before, I had been listening to the CEO of an Islamic bank
deliver a public lecture at INCEIF. His presentation focused on reforms to
Malaysia's Islamic banking laws that had been passed earlier in the year by
the country's parliament, but toward the end of his remarks he expressed
what I recognized as a familiar frustration with what he saw as a contradiction

in the piety of those he sought to attract to his bank. With no shortage of exasperation, he said, "Malaysian Muslims go out of the way to consume halal
food. They're always checking the labels for a halal logo, but then they walk
into a conventional bank and don't blink an eye." Frustrated by the general
ignorance about the religious permissibility of certain economic practices,
he related what happened following a presentation on Islamic finance he
had delivered. "A man came up to me afterwards with a shocked expression
and told me, 'I took a conventional loan to finance my son's studies at Al-
Azhar!' "[1] The audience chuckled smugly as he described the man's worried
expression upon realizing that he had contravened Qur'anic injunctions by
funding his child's education at one of the world's most renowned centers of
Islamic scholarship with an interest-based loan.

Both Sameer's question and the exasperated invocations of the CEO illuminated a central problem invoked by Islamic finance professionals. As
the industry has expanded and Islamic financial institutions survived the
2008 global financial crisis relatively unscathed, a spirited debate erupted
about the implications of the adjective "Islamic" for the noun "finance."
This problem was often expressed in the comparison of dietary habits to
commercial practices. Like the CEO, many other financial professionals
lamented the fact that although they thought Malaysian Muslims were
fastidious regarding religious prescriptions in consumption, they were far
less observant when it came to commercial matters, especially when it
came to financial practice. They regularly referred to the fact that many
of their compatriots avoided alcohol and pork with steadfast determination and doggedly inspected the labels of packaged food for the halal logo
that certified approval by Malaysia's Islamic Development Department
(Jabatan Kemajuan Islam Malaysia). However, finance practitioners were
flummoxed by the ignorance of these ostensibly pious Muslims when it
came to religious prescriptions for economic action, especially the strongly
worded Qur'anic injunction against interest. They felt that these citizens
showed markedly less concern for religious probity when it came to opening a bank account, researching a home mortgage, or applying for a credit
card compared to when they were making dietary decisions.

This chapter argues that Malaysia's Islamic finance project has made
the economy a domain in which debates over the integrity of Islamic practice are conducted. It describes how Islamic finance professionals such
as the CEO frequently make analogies between Islamic economic action
and Islamic dietary practices. It details how these experts compare the
prohibition against interest (riba) to restrictions on the consumption of

meat that is not slaughtered according to religious prescriptions. I illustrate how Islamic finance in Malaysia (and beyond) is riven by questions over the extent to which compliance with economic directives in Islam's key texts, the Qur'an and the hadiths, is necessary to proper religious comportment. The comparison between consuming Islamic financial products and maintaining a halal diet offers a window into the broader debates in which Muslims are enmeshed as they seek to reconcile Islam with various dimensions of modern life. I conclude that the apparent paradox between inattention to Islam in economic action and hyperattention in dietary practice is rooted in the relative complexity of the practices of creating halal financial products as opposed to halal food and uncertainty about the Islamicity of Islamic finance stemming from the common criticism that it is "not really Islamic." Ultimately, the difference in the respective consumption of halal food and Islamic financial products reveals the challenge to devising alternative financial infrastructures.

As Islamic finance has expanded rapidly in Malaysia and other Muslim-majority countries, this growth has been accompanied by a broad reflection over the relation between Islam and Islamic finance. Ethnographically, these questions were evident in two distinct problematizations. On the one hand were the questions that employees of Islamic financial institutions, such as the CEO, raised about the sincerity of the piety professed by Malaysian Muslims who sought to keep halal diets but did not participate in halal banking. On the other hand, some Islamic scholars and Islamic economists argued that Islamic finance itself was insufficiently Islamic. Shariah schol-·ars invoked the failure of Islamic finance to fulfill the maqasid (objectives of shariah), whereas Islamic economists argued that Islamic finance failed to meet religious prescriptions for economic action evident in the Qur'an.

Through examination of debates over the Islamicity of Islamic finance, this chapter argues that the spectacular growth and rapid development of Islamic finance in Malaysia has made economic action a site for the articulation of debates over proper religious comportment. These debates, in part, differentiate Islamic finance from conventional finance. For example, in North America or Europe it is virtually inconceivable to question the religious morality of a home mortgage or hear the CEO of a major bank discussing the finer points of religious law. However, in Malaysia these are relatively common occurrences at Islamic financial institutions, and Muslim dietary prescriptions constitute a key reference point for debating the Islamicity of Islamic finance.

Islamic finance also questions the presumption that economic action is necessarily secular. The anthropologist Talal Asad pointed out that modernity was premised on the designation of distinct spheres of life in which religion could be neatly cleaved from domains such as politics or economics (Asad 1993). Contemporary Islamic finance calls this separation into question, as institutions (such as banks and insurance companies) and domains of action (such as commerce and business) that once may have been presumed to be secular are subjected to the intricate task of reconciling domains of knowledge and practice. Contemporary Islamic finance is a practical outcome of what has been called the "Islamization of knowledge" (al-Attas 1978). Originally proposed by the Malaysian scholar Syed Muhammad Naquib al-Attas,[2] this intellectual movement sought to conjoin various fields of modern knowledge, such as science or economics, with Islamic religious principles. Malaysia's Islamic finance project is a practical effort to "Islamize" modern knowledge.

Ritual Form and Islamic Designation

The tension between form and content is evident in both financial action and dietary practice. As the anthropologist Bill Maurer has shown, one of the most contentious issues in contemporary Islamic finance is whether it is Islamic in form, in substance, or in both (Maurer 2010). As recounted in earlier chapters, the prevailing standard for Islamic finance has been formal compliance with a literal reading of Islamic texts, but reformers and critics seek to create a more authentic Islamic finance that conforms with the substantive principles of Islam. Halal designation was a frequent subject of analogy in discourse regarding whether Islamic finance met religious requirements in form or in substance.

In Malaysia the halal designation is being deployed in a multibillion-dollar food industry in which halal labels are mobilized to instill and sustain Muslim subjectivities (Fischer 2011). As Johan Fischer has shown, halal labeling—a practice whereby institutions granted authority by states to denote food and other commodities as permissible for consumption by Muslims—has become a potent means by which the Malaysian state has sought to confer a pious Islamic identity on so-called indigenous Malaysians. Even expatriate Malaysians living as far afield as the United Kingdom are interpellated as Muslims by the state through the halal label (Fischer 2011, 69–88). The state has further sought to capitalize on halal labeling by making the country a global center for halal certification.

The designation of halal food served as an important precedent in formalist arguments in support of Islamic finance. Often poultry, especially chicken, figured as the analogical point of reference in these discussions. Nuraini, a former high-level Islamic banking executive, told me that she would often argue about the integrity and legitimacy of Islamic finance with her husband. She recalled him protesting, "Look, this Islamic banking is the same as the conventional one." In turn she would respond by distinguishing the substance of a chicken dinner from the ritual practices that made it halal, replying, "You may be eating the same kind of chicken, but one is halal and one is haram. . . . You may think it is the same—the chickens look the same—except that one is slaughtered using the phrases of Allah and the other one is not." Just as halal chicken might look the same as a nonhalal chicken, an Islamic financial instrument might look the same as a conventional one. However, the Islamic version is transformed into something else through speech acts that distinguished it from the conventional version. The context in which a particular comestible was turned from a natural object into a cultural one made all the difference in enacting these distinctions (Lévi-Strauss 1969; Ortner 1972).

Defining the authenticity of Islamic finance in terms of form and substance was commonly invoked in the discourse of experts in the field. Hamza, a CEO at one of Malaysia's largest Islamic banks, also invoked halal butchering in revealing how formal practices were deployed in Islamic finance. He explained to me that the only difference between a halal chicken and a nonhalal chicken is the manner in which it was butchered. He said, "The taste is the same, the chicken looks the same; the only difference is that a prayer was recited during the slaughter and the animal was killed in a particular way." But once the two chickens "get to the supermarket they are virtually identical. . . . If it tastes the same, why bother buying a halal chicken?" Hamza felt that this focus on form was not sufficient to differentiate Islamic finance from its conventional counterpart, noting that "where Islamic finance wants to go is to reach beyond form to substance." In his eyes Islamic finance had to go beyond the superficial methods of the halal food industry that created permissible consumables through ritual forms such as prayers and butchering but in the end created products that looked and tasted the same as their conventional counterparts.

Hamza looked to the organic food movement as a model for how the Islamic financial industry might "reach beyond form to substance." He suggested that the justification for Islamic finance should not be based on claims to religious authenticity but rather on the fact that Islamic economic principles improved human life. Rather than creating a halal chicken, Islamic finance should in his words endeavor to create a "free-range chicken," which "tastes better, is better for you, and is better for the environment." With the utmost sincerity he cautioned that a free-range chicken was "more expensive" than a factory-farmed chicken, but he argued that higher-quality meat consumed less frequently would have a cascading series of effects overall. He said:

> The point of Islamic banking is, why eat chicken every day? It's expensive, so you have to eat caged chicken! Now I only eat chicken twice a week, but it's healthier, tastier chicken. So it's a choice. Whether you want chicken every day or two or three times per week. Healthier chicken [once in a while] or unhealthier chicken every day. I think our [parents] chose the second option . . . [but] eating meat every day means the quality of the meat can only come down. . . . By eating less we can give a chance for the farmers to achieve the same profitability but less volume, more space for the chicken, and better quality chicken. So less is more.

By changing the point of comparison from halal chicken to free-range chicken, Hamza was making an important point. Free-range chicken, in his words, reached "beyond form to substance" because it was healthier and more environmentally sustainable, whereas halal chicken differed only superficially from factory-farmed chicken. His point was that Islamic finance should become a true alternative to conventional finance rather than simply offer a formal veneer under which lay conventional financial operations. However, he was also suggesting that this development would come at a cost: a truly alternative finance would require a price premium. Just as one expected to pay a bit more for sustainable food, one should expect to pay a bit more for an Islamic financial product. Furthermore, Hamza implied that just as a more sustainable economy would mean certain material sacrifices (such as consuming less meat), so too would an Islamic economy. In an Islamic economy, with less ready credit and slower if steadier growth, citizens would likewise have to make material sacrifices, just as they might already be doing by eating organic food.

Hamza echoed a commonly articulated contention that the application of Islamic knowledge to finance had focused too much on questions of form and not enough on the actual content of Islamic financial devices. In so doing, he drew out the analogy between Islamic banking and gastronomy further by suggesting that there were different ways of applying Islamic knowledge to both finance and food. Hamza articulated this distinction by contrasting the formalist fiqh orientation with one that focused on maqasid. Scholars who used an approach based in fiqh to determine the Islamicity of an object only addressed the "letter of the law": whether an action or object was permissible or impermissible. In contrast, reasoning on the basis of maqasid addressed the spirit of Islamic law: whether an action or object fulfilled the moral and ethical imperatives inherent in Islam. He said that the legalistic, fiqh orientation "just looks at how the chicken is being slaughtered. If you take the chicken and you deep-fry it in hydrogenated oil and it has a high calorie content it is still halal, from a fiqh perspective." In contrast he argued that Islamic finance should embrace a more encompassing perspective that sought to implement the moral vision of Islam. He said:

> From a higher objective, from a maqasid perspective, [deep-fried chicken] is very unhealthy for you. So what is the role of shariah scholars, should they look at just the object or should they look at the process? . . . What about the front end? Are you looking at the slaughter only or are you looking at the fact that the chicken never touched [the earth]—from the time it was incubated to the time of the slaughter it just stayed in a cage? Did [that] violate the rights of the chicken? . . . The problem is the fiqh only looks at whether it is slaughtered properly. That is why there is a standard called *tayyab*, [which means] wholesome. . . . Fiqh looks at the slaughter; tayyab looks at how the chicken has been bred and how it has been cooked. So if you want Islamic banking to move—this is what I have been telling for the last two years—you bring in the standard called tayyab. Halal is just certification. But those that want a higher standard [want] tayyab!

In his eyes a more authentic Islamic finance would be more holistic in its orientation rather than simply testing instruments for their compliance with shariah.

Usman, an Islamic banker of Pakistani descent from Canada who regularly came to Malaysia on business, also made an analogy between food and finance. He said that he thought that ultimately both conventional and Islamic finance would converge around the Islamic version because such a configuration would meet the criteria for efficiency demanded by industrial food production and thus would appeal to both Muslims and non-Muslims. He drew on an analogy from the meat-processing industry to make this argument. He said that the Canadian company Maple Lodge switched its processing system so that all its meat is halal, because it "doesn't matter for a non-Muslim whether meat is halal or not, because the meat is the same." Apparently oblivious to the furor sparked during the 2012 French presidential campaign when the far-right politician Marine Le Pen proclaimed that non-Muslims in France were eating halal meat, Usman suggested that the convergence of conventional finance with Islamic finance was inevitable. He noted that Maple Lodge solved the problems of inefficiency by creating "two separate packaging streams, one with a halal label and one without" but "all the meat was halal." Usman noted that in countries like Canada, Islamic financial products could be priced higher than equivalent conventional products because "the community is willing to pay a premium" for a "halal product" such as meat.

Malaysia's effort to make itself the hub of both halal food and halal finance and the ways in which Islamic finance experts compared these two domains revealed a key aspect of its development strategy. Both food and money are absolutely essential and inescapable features of modern life. Indeed, contemporary human life is hard to envision without either. Food is an obvious subsistence necessity for human life, and money has become one. It is virtually impossible to imagine a system of economic exchange in mass societies without money in some form. Thus the state sought economic growth by making itself a central site for the certification of what made food and money Islamic. Previously, in the 1990s, the state embarked on a series of ambitious development projects (Baxstrom 2008). This included the ambitious and expensive Multimedia Super Corridor (MSC), which was conceived as a hub to incubate information and multimedia technology. The MSC included sites like Cyberjaya, which was intended to become the Silicon Valley of Southeast Asia (Bunnell 2004). The very name, Cyberjaya, spoke to the state's ambitions. "Cyber" refers to the internet, as in cyberspace, and "jaya" is a Malay word that can mean either victory, glory, or prosperity. The site spoke to the state's desire to become a major cybertechnology hub. In addition, the state developed BioValley, a biotechnology hub that was designed to capitalize on the country's abundant biodiversity (Smeltzer 2008). By locating pharmaceutical and other scientific research and development initiatives in Malaysia rather than the North Atlantic, the state sought to reverse a colonial and postcolonial pattern in which developing countries provide the raw materials for scientific and technological advances, but the knowledge work is conducted in the former colonial metropoles (Hayden 2003). Much to the dismay of planners, Cyberjaya and BioValley never lived up to the grand expectations placed upon them. In the business meeting I attended with Uzair described in chapter 4, one Islamic finance professional went on a long tirade about the failure of Cyberjaya, saying that it was a "total waste of money. . . . The government spent billions of dollars and nothing happened. The only achievement was to set up a bunch of call centers." He concluded, "We failed in high tech," noting that even in the relatively low-skilled market of offshore call centers, Malaysia had been surpassed by countries such as India and the Philippines.

Given these failures, plans to transform Malaysia into a center of Islamic food and finance were part of a broader shift in development strategy. Whereas in the 1990s the state had sought to mimic trends in development that had been lucrative in the global North, such as cybertechnology and biotechnology, by the 2000s it became apparent that neither initiative had been successful in Malaysia. Instead, the state identified the elements constitutive of modern life, food, and finance as domains that, marked in religiously distinctive terms, could stand as sources of revenue in a global economy. Rather than representing the media of development as uniform across a global space, as did the Cyberjaya and BioValley initiatives, efforts to identify specific sectors, such as food and finance, as marked by distinctive religious norms, represents a distinctive spatiality for development. Islam is the sign under which an economic space is marked as operating according to separate norms from other sectors. Rather than trying to compete in the global food or financial sectors, with their long-established dominant players, efforts at creating halal finance and food draw boundaries around particular populations and mark them as part of distinct economies. By positioning Kuala Lumpur within a network of Islamic global cities, the state seeks to create an alternative global development network under the sign of Islam.

Questioning Monetary Representation

While the idea of an Islamic banking system based on equity rather than debt investment may seem to stretch the limits of the economic imagination, in Malaysia proponents of such a reform enthusiastically endorsed a 2012 working paper titled "The Chicago Plan Revisited" and written by researchers at the International Monetary Fund (Benes and Kumhof 2012). Hannah Appel has described how the same document inspired the economic imagination of the ex–financial district employees who made up the Alternative Banking working group of Occupy Wall Street (Appel

2014, 617–618). The working paper endorsed the so-called Chicago Plan, a proposal for a set of banking reforms composed following the Great Depression for which Henry Simons, a University of Chicago economist and intellectual godfather to Milton Friedman, was the principal advocate.

The Chicago Plan was a program for monetary reform that proposed the separation of the monetary and debt functions of the banking system. This was to be accomplished "first by requiring 100% backing of deposits by government-issued money, and second by ensuring that the financing of new bank credit can only take place through earnings that have been retained in the form of government-issued money, or through the borrowing of existing government-issued money from non-banks, but not through the creation of new deposits . . . by banks" (Benes and Kumhof 2012, 4). This would end the ability of commercial banks to create money by leveraging the funds they hold on deposit. Instead, they would only be able to lend out funds that were already on deposit. Dr. Mustafa, the Islamic economist, argued that this was identical to Islamic banking. He said that the Chicago Plan, with its call for a one-to-one ratio of assets to liabilities for banks, mirrored the "wisdom of Islamic institutions such as *wadiah*." Wadiah is a "safekeeping" contract in which an "asset is placed with another party on the basis of trusteeship for safekeeping purposes." In such a safekeeping arrangement, a bank would take a deposit, guarantee it to the depositor, and be responsible for returning exactly that sum on demand to the depositor. Mustafa had concluded that the problem with debt-based banking was the "the ability to create credit through the fractional reserve system [because this] is what led to leverage and instability."

Rizal, an Islamic finance researcher, enthusiastically told me that the IMF working paper "challenged the fractional reserve system," which allowed banks to effectively create money. Fractional reserve banking is a practice by which banks accept deposits but lend funds far in excess of their deposit liabilities. Under the Basel Committee banking regulations discussed in chapter 1, the capital adequacy ratio (the amount of funds that banks were required to hold in reserve) for conventional banks was set at 8 percent. This means that for every dollar that a bank lent out "on the street," it was only required to hold eight cents on account to cover future withdrawals. Rather than the one-to-one ratio called for in the Chicago Plan, the Basel regulations allowed banks essentially a 0.08:1 ratio of funds on deposit to money created by banks through debt. While in most nations only sovereign states have the authority to manufacture physical currency in a conventional financial system any bank that takes deposits and makes loans of greater value than funds deposited essentially creates money. In a stable economy, fractional reserve banking is not a problem, as customers are usually content to store their deposits in banks for the long term if there is no risk of losing those deposits. The ratio of assets to liabilities becomes a problem when there is a perception of economic instability inciting customers to demand their deposits en masse, thus precipitating a bank run. However, Islamic finance experts viewed fractional reserve banking as a structural vulnerability that illustrated the fundamental instability and injustice of conventional finance.

Rizal marveled at the fact that a critique of the fractional reserve system had made it through IMF "filtration," because the structure of the production of knowledge at the IMF is confining, containing multiple layers of bureaucratic approval. He also noted to me that discussion of the issue of fractional reserve essentially "was off limits" in Malaysia because the Central Bank did not want the issue to be raised. While the Central Bank encouraged experimentation in many other aspects of Islamic finance, state officials were unwilling to countenance questioning of fractional reserve banking. And yet the fact that the IMF, at a central node in the global financial system, had problematized fractional reserve banking in a working paper demonstrated that the topic was not entirely beyond the limits of financial thought.

Social Finance

The argument that Islamic finance is Islamic only in form but not in substance is perhaps most evident in the allusion that Hamza made to the maqasid or "purposes" of shariah law. The maqasid defines the shariah by five foundational goals: the preservation of religion, life, progeny, intellect, and wealth. A methodological privileging of the maqasid entailed examining Islam's key texts, the Qur'an and the hadith, with the presumption that the ultimate purpose of these texts was to fulfill these foundational goals. Thus, rather than resorting to the simple binary of permissibility and impermissibility on which the notion of halal was based, the maqasid sought to extract the meaning underlying the directives set forth in shariah.

Drawing on a renewed interest in the maqasid in Islamic studies, especially within the Muslim world, experts who advocate that Islamic finance should meet the maqasid objectives see this as means of remaking society in broad terms (Kamali 1999). The demand that Islamic finance should realize the maqasid was evident in a variety of public forums that I attended in Malaysia. One such forum, consisting of papers delivered by shariah scholars, a number of whom served on the shariah boards of Islamic banks, was titled "International Conference on Sharia Objectives in Muamalat and Contracts." The forum was sponsored by the Securities Commission and was hosted by the International Institute of Advanced Islamic Studies, a think tank based in Kuala Lumpur and directed by the renowned scholar of Islamic law Hashim Kamali.

Younes Soulhi, a senior scholar who served on the shariah board of HSBC Amanah and was also a professor at the International Islamic University of Malaysia, captured a broadly held sentiment at the forum. Soulhi, who hailed from Algeria but had lived in Malaysia for over two decades, argued that a focus on the objectives of the shariah would mean shifting away from formal complicity to a focus on the substantive content of religious injunctions:

> Thirty years ago the industry was just starting and we let form override substance, but today the industry is in a state of refinement. A focus on maqasid would take the industry back to its intentions, on the substance, not the form. If we can develop a framework . . . we will see Islamic finance is moving in the right direction. When the corporate sector is maqasidi oriented, that will be an indication we are moving there. It would show that the Islamic finance industry would be more substance based and prove that Islamic finance is doing the right thing.

Invocations of maqasid are one means by which shariah scholars seek to remake Islamic finance to make it stretch beyond mere economic functionality and to instead become a force for social justice. By arguing that it should embrace extraeconomic goals such as the preservation of religion, life, and knowledge, these experts sought to stretch Islamic finance beyond its initially narrow mandate of investment, costs, and profit. However, as one Islamic finance researcher explained to me, this directive went against prevailing economic convictions insofar as it was dedicated to the preservation of wealth, not its expansion and growth. In this respect, many of those seeking to reform Islamic finance saw common cause with environmentalists advocating sustainable development and a "green" economy (Jacobs 1993).

Maqasid was often invoked as a barometer against which proper Islamic piety could be measured. An individual could be represented as an observant Muslim if his or her actions were identified with the maqasid. State officials sometimes merged the ethical imperative of fulfilling the maqasid with the bureaucratic rationality of the state. In 2010 the Malaysian state launched the Government Transformation Program (GTP), which sought to achieve Malaysia's goal of becoming a developed nation by achieving excellence in seven "National Key Result Areas" (NKRAs): reducing crime, fighting corruption, improving student outcomes, raising living standards of low-income households, improving rural basic infrastructure, improving urban public transport, and addressing the cost of living (Yehambaram 2012, 63). At the same conference where Soulhi discussed efforts by Islamic financial institutions to fulfill the maqasid by focusing on the substance of Islamic ethics rather than its formal rules, the keynote address was delivered by the former prime minister of Malaysia, Abdullah Badawi. Badawi argued that the Malaysian state was working to fulfill the maqasid through its obsession with achieving "performance indicators":

> The Malaysian government recognizes the need to observe the five essential elements: preservation of religion, life, intellect, wealth, and progeny. Our government intended to bring these objectives into existence through development programs: the NKPIs [National Key Performance Indicators] and NKRAs of the GTP. [We] may . . . achieve the maqasid through performance indicators. Preservation of life is achieved through reduction of crime. Preservation of wealth is achieved through alleviating the low living standards for low-income households.

What is especially salient in Badawi's invocations is the way in which the rational bureaucratic objectives of the modern state were redefined as a yardstick against which fulfilling Islamic moral objectives could be measured.

Those embracing the maqasid approach often framed their favor in terms of social justice. Indeed they saw Islamic finance as a means to further Islamic ideals, such as reducing poverty and increasing equality of opportunity. In contrast, Islamic economists who sought to extract the economic logic of shariah directives did not emphasize the social justice outcomes. They acknowledged that these might be a secondary effect, but they did not see them as the primary goal. Instead, these economists saw the primary objective of the prohibition on interest as an endorsement of sharing risk equitably among members of society. This led them to their critique of debt, which they held disproportionately allocated risk to borrowers and taxpayers, and to their endorsement of equity financing, which they saw as a superior tool for sharing risk. The endorsement of equity also coincided with their economic philosophy, which embraced free markets and risk-taking principles that, as I discuss in chapter 8, also converged with certain strands of neoliberalism.

Signs of Halal Recognition

A few conclusions can be reached about debates over the Islamicity of Islamic finance and how they were evident in discussions on the oppositions between halal and sustainable food on the one hand and between fiqh and maqasid on the other. First, it is important to note that of the four groups of experts with whom I conducted research, the group that most often compared Islamic finance and halal food was Islamic finance professionals. This may have been because, of the four groups, they were the only ones who regularly had to explain Islamic finance to a public with limited understanding of how it worked. Food was an easily interpretable means of making finance comprehensible. It also served as an already-existing domain in which one dimension of modern life had been "Islamicized." In earlier times, most food Malays consumed was locally produced, and one did not have to worry about whether it was permissible. It was halal by default. However, industrial food created a problem of recognition in which one could not be sure whether packaged food was permissible. The state created licensing boards that resolved the problem of dietary permissibility through an official certification process. Islamic bankers hoped that consumers would transfer their efforts to keep a halal diet to their financial practices.

These experts invoked halal food to argue that although instruments used in Islamic finance appeared to be the same as instruments used in conventional finance, the context of their creation marked their difference. Both a chicken and a bond could be deemed permissible through the endorsement of a religious authority endowed with the power to designate what complied with shariah and what did not. Hamza, the CEO, took this a step further when he pointed out the limitations of this logic, stating that Islamic finance should not be content with the mere designation of permissibility but should instead seek to achieve social and moral benefits. He couched this in terms of achieving fulfilling the maqasid (the intent of the shariah), rather than merely fiqh requirements.

Debates over whether Islamic finance is halal reveal how Muslims are asking themselves and each other about what denotes authentic Islamic practice. Scholars have focused on the key role of orthopraxy as a defining feature of Islamic piety, which emphasizes practice over belief (Asad 1986; Bowen 2012, 53; Smith 1957, 28). That is to say, they have asserted that proper Islamic practice is more dependent on what one does (prays five times a day, avoids pork and alcohol, fasts during Ramadan) than what one believes. This contention has its roots in the contention in some schools of Islamic jurisprudence that internal states are ultimately unknowable to others except Allah. This perspective has enabled arguments that privilege form over substance and context over content. However, the recurrent reflection on authenticity in Islamic finance (evident in comparisons to halal food) indicates a discontent with a formalistic approach to Islam. Indeed, efforts to ground Islamic finance in the maqasid (the purposes of the shariah) reveal a concern that external appearances be aligned with internal intentions and states (Siegel 1969). In making recourse to halal food as a point of reference for Islamic finance, Muslims ask whether the latter might reach beyond form to substance. Efforts to shift from debt-based finance to equity and investment-based finance represent efforts to reach beyond form by making risk sharing the substance of Islamic finance. These efforts are addressed in the next two chapters, where I describe efforts to devise equity-based devices and how they were embraced by the Malaysian state.

PART III
Problematization

CHAPTER SEVEN

Experimenting with Risk

In November 2013, I sat in the audience while Ridzuan, the CEO of Mega Islamic Bank, one of Malaysia's largest Islamic banks, addressed an audience at INCEIF. He was delivering what the university called an "industry talk" to faculty and students about extensive reforms that the Malaysian parliament had made to the country's laws governing Islamic finance. Ridzuan spoke carefully: many of the faculty and students he was addressing were critical of the practices of Islamic financial institutions such as Mega Islamic, despite the fact that many of the students hoped to start careers in Islamic banking following their graduation from the university. Ridzuan's remarks were prompted by the 2013 Islamic Financial Services Act that had recently been passed by Malaysia's parliament at the behest of the Central Bank. The new act promised far-reaching changes to Malaysia's Islamic finance industry. IFSA was far more comprehensive in both scope and detail than the relatively thin Islamic Banking Act it replaced, which had first authorized Islamic banking operations in Malaysia thirty years earlier. Ridzuan launched into an analysis of the impact of the new legislation that echoed the sentiments of many industry practitioners.

At the outset of his talk, Ridzuan said that the new law portended many changes for the industry, "some brilliant, some troubling." He bristled at the fact that the law was "passed with little industry consultation," suggesting that regulators at the Central Bank had not adequately engaged financial professionals in the recent legislative changes. This was a common perception. In private conversations I had with several of Ridzuan's colleagues, they strenuously objected to the new laws and what they perceived as a lack of industry consultation in their formulation—although they always requested that their objections be kept anonymous out of fear of retribution by officials from the Central Bank. Like their conventional counterparts, Islamic bankers often spoke out against government regulation of the industry and frequently criticized efforts at supervision. Ridzuan interpreted the legal changes as an effort by the Central Bank to spur change in the industry, intoning that "regulators say that they want to push Islamic finance to the next stage. They say that Islamic finance is the same as conventional finance." Industry professionals sensed that regulators, especially officials in the Islamic Banking and Insurance Department, were attentive to the widespread criticism that Islamic finance merely mimicked conventional finance by replicating its devices and failed to offer a "true" alternative. In response, finance professionals believed that the Central Bank was seeking to move the industry toward what reformers saw as a more authentic version of Islamic finance focusing more on equity than on debt.

Midway through his remarks Ridzuan came to what he saw as the central issue in the debate over the present and future of Islamic finance, namely, how risk should be allocated among financial actors: "The goal of IFSA is to move from risk transfer to risk sharing." The fact that the CEO of a major Islamic bank saw the transformation of Islamic finance in these terms illustrated the national impact made by those seeking to reform Islamic finance. The widespread debate over the definition and future of Islamic finance was one in which the Central Bank was actively engaged. This debate turned on the question of the sociality of risk, that is to say, how risk should be apportioned among members of a collectivity. Reformers argued that the tenets usually deployed to define Islamic finance—most notably the prohibition of interest, but also injunctions against ambiguity (gharar) and gambling (maysir)—are surface manifestations of an underlying principle that stands at the root of Islamic economic action: the equitable distribution of risk. In so doing they suggest that contemporary social inequality is less the effect of the distribution of wealth than of the distribution of risk (Beck 1992). Their primary contention was that risk sharing could resolve conflicts over the distribution of risk. This would be best achieved through equity-based devices premised on partnership rather than debt-based ones such as bai al inah.

Nonetheless, the desire for a shariah-based Islamic finance that deployed equity contracts, instead of shariah-compliant ones still largely premised on debt contracts, was not only grounded in their conviction regarding the social benefits of risk sharing. Reformers and critics claimed it also had economic advantages. Most notably, they argued that Qur'anic directives for financial action would reduce the propensity of leveraging in financial markets. "Leveraging" refers to the practice of borrowing for investment under the belief that the profits generated through an investment will outpace the interest payments due on a loan. Leveraging is a high-risk financial strategy that can lead to immense profits but also can precipitate equally massive losses. Islamic finance experts argued that an emphasis on investment and equity financing (which they saw as the logical result of Qur'anic prescriptions against interest) would create greater financial stability and reduce the propensity of finance capitalism to effect economic crises. In detailing these debates this chapter depicts the viewpoint of critics and reformers who argue that the promise of Islamic finance lies in its critique of the widespread deployment of leverage in finance capitalism.

Risk Transfer and the Techniques of Replication

The notion that risk sharing is a constitutive feature of Islamic economic ethics is a commonly expressed sentiment, especially among reformers, but it is also widespread enough to appear on ads for Islamic banks (see figure 14). Nonetheless, in practice the majority of the contracts used by Islamic financial institutions essentially replicate the risk transfer features that reformers argue are a hallmark of "debt-based" conventional finance. Critics of Islamic finance argue that equity-based contracts are representative of Islamic finance in its purest form. Whereas sale-based contracts dominate the Islamic finance industry, reformers hope that in the future they will be replaced by these equity-based contracts. Historically, due to the strict Qur'anic prohibition on interest, those seeking to comply faithfully with religious prescriptions have resorted to other basic methods for financing: partnerships and sales.

While partnership contracts are viewed as the epitome of Islamic finance, sale-based contracts underlie most of the actual day-to-day operations of Islamic banks. As noted previously, shariah scholars in the Middle East have come to a different conclusion regarding the sale-based bai al inah contract that is permissible in Malaysia. Islamic banks in the Gulf region and elsewhere in the Middle East use a different sale-based contract called tawarruq to facilitate financing. Also referred to as a commodity murabaha, tawarruq differs from bai al inah in that the asset is not sold and repurchased by the same two parties. In a tawarruq contract, a

FIGURE 14. An advertisement for the Saudi-owned Al Rajhi Bank. The copy alludes to the prominence of sharing as a key principle of Islamic banking. Reformers contend that risk sharing and profit-and-loss sharing are central aspects of Islamic banking. The ad is further significant because the three boys in the photograph appear to be of Malay, Chinese, and Indian descent, the three major ethnic groups in Malaysia. Tension between these groups has been a recurring feature of modern Malaysian history. In addition to evoking risk and profit sharing as central principles of Islamic finance, the jovial scene in which the boys are sharing a cake could be read as a comment on the importance of national unity and reciprocity between citizens in contemporary Malaysia. Photo by author.

customer purchases a commodity from a bank at the market price plus a markup and then sells the asset for cash on the spot to a third party (see figure 15). The bank, in turn, may have originally purchased the commodity from a fourth party. As in bai al inah, the buyer generally does not intend to actually utilize the commodity but rather to resell it as a means to raise capital. Tawarruq is viewed as more shariah compliant than bai al inah because the seller does not repurchase the physical asset from the buyer. Scholars in the Middle East have deemed it permissible because it involves a transfer of ownership rights: after the initial sale the buyer is theoretically able to use the asset or sell it to another party. Thus the first sale in tawarruq is viewed as a true sale, whereas in bai al inah the fact that the asset is sold and then repurchased by the same party casts doubt on the validity of the sale. Middle Eastern scholars from the Hanafi and Hanbali schools ruled that the objective of the bai al inah transaction is not the transfer of ownership rights but rather to facilitate financing.

The popularity of sale-based contracts among Islamic banks is attributable to the fact that they effectively replicate the interest-based debt devices with which conventional bankers are familiar. This is accomplished through a reverse calculation of the necessary markup on the sale over a given period of deferred payment to yield a "profit rate" that effectively mirrors the prevailing interest rate. Indeed, Islamic banks advertise the profit rate in such a way that it is virtually indistinguishable from an interest rate in conventional finance (see figure 16). As one reformer mentioned to me, the evidence that, in practice, Islamic financial institutions use sale-based contracts to "back-calculate" profit rates that mirror interest-based loans can be drawn from the fact that Islamic banks that are subsidiaries of large conventional banks in Malaysia use the same computer software for both their conventional and their Islamic operations.

Islamic bankers who came to the industry from the conventional side prefer sale-based contracts to partnership-based contracts because they do not have to change their methods of risk measurement. Indeed, sale-based contracts can be executed with credit risk evaluation procedures drawn from conventional banking. Partnership contracts would require a

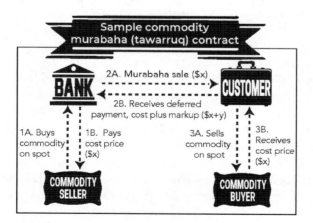

FIGURE 15. A sample tawarruq contract structure. This structure is used by Bursa Suq Al-Sila' to facilitate liquidity management in the Islamic banking system. Credit: Jos Sances.

FIGURE 16. An advertisement by Al Rajhi Bank that publicizes the bank's profit "rate" for auto financing. Note that the script "i" following the product name indicates that the product is Islamic in origin. Photo by author.

new kind of expertise to evaluate the probability of success for a particular business undertaking. Islamic bankers expressed considerable anxiety about efforts to increase the use of equity-based partnership contracts and make them more faithful to authentic Islamic principles. Addressing legal reforms instituted at the behest of Bank Negara, Ridzuan suggested that evaluating the commercial potential of entrepreneurs exposed the limits of knowledge in Islamic banks. His voice betraying considerable stress, he explained, "Banking doesn't recognize a skill or an idea. This is the sphere of private equity and venture capital. We don't have the technical know-how to manage these kinds of risks. . . . When we lend a dollar, we expect to get a dollar back." In this sense, he viewed the main obstacle to the adoption of equity-based contracts as the lack of expertise necessary to evaluate the

risks inherent in them. He appeared frustrated by the Central Bank's efforts to push his firm toward a fundamentally different logic of banking.

The ambiguity regarding sale-based contracts became apparent in a
conversation I had with Nuraini, a former high-level Islamic banking executive, about her career in and opinions about Islamic finance. She was
one of the so-called national "pioneers" of the industry and had helped
to create some of the early knowledge infrastructure for the country. Although she had worked in an influential capacity at several key Islamic
financial institutions, by the early 2000s, just as Malaysia was seeking to
scale up its domestic financial industry to become a global hub for Islamic
finance, Nuraini became disillusioned with the industry. By the 2010s she
was a vocal critic of Islamic finance in Malaysia.

Nuraini told me that the techniques to avoid interest on debts were a
major reason she had become critical of Islamic finance. With no shortage of sarcasm, Nuraini provided a vivid example of how Islamic banks
had developed techniques to evade the Qur'anic prohibition on interest
by using a "paper sale." In the mid-1990s she was working in an executive capacity at a state-owned development bank, which was looking to
raise capital to in turn provide financing for small-scale enterprises. She
described how a bai al inah contract was used to generate the capital the
bank needed for financing small-business loans:

> We [owned] a building that was priced at 600 million . . . then we sold the building
> to the Ministry of Finance. Then, the second transaction was when the ministry
> sold the building back at, say, for example, 700 million [on a deferred payment
> basis]. So it became a transaction of sale and purchase. . . . The shariah part
> was, they said, that you cannot have two contracts in one . . . so what we did, in
> order to have . . . a separate agreement, was have two distinct events. At the first
> event we had representatives of the bank and representatives of the Ministry of
> Finance. Here we had the chairman of the Islamic development bank and here
> we had the vice president of the ministry. They came and met and exchanged
> the key to the building. They were shaking hands and they were transferring
> the key. One said, "I am selling you the building for 600 million"; the other one
> said, "I accept this transaction." So we did that in one room witnessed by the
> muftis![1] We had the mufti of Penang, the mufti of Selangor, the mufti of Perak,
> and we had the mufti of Perlis.[2] They came to witness the whole ceremony.
> Then the whole transaction was adjourned. . . . We went for tea. Later we came
> back again and we did the reverse! It became like a show! And this we called
> Islamic financing.

The asset used in the transaction was the headquarters of the bank, which is now the Small and Medium Enterprise Development Bank building on Jalan Sultan Ismail in central Kuala Lumpur (see figure 17). The bank sold the headquarters on a spot basis to the Ministry of Finance for 600 million ringgit and then bought it back at 700 million to be paid in installments. The presence of a group of prominent muftis and other Islamic officials endowed the transaction with the trappings of religious authenticity. Nuraini said that at the time she felt that although the effects of such contracts were the same, the differences in form marked Islamic finance as distinct from its conventional counterpart. However, it gradually became apparent to her that Islamic finance, as practiced, deployed loopholes to mimic conventional finance.

FIGURE 17. The headquarters of the development bank at which Nuraini worked and which facilitated the bai al inah contract between the Ministry of Finance and her bank. Photo by author.

These kinds of sale-and-buyback transactions could be used to facilitate all sorts of financing, from big corporate deals to retail purchases. Nuraini provided another example. She had been in search of financing for a small business she was launching with her husband. She sought to obtain capital from Bank Rakyat; to facilitate the financing, the bank used a bai al inah contract based on the sale and repurchase of an office computer. For the "profit rate" on the deferred payments that Nuraini would have to make, bank staff "back-calculated" the markup based on the prevailing interest rate on the Kuala Lumpur Interbank Offer Rate.[3] She explained:

> I told them I wanted to borrow RM10,000 So they said to me, "OK, you sign this contract." I said, "What is this contract?" They said, "Well, you just sign here, on this line." So I said, "Let me read it first." What it said was that I was purchasing a computer for a certain price. The computer belongs to the bank. So I said, "No I don't want to buy a computer!" They said, "No, never mind, I know you want to borrow money, so you just sign here." So I said, "But it says here that I am buying a computer." They said, "It's just one of our ways of doing things." So I signed. Next they handed me another contract that said now I am selling the computer. I said, "In the first place I don't want to buy a computer and there is no computer in front of me." They said, "Never mind, don't worry about it. Just sign!"

Nuraini said that Islamic banks in Malaysia relying on sale-and-buyback transactions would "sell the same computer thousands upon thousands of times" with numerous different clients in order to facilitate financing. The bai al inah contract provides a simple way to circumvent the Qur'anic prohibition on interest by using two sales to replicate what is essentially an interest-bearing loan: a customer in need of financing would come into the branch, buy a computer owned by the bank on a deferred payment basis (for example, RM3,240 payable over three years at RM90 per month), and then immediately thereafter sell the computer back to the bank for cash on the spot but at a reduced price (for example, RM3,000). One could view such a transaction as essentially the same as a loan with an interest rate of roughly 5 percent per year, or one could view it as two distinct sales of the same good for two different prices justified on the basis of the time lag between the sale and resale payments.

By the 2010s there was evidence that criticism of the paper sales practiced by Islamic banks and the bai al inah contract had not fallen on deaf ears. In late 2012 Bank Negara required Islamic banks to remove the so-called interconditionality clause from bai al inah contracts. The head of one Islamic bank provided a dramatic account of how Islamic banks were notified of the change: "It was December 2012 and all CEOs were called away from their London homes at Christmas by the Central Bank. We were told that we had to revamp our contracts to account for the new structure. It ruined our holidays!" Not only were the holidays ruined, but the irony of Islamic bankers celebrating Christmas in London was also lost on the CEO. Prior to this new regulation Islamic banks in Malaysia routinely required that the first of the two sales in a bai al inah transaction be conditional on the second. But the new regulation broke this link, imposing a period of time when the bank would have to hold the asset. This presented a nonzero chance that the two sales in a bai al inah or similar sale-based transaction would not both be completed. A customer could sell an asset to the bank and then abandon the deal without buying it back from the bank at an increased price, leaving the bank holding the bag. This simple change increased the risk associated with bai al inah and caused a great deal of consternation among executives at Islamic banks.

Saif, a shariah scholar, told me that the rationale for moving away from interdependent sales was based on the fact that Malaysia had frequently been "criticized by [shariah] scholars" from the Arabian Gulf region. They viewed the clause as contrary to shariah on the premise that "there should be no conditions on a sale . . . [because this] affects the free will of the buyer or seller." The interconditionality clause contributed to the opinion that the validity of bai al inah was hiyal, because it bent Islamic prescriptions on economic action to enable Islamic banks to act in essentially the same manner as conventional financial institutions. He attributed the removal of the clause to an effort to deploy "universally accepted contracts" in Malaysia, as part of a broader effort to make Kuala Lumpur a hub for Islamic finance. He reasoned that only by eliminating contracts that were viewed with suspicion in the Gulf region would it become an appealing destination for Middle Eastern capital.

Nuraini and Saif were not alone in their criticism of the paper sale arrangements that most Islamic financial institutions in Malaysia use to facilitate financing that meets the letter of Islamic law if not its spirit. In addition to changing the rules governing the use of these contracts, there were extensive efforts to replace the sale-based arrangements with equity devices based on principles of partnership and "risk sharing," as opposed to "risk transfer" or "risk shifting." In general, most Islamic finance experts acknowledge that equity devices are most in keeping with both the spirit and the letter of Islamic law. The greater religious authenticity of these contracts was often articulated in an idiom of purity. For example, in a workshop for central bankers that I attended at the IFSB headquarters in Kuala Lumpur, a regulator formerly employed by the Central Bank of Sudan described partnership contracts as "pure Islamic finance from the time of the prophet." In his remarks at INCEIF, Ridzuan said, "People feel that the only pure form of Islamic banking would be equity based." This perspective was widely shared, not only by Islamic economists and shariah scholars but by some regulators and industry professionals as well.

The Morality of Profit

To achieve "pure" Islamic finance, reformers sought to substitute equity and partnership contracts for debt-based contracts. The contract that these reformers most favored is called a mudaraba, the partnership contract described above in which the capital provider invests in an enterprise and then is granted an agreed-upon percentage of the profits from the entrepreneur. Mudaraba contracts actually date from before the time of the prophet Muhammad and were widely used in the classical Islamic world (Udovitch 1970, 170–248).

Mudaraba contracts were particularly suited to the trading economy of the Arabian Peninsula that was common around the time of the birth of Islam. In the caravan economy, a prosperous merchant would commonly contract with a younger or less prosperous partner to finance a trading voyage. The wealthier merchant would pay for all the goods up front, and the junior party would be responsible for their physical transport and delivery. However, if the goods were lost due to robbery or some other misfortune, the capital provider would bear the financial loss, while the junior member in the relationship would lose only his time and labor. Several participants in my research enthusiastically regaled with me tales about how the prophet Muhammad had used these contracts as a young merchant. One told me that, before Muhammad had wed his first wife, Khadija, the two of them had been in business together on the basis of mudaraba contracts. Khadija would put up the capital and Muhammad would traverse the Arabian desert in the caravan trade.

Exponents of mudaraba liken these contracts to the venture capital arrangements that have financed Silicon Valley firms such as Facebook, Twitter, and Google. These advocates argue that they could facilitate similar entrepreneurial dynamism in the Muslim world. In a lecture I attended at INCEIF, an Islamic economist extolled the virtues of this contract, saying, "I became aware of venture capital in 1982, when I learned about mudaraba. Venture capital has been applied with enormous success . . . but it turns out we are talking about a classical Islamic partnership that was practiced by Muhammad. And today [in] twenty-first century California, Silicon Valley is doing the same thing. . . . They learned it from us, but we have forgotten it!" In so doing, he likened a fundamental contractual instrument of the golden age of Islam to the venture capital agreements that, so we are told, have underwritten the halcyon age of the internet.

As bankers such as Ridzuan revealed, the primary obstacle to widespread adoption of equity-based partnership contracts is that they entail a dramatically new method of calculating risk compared to conventional banking contracts. A central instrument of banking since the time of the Medici has been the interest-bearing loan in which a bank lends capital at a certain rate of interest and makes a profit from the interest paid, as well as receiving the initial (principal) funds over time. Most loans in the conventional interest-based system are secured, meaning that the bank has obtained a guarantee for the loan, usually in the form of collateral. If the debtor is unable or refuses to pay back the loan, a conventional bank can simply liquidate the collateralized asset and thus recoup the initial funds extended.

Proponents of equity-based Islamic contracts argue that the widespread use of collateral in conventional banking loans makes debt contracts "risk free." They aver that these contracts are characteristic of conventional finance at large, which they argue is premised on "risk transfer" rather than risk sharing, and thus not compatible with Islam. The root of this critique of conventional finance is based in two Islamic legal maxims that suggest that profit is morally justified only if it is earned while incurring risk. The first, *al-ghurm bil-ghunm,* means "there is no reward without risk"; the second, *al-kharaj bil-damam,* translates as "there should be no guarantee of profits" (Rosly 2005, 405). Islamic finance experts invoke these maxims in distinguishing Islamic from conventional finance, as they object not only to the payment of interest but also to other routine mechanisms such as government-guaranteed deposit insurances. Interest payments contravene this principle because they are guaranteed payments and the payee does not risk the possibility of loss. Reformers argue that in a financial system run purely according to Islamic norms, institutions such as the US-based Federal Deposit Insurance Corporation (FDIC) or the United Kingdom's Financial Services Compensation Scheme would not be permitted because they offer no-risk guarantees to depositors.

A partnership contract entails a great deal more risk than an interest-bearing loan. In the latter the principal is guaranteed by the debtor's collateral, and the interest profits are guaranteed in the sense that the rate is fixed. In contrast, the proceeds an investor might get from a partnership contract are subject to market fluctuations, and, in the event of an economic downturn or worse-than-expected performance, there may be no profits. Furthermore, the investor might even lose his or her investment should the company in which he or she invested go bankrupt. Expressing anxiety about new legal requirements regarding the ways in which Islamic banks could use partnership contracts, Ridzuan said, "At its core, banking is the business of risk management, and we have no idea how to manage risk in an equity-based contract." Ridzuan's anxiety showed how the legal reforms prompted by the Central Bank and implemented in IFSA created uncertainty for Islamic bankers. Since most Islamic bankers started their careers as conventional bankers, shifting from a framework based on debt to one based on equity profoundly challenged their underlying perspective on banking.

During the 2000s many Islamic banks in Malaysia developed mudaraba accounts and used them in lieu of interest-bearing deposit accounts to comply with the Qur'anic prohibition on interest (see figure 18). In these schemes depositors are designated "investors" and the bank adopts the position of the entrepreneur. The depositor "invests" money in the bank, which then in turn reinvests the funds in projects such as real estate development or commercial ventures. However, reformers argued that Islamic banks had essentially reengineered these contracts to replicate interest-bearing accounts.

Replication was accomplished through several means. First, the principal amount was guaranteed, which reformers argued was contrary to Islamic economic ethics. Interest payments violate this dictum because they are guaranteed payments in which the lender does not bear the risk for the possibility of loss. Second, not only did Islamic banks guarantee the principal in mudaraba savings accounts, but they also used various techniques to keep the "profit rate" paid to depositors relatively consistent, again mirroring fixed interest rates. This was accomplished through techniques such as "profit smoothing" whereby the proceeds due to an investor were held at a constant rate from year to year and any excess was

FIGURE 18. An advertisement for a banking product based on the mudaraba offered by May-
bank Islamic, Malaysia's largest Islamic bank. Photo by author.

held in a "profit equalization reserve." Through these techniques, if the
actual rate of returns did not meet the expected rate, then the funds held
back could be disbursed to "smooth out" the profits. This practice also
violated the principle of "no reward without risk" because it distorted the
relationship between the investment and the actual effects of market gains
and losses. According to critics of the existing Islamic financial system in
Malaysia, Islamic banks were unscrupulously manipulating traditional Islamic equity and investment devices to make them virtually undistinguish-
able from conventional debt-based ones.

Syed, a shariah scholar at one of Malaysia's largest Islamic financial
institutions, told me that product managers at Islamic banks preferred
mudaraba accounts because they allowed the bank to transfer a "benefit"

to depositors. He explained that Islamic banks most often used two different kinds of contracts to attract depositors: mudaraba and wadiah. Bank Negara defined "wadiah" as "a contract by which an owned asset is placed with another party on the basis of trusteeship for safekeeping purposes." In such a safekeeping arrangement, Syed said, "There are not supposed to be any promotions": the bank takes the deposit, guarantees it to the depositor, and is responsible for returning exactly that sum on demand to the depositor. He further explained that mudaraba contracts were very popular because they enabled banks to offer "various kinds of promotions, such as giving customers trips for signing up for accounts." In contrast, promotions are not allowed on wadiah because they are to be based on qard al hasan, in which the depositor is considered to make a "benevolent loan" to the bank. Any promotions "would be considered riba from a shariah perspective" and would therefore be impermissible.

In response to criticisms of the ways that the mudaraba had been remade to mimic a conventional interest-bearing deposit account, regulators at the Central Bank sought to clearly differentiate it. Ridzuan referred to one move in this regard that was contained in the Islamic Financial Services Act. In a level of detail that was unprecedented in parliamentary legislation regarding Islamic finance in Malaysia, IFSA distinguished "Islamic deposits" from "investment accounts." According to the law, an investment account is defined as an

> account under which money is paid and accepted for the purposes of investment, including for the provision of finance, in accordance with Shariah on terms that there is no express or implied obligation to repay the money in full and: (a) either only the profits, or both the profits or losses, thereon shall be shared between the person paying the money and the person accepting the money; or (b) with or without any return. (Legal Research Board 2013, 2.1)

Thus an investment account is defined in terms endorsed by those seeking to reform Islamic finance, insofar as it preserves many of the features of a mudaraba: no principal guarantee and a variable return based on the actual profits (or losses) on the investment made with the funds. In contrast, an Islamic deposit is defined as

> a sum of money accepted or paid in accordance with Shariah: (a) on terms under which it will be repaid in full, with or without any gains, return or any other consideration in money or money's worth, either on demand or at a time or in

circumstances agreed by or on behalf of the person making the payment and person accepting it; or (b) under an arrangement, on terms whereby the proceeds under the arrangement to be paid to the person paying the sum of money shall not be less than such sum of money. (Legal Research Board 2013, 2.1)

An Islamic deposit, in contrast to an investment account, is a guaranteed credit in which the depositor is entitled to repayment in full. Whereas the investment account is based on the principles of a mudaraba, an Islamic deposit is premised on those of the wadiah.

Technologies of Risk

Islamic finance professionals interpreted the legal restrictions placed on mudaraba accounts as an effort by the Central Bank to increase shariah compliance and, in Ridzuan's terms, "to move from risk transfer to risk sharing." It was not just those in the industry who held this opinion. Syed, the shariah scholar, told me that the goal of a separation of investment accounts based on mudaraba from Islamic deposits based on wadiah was "to promote profit sharing and risk sharing. This will require a rethinking to make people aware that those who partake in investment accounts are not depositors but investors. Depositors will still be protected, but not investors." In his eyes Bank Negara revised the rules on investment accounts to make them "more truly representative of shariah contracts."

By the mid-2000s Bank Negara had already started to try to move from debt-based to equity-based contracts. Umar, a senior employee in the Islamic Banking Department, told me that Bank Negara had issued guidelines for profit-sharing contracts in 2007 because banks had until then relied mostly on sale- and trade-based contracts, despite being strongly urged by the central bank to "experiment with musharaka and mudaraba." Heeding the calls of Islamic economists, Umar said that the bank had sought to increase risk taking by banks to fulfill their religious obligations. "If you ask the academicians, everyone is talking about risk sharing, but our banks are not doing it; they are very risk averse. . . . We thought that maybe they weren't doing risk sharing because there weren't any guidelines, so we issued the guidelines. . . . [But] even though we did that, the take-up rate was very low."

It is hard to understate the dramatic extent of the changes that the new law demanded of Islamic banks. IFSA represented a bold effort to move the industry toward a shariah-based system by upholding what reformers saw as the authentic principles of equity finance. Umar told me that legal changes to mudaraba accounts were needed because, in practice, techniques such as profit smoothing had made deposits in Islamic banks almost identical to those in conventional banks. Furthermore, until 2013 all "customer placements" were defined as deposits, but the new law made a distinction between deposits and investments. Furthermore, he argued that the profit equalization reserve made "the rate [paid by the bank] very similar to the conventional rates." Because of this Bank Negara decided to make a radical intervention that Umar called a "paradigm shift":

> We said, "No, not anymore. If you make a bigger profit, you pay higher. If you make a lower profit, you pay a lower rate." We just want the banks to start thinking differently from what they have been doing before. I mean, this is a paradigm shift for the bank. . . . For a deposit, yes, you can make it as competitive as the conventional. But when you talk about investment, it should reflect the actual performance of the investment.

Umar told me that 60 percent of deposit accounts in Islamic financial institutions were mudaraba based, so it was the most popular contract for an Islamic deposit instrument. He said that the goal is to make the individual customer judge for him- or herself what kind of "risk appetite" they have. He explained that the goal behind some of the changes was to make the banks more innovative in their practice of Islamic banking:

> This is a whole new game for the banks. They complain, saying they are not investment banks. We told them, "This is the opportunity for Islamic banks to do something bigger than what the conventional banks can do. The conventional banks can only do deposits and lending, but Islamic banks can do more than that! You can do lending, you can do financing, you can do venture capital, you can do a lot of things under these regulations." . . . So we see a lot of potential, but it takes time for [the banks] to see the potential. . . . Some banks are very risk averse, but some banks are willing to do some risk taking.

Here Umar illustrated the pastoral role that the Central Bank takes in Islamic finance. It acts not only to regulate Islamic finance but, more important, to foster its growth. In this regard one key role is to get the Islamic banks to heed the calls of critics who saw them as "merely replicating" the instruments of conventional banks. The sentiment that banks were too conservative and needed to be spurred toward innovation was widespread among regulators.

However, encouraging risk sharing was not merely a means of producing an identity for Islamic finance distinct from conventional finance. Caitlin Zaloom has emphasized the "productive dimensions of risk" (Zaloom 2006, 109) and described how traders in Chicago securities markets form themselves through "turning risk into profit." Thus risk taking is a practical activity through which a "capitalist ethic" is enacted (Zaloom 2006, 94). Zaloom shows how inculcating risk calculation produces a distinct kind of subject finely attuned to the mechanisms of the market. Along analogous lines, by transforming depositors into investors and subjecting these customers to new risks by forcing them to "share risk" with banks, the Central Bank also sought to attune the customers who used mudaraba to the market. Rather than having their balance guaranteed and receiving a fixed return, in the new regime of risk sharing those who used mudaraba would have to be better attuned to calculating risk and more attentive to market movements.

Furthermore, bank officials emphasized the "upside" of risk: the fact that risk taking had the potential to generate greater profits. A lower-level employee in the Department of Islamic Banking and Takaful, Shamsul, told me that Islamic banks and their customers had to reconceptualize how they thought of risk. He explained, "We typically think of risk in terms of losses, but there might be benefits too. Everyone sees risk in terms of the possibility of losses," but it could also be thought of "in terms of profits." By producing subjects better at calculating risk, the state could elicit entrepreneurial citizens better capable of competing in a global economy, a subject to which I return in the next chapter.

Testing Stress

Shifting Islamic finance from a reliance on debt-based devices to increased use of investment-oriented ones required experimenting with risk calculation. This substitution required a fundamental rethinking of devices for the provision of capital in general, which was apparent during a weeklong workshop I attended titled "Liquidity Risk Management and Stress Testing Standards for Islamic Finance" at Sasana Kijang in late 2013. The workshop was hosted by the IFSB and was part of a series of special sessions designed to facilitate the implementation of the standards it had developed through national banking regulators. Around twenty representatives from central banks and monetary authorities attended the workshop. They were tasked with the regulation of Islamic finance and hailed from countries across the Muslim world, including Bahrain, Egypt, Nigeria, Sudan, Oman, Indonesia, Malaysia, Turkey, and Bangladesh. The central objective of the workshop was to help regulators effectively implement some of the standards that the IFSB had developed. The bulk of the workshop was dedicated to the problem of "stress testing" Islamic banks. Stress testing had emerged as a hot topic in European and North American banking regulation but, as described below, it presented a unique obstacle to Islamic banks.

In the wake of the 2008 financial crisis in the United States and ensuing near collapse of the banking infrastructure in the country, plans by the Federal Reserve to "stress-test" American banks attracted a great deal of popular media coverage. Stress tests are simulations that determine the ability of a given financial institution to withstand the capital demands precipitated by an economic crisis. The stress tests launched by the Fed were in part intended to tighten oversight of financial institutions following the crisis. Typically, a stress test determines whether a financial institution possesses sufficient resources to ensure solvency in the event that the institution is faced with a financial "shock." In conventional finance, stress tests focus on the implications of various scenarios for the stability of financial institutions, including, for example, a precipitous drop in real estate values, a steep rise in energy prices, a stock market crash, or an abrupt increase in interest rates. All of these events could not only bring down individual financial institutions but also might pose "systemic risk" to the financial system at large. Prior to 2008, banks in the United States had conducted stress tests internally as part of their risk management strategies. However, following the crisis, the 2010 Dodd-Frank Act authorized the Federal Reserve to independently apply stress tests to American banks. In early 2009, the first round of stress tests was breathlessly covered by the US media as the Fed sought to discern the ability of financial firms to withstand a future economic shock. Since then US regulators have required large American banks (those with over $50 billion in assets) to conduct stress tests two times per year to ensure the US financial system continues to function smoothly.

At Malaysia's Central Bank and at the IFSB, those tasked with regulating Islamic finance likewise considered the possibility of catastrophic failure in the Islamic financial system and sought to devise a model to subject them to stress tests analogous to those used in the conventional system. However, the particularities of Islamic finance meant that the methods of stress testing developed to evaluate the health of conventional banks could not simply be translated wholesale to determine the solvency of Islamic banks, because their balance sheets differ in key ways from those characteristic of conventional banks.[4] This is mainly due to the presence of equity-based devices in Islamic finance, as opposed to the debt-based instruments that predominate in conventional banks. As regulators sought to shift toward more equity-based devices, the problem of how to stress-test Islamic banks required attention.

On the balance sheet of a conventional bank, assets can be neatly cleaved from liabilities. Banks must ensure they have enough capital on hand to meet projected obligations. Any funds loaned by a bank are considered assets, and funds held on deposit are considered liabilities. However, an Islamic bank reliant on equity-based instruments operates according to a wholly different logic. Rather than making loans on which interest is charged and holding deposits on which interest is paid, an Islamic bank serves as a sort of middleman between those who hold excess capital and the businesses in need of it. In their everyday operations, banks reliant on equity devices use a "double mudaraba" system of financing whereby on one side of their balance sheet they assume the role of the mudarib (entrepreneur), partnering with a rabb al maal (capital provider); on the other side of their balance sheet, using the capital raised as mudarib, they assume the role of the rabb al maal and form partnerships with entrepreneurs in need of capital under a completely separate mudaraba contract.

The use of equity-based instruments in a double mudaraba banking system raises a profound question for Islamic financial institutions when it comes to performing a stress test: How should risk be allocated in a partnership based on investment and profit sharing? In the conventional system, the answer is clear. The risk is borne in the first instance by the bank because it is considered the risk-bearing agent. In the event of a default on a loan, the bank is still responsible for settling with its depositors. In the event of a catastrophic failure with multiple defaults resulting in the insolvency of the bank, deposits are still guaranteed by deposit insurance provided by the state. However, in an Islamic system, the allocation of risk and responsibility is not so clear cut because, under the Islamic principle of risk sharing, the risk-bearing agent is the capital provider who accepts the possibility of losses in making an investment. Indeed, it is only through taking risk that profit is morally justified under the principle of "no reward without risk." In a bank deposit structured according to a mudaraba, the depositor occupies the position of capital provider and therefore (unlike in the conventional system, in which deposits are guaranteed) the depositor is responsible for the risks that he or she undertakes.

The problem of allocating risk was presented in the context of profit-sharing investment accounts (PSIAs) and was a central focus of concern at the IFSB workshop for central bankers that I attended. These instruments are deposits in Islamic financial institutions structured according to the risk-sharing principles of mudaraba. Unlike conventional deposit accounts, which are typically guaranteed through deposit insurance provided by the state (like FDIC insurance in the United States), Islamic scholars contend that there should be no insurance or other guarantee for a PSIA. Thus, a PSIA holder is considered a capital provider and accepts the possibility that his or her investment could be reduced or disappear completely.

The question posed at the IFSB workshop in seeking a method for stress-testing Islamic financial institutions was how PSIAs should be reckoned on an institution's balance sheet: Were they liabilities for which the financial institution was responsible, or were the PSIA holders responsible for these instruments? Strict religious interpretations of mudaraba argued that the capital provider held all liability for the risk incurred in an investment. However, as discussed previously, in practice some Islamic financial institutions had introduced various schemes, both to guarantee the balance and "smooth" the returns, so that they were consistent from year to year. Reformers had become increasingly critical of these practices because they did not comply with the principle of "no reward without risk." In sum, the problem with stress-testing an Islamic bank lay in the expectation that the depositor would bear some of the risk. Presented with this challenge, the final three days of the workshop entailed learning the methodology that IFSB experts had created to address how to conduct stress tests in an equity-based system. Participants then completed a simulation in groups to apply these techniques to an actual case study.

For the duration of the workshop the attendees sat at six clusters of tables that were spread out around the room. The air-conditioning blew through vents in the floor and created frigid temperatures, especially in contrast to the tropical heat outside the building. By the latter stages of the meeting several of the attendees from midlatitude countries, unaccustomed to such industrial cooling, took to placing briefcases or bags on top of the vents to block the unrelenting stream of frosty air. The attendees were well-educated technocrats who had worked at the various central banks and monetary authorities that they represented for several years. All had university degrees in conventional banking and finance but had limited experience with Islamic operations. They were skilled at using the mathematical formulas to which we were introduced and at completing the computations necessary to execute them, many of which were quite technical and went beyond the calculus I remembered from high school. However, they had much more limited understanding of the core concepts and religious principles of Islamic finance and the key differences between Islamic and conventional finance. In the afternoon of the first day of the workshop, Erkhan, from the Banking Regulation and Supervision Agency of Turkey, turned to me and asked me if I could recommend a good introductory textbook on Islamic finance.[5]

One of the main objectives of the IFSB was to build capacity among national financial authorities to regulate Islamic finance. The workshop was in part intended to bring regulators relatively new to the industry up to speed. The discussion of stress testing and the tools to implement it were a key part of the workshop. After introducing the concept of stress testing on the third day, the main facilitator of the workshop, Rashid, led into the methods that he had developed for stress-testing Islamic financial institutions. He was a bright young Pakistani who had been employed at the IFSB for nearly ten years. A math whiz, he had worked on several of the teams responsible for developing the standards that the IFSB produced. He explained the method he had developed for stress-testing Islamic banks with a mixture of earnestness and bravado.

On the morning of the fourth day he got to the main issue at stake in trying to apportion who was responsible for the risk in bank accounts structured according to mudaraba principles. In a rising voice, he rhetorically asked the group, "How are PSIA holders treated? Are they investors, like a liability [deposit], or both?" He answered his own question, "In theory, investment account holders are actually liable for investment losses, because they are the rabb al mal. If there is a profit, they will receive profit according to profit-sharing ratio." He then noted that "many banks said it is very hard to keep the PSIA holders as customers." Banks had found that their depositors did not like the variable returns generated in these accounts. In response, he said, "Over the past few years the banks [have decided to] smooth the returns," referring to the practice of averaging the returns paid to account holders so that the proceeds were consistent from year to year, like interest rates, rather than calculated according to the fluctuating profits generated by the investments banks made with their depositors' funds. He noted that different jurisdictions have varying regulations regarding the way risks are distributed on banking deposits and described the recent changes to Malaysia's laws due to the implementation of IFSA.

Then he shifted to discussing the operations of Islamic banks elsewhere, where mudaraba principles were expressly prohibited in the country's banking laws. He said, "Some countries, such as the UK, do not recognize PSIAs in the law. Any funds deposited in a UK bank are considered deposits. They are guaranteed liabilities for the bank and they fall under Basel. Basel treats all deposits as liabilities, and the banks must consider all funds from customers as deposits. If all the risk is borne by the investors, then the bank is not facing the risk." The central problem banks faced was how risk should be apportioned in risk-sharing contracts and how it might be allocated in a stress-testing exercise implemented at an Islamic bank using mudaraba contracts.

Rashid's innovation was to create a variable, α ("alpha"), which was an indicator of the proportion of a bank's assets that were held in the form of unrestricted PSIAs.[6] Alpha was a ratio in which a value near zero reflected an "investment-like product, with the investor bearing the commercial risk, while an 'alpha' close to one would reflect a deposit-like product with the depositor effectively bearing virtually no commercial risk" (IFSB 2011, 1). Rashid explained that the creation of the alpha variable essentially allowed regulators to accurately apportion risk between depositors and banks. Responding to a question from a regulator from Sudan, he said, "If in Sudan alpha is 50 percent, it means the risk is distributed fifty-fifty." The value of alpha indicated the relative proportions of risk carried by depositors and by the institution. A lower alpha would mean that the risk was primarily held by depositors but also that institutions must have a higher capital adequacy ratio to withstand the pressure of an economic shock. The alpha variable was key to enabling the application of a stress-testing framework in Islamic finance because it could measure the distribution of risk between depositors and financial institutions.

In sum, efforts to create a financial infrastructure premised on equity rather than debt required innovative thinking and experimenting with risk. The tools developed for conventional finance could not necessarily be translated wholesale into an Islamic financial system, especially one with extensive use of equity-based devices. As Ridzuan's remarks presented at the outset of this chapter demonstrated, conventional bankers who had migrated to Islamic finance were not accustomed to a financial

system premised on risk sharing. A mudaraba-based, profit-sharing investment account exhibited a far different risk profile than a conventional
deposit account. It was up to institutions such as the IFSB to synthesize instruments and techniques that could enable an Islamic financial system to
function. This was accomplished through innovations such as the creation
of alpha, a variable that reflected the distribution of risk in a PSIA. The
ethic of innovation and experimentation evident in the creation of alpha
is characteristic of Islamic finance. What Islamic finance will ultimately
become is the subject of such experimentation, as experts within the field
of Islamic finance debate what its core principles should be. This account
of devising a stress-testing model for Islamic finance and its resolution
demonstrates the emergent nature of this domain and the ways in which
experts within it are engaged in the process of producing new knowledge.

Provincializing Leverage

Midway through the IFSB workshop, a "market risk specialist" from Malaysia's Central Bank made a technically sophisticated argument for the
promise that equity-based finance offered in comparison to debt-based finance. The argument was made in the context of an address on liquidity
risk management supervision and was not based on the inherent superiority of religious principles but presented in solely deductive terms. The
speaker was describing the Malaysian Central Bank's "supervisory risk-
based framework," which he referred to as "SuRF." It was shortly before
lunchtime, and the energy in the room had begun to flag. Given the time of
day and the fact that many of us were still affected by jet lag, the attention
of many of the participants in the workshop, myself included, had begun to
fade. However, my focus quickly returned when the market risk specialist,
Nazmi, departed briefly from his expertly choreographed PowerPoint presentation and starkly contrasted Islamic with conventional finance. Much
as I had heard from many experts before, he averred that their essential
difference is that Islamic financial instruments should be equity based
rather than debt based. However, what especially piqued my interest was
his explanation of why financial systems based on equity are more fundamentally sound and less prone to crisis than those based on debt.

Nazmi's presentation crystallized a central conviction among experts
regarding the advantages of Islamic finance. It was one of the pivotal mo-
ments of my fieldwork: some of the central questions with which I had

been preoccupied came sharply into focus at this moment. Nazmi distilled the essential difference between conventional and Islamic finance down to the relative difference in the presence of a single financial quality: *leverage*. In relatively simple terms, he asserted the superiority of an equity-based Islamic financial system due to the stability it maintained through constraining leverage. He explained, "What caused the crisis is excessive leverage . . . , but the PSIA minimizes excessive leverage. . . . [In an Islamic system] if the banks fail, there is no need to step in to bail them out." This was because, he explained, in an equity-based system depositors bear a larger share of the risk than do banking institutions in the provision and circulation of capital. A number of observers have pointed to the role of leverage in the financial crisis, including that of former Federal Reserve chairman Alan Greenspan himself (Stein 2010). In corporate finance, leveraging refers to the practice of purchasing the assets with a combination of equity and borrowed funds (or "debt"), under the presumption that the income generated by the asset will exceed the cost of borrowing those funds. Higher leverage necessarily means more debt. A common measure of leverage for a corporation is its debt-to-equity ratio (also known as the leverage ratio).[7] Leverage greatly multiplies the risk in a given financial strategy. The widespread use of credit default swaps to insure collateralized debt obligations precipitated the near collapse of insurance giant AIG at the height of the 2008 financial calamity is an example of high-risk leveraging (Roitman 2014, 51–53).

Nazmi's intervention was striking because he offered a concrete rationale for reducing leverage that was grounded in Islamic principles of equity investment and risk sharing. He argued that a financial system based on equity would not be subject to the same fierce fluctuations that plagued debt-based economies. In a financial system operating according to principles of equity investment, one can only venture the capital that one already has in hand. In contrast, in a financial system where the provision of capital occurs through debt, interest-based borrowing to chase financial returns can easily become speculative. The US mortgage crisis of 2008 was a paradigmatic example of this, as banks made massive amounts of debt financing available to home buyers, who borrowed under the presumption that real estate values would continue to rapidly escalate. Home buyers speculated that the increase in home prices would outpace the loans they were taking. While for a time the increase in home prices exceeded the cost of borrowing, as house prices increased, borrowers became overleveraged and ultimately had no recourse but default when the housing bubble burst.

BOX 2. **The Upside and Downside of Leverage**

Leverage refers to the use of equity and debt to purchase assets with the expectation that the income generated by the asset will exceed the cost of borrowing those funds. Proponents of Islamic finance argue that part of its advantage is due to the fact that it limits leverage, as leveraging can rapidly multiply both profits and losses. For example, take the hypothetical case of two investors, Ameena and Naailah, who both have $200,000 to invest. Ameena uses $200,000 of her cash to purchase twenty acres of land with a total cost of $200,000. Ameena is not using leverage. In contrast, Naailah uses $200,000 of her cash and borrows an additional $400,000 to purchase sixty acres of land having a total cost of $600,000. Naailah is practicing financial leverage by obtaining $600,000 worth of land with only $200,000 of her own funds.

If the properties owned by Ameena and Naailah increase in value by 25 percent and are then sold, Ameena will have a $50,000 gain on her $200,000 investment, a 25 percent return. Naailah's land will sell for $750,000 and will result in a gain of $150,000. By using leverage Naailah has multiplied the value of her return: the $150,000 gain on her $200,000 investment results in a 75 percent return for Naailah. When assets increase in value, leverage offers tremendous financial benefit.

When assets decline in value, the use of leverage can have sharply adverse consequences by multiplying losses. For example, suppose the properties owned by Ameena and Naailah decrease in value by 10 percent from their cost and are then sold. Ameena will bear a loss of $20,000 on her $200,000 investment—a decline of 10 percent on her investment. In contrast, Naailah's losses will multiply because she has leveraged her initial funds to purchase three times as much land. She suffers a loss of $60,000 on her $200,000 investment, a loss of 30 percent ($60,000 divided by $200,000). A decline of 20 percent in land values would have even more disastrous consequences for the leveraged investor. Whereas Ameena's loss would only be $40,000, a 20 percent decline for Naailah would mean a loss of $120,000, or 60 percent of her original $200,000 investment.

In an equity-based Islamic system, by contrast, one cannot invest what one does not own: investment is much more closely tied to what Islamic finance experts call "the real economy." When I asked the former CEO of a Malaysian Islamic bank what he meant by the real economy, he answered, "Railroads, infrastructure, hospitals . . . investments backed by real assets." He contrasted the "real economy" with what he called "vapor ware," which he clarified referred to "speculative investment." Of the $33 trillion raised in US capital markets each year, less than 1 percent, he said, "goes into real assets." The remainder, he claimed, is invested in speculative instruments, such as derivatives.

The PSIA puts limits on leverage because a depositor makes a deposit to a bank, which the bank then invests. The depositor and the bank are effectively partners in a mudaraba contract. The two share any proceeds from the investment based on a previously arranged profit-sharing agreement, while the depositor is strictly responsible for any losses. The bank's profits are limited to the funds it can attract through investment, and the depositor/investor is limited to investing money already earned. Neither party can resort to credit markets to invest borrowed funds speculatively, and, similarly, leverage is absent because neither party can invest funds that it does not already hold.

When pressed, proponents of equity finance admitted that economic growth in an financial system based on equity investment would likely be more modest, but they felt that this would be a small price to pay for greater stability and coherence. The recognition of slower but more sustainable growth echoed Hamza's plea for sustainable agriculture that is detailed in chapter 6. Furthermore, slower growth would likely lead to less economic inequality, as elites would not be able to multiply their wealth as quickly. Nazmi argued that in a debt-based system risk was also distributed across society, such as when taxpayers were compelled to bail out large banks. However, he noted that the benefits of such an economy were not distributed evenly: "The taxpayer doesn't get to enjoy the upside in the debt-based model of 'too big to fail.'" In his opinion the crisis demonstrated that in a speculative, debt-based economy, profits were individualized, but losses were socialized because large banks threatened to bring down the economic system as a whole if taxpayers did not bail them out. Thus, debt-based economies were more prone to "systemic risk" than equity-based ones in which there would be less speculative investment and a lower likelihood of financial crisis.

The critique of leverage and the conviction that equity-based financial arrangements reduce volatility is not limited to those seeking to reform Islamic finance. Indeed in Malaysia reformers were heartened by the 2009 publication of *This Time Is Different* by the Harvard University economists Carmen Reinhart and Kenneth Rogoff, which argues that financial markets "reliant on leverage . . . can be quite fragile and subject to crises of confidence" (Reinhart and Rogoff 2009, xxxix). During my fieldwork, Reinhart and Rogoff's argument that recessions are caused by high levels of leverage was often invoked as evidence supporting equity- and investment-based Islamic finance. Furthermore, Islamic finance experts were emboldened by an influential economist at a world-renowned university such as Rogoff taking a strong position over the course of his career against debt and in favor of equity finance (Rogoff 1999). Although Reinhart and Rogoff do not refer to Islamic finance per se, the endorsement of equity finance and critique of leverage by prominent Harvard economists greatly emboldened those seeking to reform Islamic finance according to equity principles. One Islamic economist suggested to me that the support for equity financing by Reinhart and Rogoff proved that the Qur'an was correct in preferring risk sharing and equity finance and enjoining against debt.

This chapter has detailed the experiments with risk that were under way in Malaysia as the Central Bank took steps to heed the calls of reformers and seek to enhance religious authenticity in the Islamic system. Officials sought to make banking products offered under the moniker of mudaraba more faithful to the principles of risk and profit sharing that reformers contend are the guiding principles of Islamic finance, and indeed the characteristics that most distinguish it from conventional finance, by demarcating Islamic deposits from PSIAs. These reforms caused a great deal of consternation among bankers in the industry, who understood the rationale for the revisions but were frightened because they appeared, as Ridzuan averred, to suggest a model that was wholly untested and experimental. The challenge that newly legislated PSIAs posed to previous Islamic banking practices was evident in the way in which a new technique for stress testing specific to these devices required invention. Nonetheless, this was a challenge that could be readily answered due to the infrastructure and expertise that had been facilitated in Malaysia through institutions such as the IFSB.

There was more at stake here than simply fabricating new financial devices and techniques. Indeed, refocusing Islamic finance around risk-sharing equity contracts, such as the mudaraba, exposes some of the central assumptions of conventional banking. Reformers in Islamic finance had come to the conclusion that leverage was responsible for the instability, crises, and inequality that plagued the conventional financial world. Reassured by the fact that some prominent North Atlantic economists had come to the same conclusion, they saw the promise of Islamic finance in the limits it placed on leverage. Interventions such as the new requirements regarding the use of the mudaraba contract illustrated that the calls of reformers did not fall on deaf ears on Malaysia. Indeed, Central Bank officials were not only listening to these calls but seemed to be actively eliciting them through their support for scholarly work that was often critical of existing Islamic financial forms and their efforts to incite experiments in Islamic finance. In the next chapter, I seek to explain exactly why the Central Bank was supportive of these initiatives rather than tolerating business as usual. This support can be attributed to the changing prerogatives of state-led development in Malaysia as well as the country's ethnic and religious composition. Ultimately, I argue that equity-based finance is more compatible with development strategies that emphasize entrepreneurialism, individual agency, and innovation and is thus broadly complicit with a neoliberal approach to development.

CHAPTER EIGHT

Subjects of Debt, Subjects of Equity

In February 2014 I sat with Farhan, the former CEO of a large Malaysian Islamic bank, in his expansive and well-appointed office. He had agreed to chat with me about the history of Islamic finance in Malaysia and the work undertaken by some of the early pioneers in the industry. He conceded that as Malaysia's Islamic finance project was first being conceptualized in the 1980s, one of the preoccupations of those involved "was the fact you had a Malay majority here who weren't economically as empowered as the Chinese community." In those early days Islamic finance was seen as a way to enhance the material well-being of Malays who were defined as Muslim in the constitution itself. Farhan described the gravity with which those involved in establishing Islamic finance in Malaysia took their work, explaining how they sought to map out what an Islamic system might look like:

> I've sat with one or two people who were working with the . . . prime minister and they were doing their day jobs and then for months none of them slept. They went to a room somewhere and worked through the night to look at "Well, what would we do? What would the central bank do? What would we do about liquidity?" . . . This all started getting put together on the back of [an] envelope with people, you know, clocking off at seven o'clock in the evening, going to *maghrib*[1] prayers, and saying, "Well, we're now on a mission of national importance."

These early pioneers in the industry attached grave significance to the task of establishing Islamic finance, due in large measure to the fact that Malays had been economically disadvantaged and excluded from colonial and early postcolonial commercial life in Malaysia. "The fundamental message [behind establishing Islamic finance]," he continued, "was about the financial inclusion of the Malays."

Building on Farhan's insights into the history of Islamic finance, this chapter argues that Islamic finance has been deployed in conjunction with two distinctive state strategies of subject formation in Malaysia. In its initial phase, dating to when the initial study group on Islamic banking was established in the early 1980s, a central goal was what Farhan called "the financial inclusion of the Malays." For historical reasons, dating back to the colonial period, citizens from this predominantly Muslim ethnic group had been mostly marginalized from the commercial life of the nation. Thus the state sought to develop Islamic finance as one technique to incorporate them into the modern economy. However, by the early 2000s the state's goal of fostering a substantial Malay Muslim middle class had largely been achieved through aggressive state affirmative action policies. Consequently, the state's objectives for Islamic finance began to shift. Islamic finance was no longer so much about the financial inclusion of a disenfranchised majority. Instead, commensurate with a shift in national politics and development strategy, it became a technique for the entrepreneurialization of the Malay population.

The Politics of Inclusion

The imperative to integrate Malays into the national economy can be traced to their economic marginalization during the colonial period. As the British intensified their occupation of the Malayan peninsula in the nineteenth century, Islam was deployed as a category through which the colonizers differentiated between the majority Malay population and inhabitants who had migrated to what is today Malaysia from elsewhere in Asia. These migrants were mainly from China and India, and their numbers increased rapidly as the colonial economy expanded and the demand for labor increased during the era of high colonialism. Due to the movement of laborers from the South Asian subcontinent and southern China, Britain's Malayan colony became a paradigmatic example of what John Furnivall called "plural societies" (Furnivall 1948, 304). Colonialism created a structural relationship in which separate cultures met "only in the market, as competitors or as opponents, as buyers and sellers" (Furnivall 1948, 311). Colonial rule was premised on a political economy in which subject populations were produced and governed through the various technologies of knowledge introduced by the British, such as the census (Cohn 1996, 8; Hirschman 1987). Although the three main racial groups produced through what Shamsul terms "colonial knowledge" were culturally and linguistically heterogeneous, prior to independence in 1957, they were incorporated into the colonial economy differently (Shamsul 2001). Indian workers were mainly plantation or public works laborers, Chinese pursued industrial and entrepreneurial activities, and Malays were overwhelmingly rural and engaged in either small-scale agriculture or fishing (Chin 1998, 41). By 1957 the "working class was overwhelmingly non-Malay" and only one out of five urban residents was Malay (Crouch 1996, 15).

As the sun set on the British Empire in Malaysia, ethnic divisions, largely produced through colonial knowledge, bred resentment. Citizens of Chinese descent were perceived to have profited more from the colonial economy and enjoyed better economic standing at the end of British sovereignty than the majority Malay population. Frustration with economic inequality culminated in the riots of May 13, 1969, which saw violent clashes in cities across the young federation, mainly between Chinese and Malay groups. For the most part, the conflict was attributed to the fact that many Malays felt that "the only ultimate weapon the ordinary Malay had against Chinese wealth was violence or the threat of violence" (Reid 1969, 269). In the aftermath of the riots, the state introduced the New Economic Policy (NEP) (Jomo 1991).

The NEP had two fundamental objectives. First, it was meant to eradicate poverty and increase economic opportunity for all communities in the nation; second, it was meant to accelerate the "process of restricting Malaysian society to correct economic imbalance, so as to reduce and eventually eliminate the identification of race with economic function" (Crouch 1996, 25). In practice, as Johan Fischer has noted, the NEP was designed to create an "urban, educated, entrepreneurial and shareholding Malay middle class" (Fischer 2008, 33) known as "new Malays" (*Melayu Baru*) (Ong 2006, 35). The creation of these "new Malays" led to the introduction of affirmative action policies that provided those classified as ethnic Malays with privileged access to resources offered by the state, such as civil service positions, business licenses, government contracts, and access to secondary education. These policies have created what has been called "the world's first affirmative action system tied exclusively to ethnicity" (Ong 2006, 80). In the 2010 census, the state identified around 67 percent of Malaysia's population of roughly thirty million as *bumiputra* (indigenous or literally "sons of the soil"), 25 percent as Chinese, and 7 percent as Indian (Department of Statistics Malaysia 2017). Most of those classified as bumiputra are further identified as ethnically Malay and are granted special rights by the state by virtue of their claims to be the original inhabitants of Malaysia (Ong 1999, 284n83). Islam is a defining feature of Malay identification, for the Malaysian federal constitution reads, "Malay means a person who professes the religion of Islam, habitually speaks the Malay language, [and] conforms to Malay custom" (Federal Constitution of Malaysia 2013, article 160). Most, although certainly not all, Malaysians of Indian and Chinese descent are non-Muslim.

After solving the problem of creating an interest-free pilgrimage savings scheme, there was little further development of Islamic finance in Malaysia until the early 1980s. Renewed enthusiasm for Islamic finance was in part due to a widespread Islamic resurgence in the country and the increasing international profile of political Islam. Politically this resurgence was made visible in the growing influence of the Partai Al-Islam Se-Malaysia (PAS), which presented an Islamist alternative to the ruling Barisan Nasional coalition headed by prime minister Mahathir Mohamad's United Malays National Organization. As Islamic piety among the country's growing middle classes increased in the country, Mahathir sought to foreclose the ability of the PAS opposition to claim the mantle of Islam. As the political scientist Joseph Liow has written, "In attempting to accord greater significance to Islamic laws, values, and practices, UMNO and PAS essentially entered a 'race' to see which of the two parties was able to package, sell, and execute its Islamization campaign most effectively in Malaysia" (Liow 2009, 43).

Experts with whom I engaged often put initial state sponsorship of Islamic finance in the context of these domestic politics. For example, Zainal, who worked at the Securities Commission, recalled that the competition between UMNO and PAS to assert their Islamic credentials was evident in Islamic finance. Zainal told me that in the late 1970s Mahathir had asked the economist Abdul Halim and some colleagues "to begin researching a banking system free of riba." Halim was an Oxford-educated former dean of the Faculty of Economics at the National University of Malaysia and an economist working for Bank Bumiputra, which had been established in 1965 in part to redress the colonial marginalization of "indigenous" bumiputra by increasing their participation in the national economy. Halim and the others wrote a paper on interest-free banking and presented it to Mahathir. As Zainal recalled, "Mahathir sat on it for a year, so Halim took the paper to PAS and their leader, Nik Aziz, took up the idea of Islamic banking and put it in their election platform" for the 1982 general election. Anxious that the political opposition would seize the initiative regarding Islamic finance, Zainal said Mahathir "very quickly produced the funds to set up Bank Islam," the first Islamic bank in Malaysia. It was established in 1983 with Halim appointed as the first CEO.

Halim and the other members of the team had also formed the core of an initial study group that Zainal and others referred to as the "pioneers" of Islamic banking in Malaysia. In the early 1980s this study group traveled to Khartoum to survey the Islamic Bank of Sudan and Cairo to undertake a similar evaluation of Faisal Islamic Bank; both were established in 1977 and were two of the first modern Islamic banks (Warde 2010, 72). Whereas these early Islamic banks in North Africa were private initiatives sponsored in large part by Prince Faisal of Saudi Arabia, Malaysia's Bank Islam was established with the full backing of the state. Unlike Middle Eastern states such as Egypt and Turkey, which were largely committed to secular nationalism and therefore sought to minimize any association with Islam, secularism never held the same sway in Southeast Asia, and in this sense the Malaysian government operated under different imperatives than did countries in the Middle East. Zainal recalled that although the banks in the Arab world were using equity-based structures premised on partnerships, Halim and his team (consisting of people with expertise in conventional banking) decided that equity finance would be too much of a stretch. Instead they chose to deploy predominantly debt-based contracts using the sale of an underlying asset to facilitate most financing arrangements. This is how the bai al inah became the prevailing contract in Malaysian Islamic finance.

The founding of Bank Islam achieved two key goals. First, it established UMNO's domestic political credibility in matters relating to Islam. As Liow writes, the "Islamic banking project . . . served as a response to criticisms by PAS and elements from the Islamic civil sphere that economic development involving a secular-banking system would incur 'riba' or profit maximization through usury" (Liow 2009, 55). Second, it served as a mechanism to incorporate Malays into the institutionalized economy of the modernizing nation. As such, the initial stage of Islamic finance fit with the state's broader affirmative action program targeting the historical economic imbalance between the majority Malay population and other ethnic groups.

Christine Chin has referred to the economic development strategy pursued by the Malaysian state as a "modernity project," insofar as it was a self-conscious effort to transform the country into a modern, developed country. Prime Minister Mahathir referred to this as "Vision 2020": the objective of achieving "a fully developed country by the year 2020" (Chin 1998, 3). Indeed, this program of state-directed economic development was phenomenally successful, as the country enjoyed some of the world's highest annual rates of growth in gross domestic product per year between 1970 and the Asian financial crisis of 1998. At the heart of the Malaysian modernity project was the economic advancement of the majority Malay population, which entailed the rapid creation of a Malay middle class that identified so strongly with Islam that a whole new market for goods and services explicitly marked as Islamic was created (Fischer 2008).[2] The robust and globally unprecedented state support for Islamic finance was a key feature of creating this new Muslim middle class in Malaysia, and participation in Islamic banking grew sharply though the 1980s and 1990s. As Liow writes, "The popularity of [Bank Islam] skyrocketed. . . . So strong was the support for the Islamic bank that it became the nation's third-largest bank within four years of its opening" (Liow 2009, 55).

Islamic finance and the goal of the "financial inclusion of the Malays" was part of a distinctive Malaysian governmentality designed to foster a productive population in the image favored by the state. As Aihwa Ong has shown, the Malaysian state under Mahathir aggressively promoted a version of Islam conducive to the production of workers who possessed the skills desired by global capital. Nonetheless, these workers were also dependent on state benevolence: the "new Malay subject—the receiver of government scholarships, credit, business licenses, civil service jobs, and innumerable other perks associated with being bumiputra—has been trained to obtain credentials, to be effective on the job, and also to view these activities as within the dictates of an official Islam" (Ong 1999, 204). Opening an account at an Islamic bank was part and parcel of the project of creating a middle-class Malay subject who was simultaneously capable of performing labor valuable in a global market and of conforming to the political and economic objectives of the state.

Entrepreneurializing Muslim Subjects

By the 2010s the state's objective for Islamic finance had shifted from financial inclusion to entrepreneurialization, by which I refer to efforts to inculcate values such as risk calculation, autonomy, and innovation into

202   CHAPTER EIGHT

a laboring population. In part this shift was attributable to both broader
changes stemming from Malaysia's changing position in the global economy and domestic political affairs. Following the lead of other "Asian
tiger" economies such as Hong Kong, South Korea, and the country's close
neighbor, Singapore, between the 1970s and 1990s, Malaysia had aggressively pursued foreign direct investment by establishing special zones for
industrial assembly where multinational firms were enticed to establish
production facilities for high-tech devices and other commodities through
tax incentives, modest wages, a stable political situation, and a well-trained
and docile laboring population (Ong 1987). However, this configuration
was threatened by the emergence of China as the foremost destination
for industrial production in Asia; competition for foreign investment from
other countries in Southeast Asia such as the Philippines, Indonesia, and
Thailand; and the increasing wage demands of a middle-class labor force
characteristic of a middle-income country.

As Malaysia's export-oriented development paradigm was put in question, the state began to develop other sectors suited to an increasingly educated and better-paid working population. Indeed, as income levels and
education capabilities in Malaysia increased, the state sought to develop
sectors to which its self-proclaimed "knowledge-based society" could add
value (Evers 2003, 355). Plans to transform Kuala Lumpur into a global hub
for Islamic finance business and expertise were part of this broader shift
in development strategy.

Alongside the shift in industrial policy away from assembly and toward
a knowledge economy, a parallel and intersecting shift was taking place in
social policy. By the mid-2000s, the affirmative action plank of the Malaysian modernity project was under reconsideration in some quarters due
to changes in domestic political concerns and the emergence of movements for change. There was a confluence of factors that precipitated reflection on Malaysia's affirmative action project. Most prominent was a
deep-seated dissatisfaction among non-Malays, especially citizens of Chinese and Indian descent, who increasingly came to object to the privileges
afforded to the Malay majority. These included benefits such as preference for positions in the civil service, subsidies for medical care and phar-
maceuticals, and priority for business licenses issued by the state. Malay
students were given precedence in accessing the state's higher education
system. Consequently, young people of Chinese and Indian descent often
felt compelled to travel overseas for their education, with large numbers
obtaining degrees abroad in the United Kingdom, Australia, the United

States, and elsewhere. Additionally, the affirmative action policies were evident in university courses, as Malay students were perceived as coddled by faculty members. One professor at an institution with a large number of foreign students told me that he felt pressure to grade Malay students more leniently than both foreign and non-bumiputra Malaysian students. Needless to say, non-Malays often grumbled about this state of affairs. Indeed, many felt compelled to leave Malaysia for careers and lives outside the country because they did not feel as if they were allowed to compete on level terms with the Malay majority.

By the 2010s there was a small but growing sense of dissatisfaction with the state's affirmative action programs even among Malay Muslims. Although they had benefited tremendously from these initiatives, they also realized that privileged access to the largesse of the state did not always work in their favor. This was due to the fact that the achievements of indigenous bumiputra were in some cases attributed to affirmative action rather than the aspirations and initiative of those who were perceived to have benefited. For example, shortly after the establishment of the Bumiputra Empowerment Program, a program designed to benefit bumiputra following the 2013 election, an editorial in the venerable *Straits Times*, one of Southeast Asia's predominant English-language newspapers, opined, "One negative perception of the community is the belief that every successful Malay who reaches the top of his career achieves it not through his own ability and merit, but through the special assistance provided for him by the state under the race-based policy" (Osman 2013). There is an abiding sense that entitlements and promotions based on social and biological considerations rather than merit might produce a complacent and entitled population and adversely impact the nation's ability to compete in a global economy. For example, none other than Mahathir Mohamad, Malaysia's former prime minister and senior statesman, criticized Malays for being "lazy" and accused them of not taking advantage of the educational privileges afforded them (Lee 2014).

Furthermore, officials worried that the state's affirmative action program would prompt non-Malay citizens to seek greater opportunities outside the country. State officials expressed anxiety about the global labor market and what one official in the prime minister's office candidly told me was the possibility of "brain drain" from Malaysia. If well-educated, non-bumiputra Malaysians concluded that opportunities in their native country were arbitrarily limited, they might resettle overseas. Especially threatening in this regard were neighboring states in Southeast Asia that aggressively pursued "foreign talent," Singapore foremost among them.

With a Chinese majority, a consistently robust economy, and generous salaries and living standards, many young Malaysians of Chinese descent saw Singapore as a better bet for their economic futures.

Such racialized economic calculations were apparent at an ostentatious wedding for two Malaysians of Chinese descent I attended at a large hotel in Kuala Lumpur in 2013. A Malaysian civil servant who had held posts in the prime minister's office and the Ministry of Foreign Affairs told me that he had attended secondary school with a number of attendees, the majority of whom were of Chinese descent. He noted that several had recently obtained lucrative, high-skilled positions in Singapore and wistfully worried about losing well-educated young citizens to Malaysia's dynamic neighbor. With mild envy he described the incentives, mainly in the form of high salaries, low taxes, and bureaucratic efficiencies that the Singaporean state provided to attract "foreign talent" from Malaysia and elsewhere. He told me that he had heard colleagues in his office privately worry that labor migration threatened to create a situation where the skills and expertise of Malaysia's highly educated, well-disciplined labor force were deployed to facilitate the economic development of a foreign country.

In this context the state began to deploy Islamic finance toward a new end. The previous objective of financial inclusion had largely been achieved. Many Malays had become solidly middle class and actively participated as producers and consumers in what the World Bank had categorized as an "upper middle-income country" (World Bank 2016). However, the specter of Malay entitlement and complacency cast a shadow over the country's lauded development legacy. The problem was no longer the integration of the Malay population into a national economy but inciting them to action—that is to say, making them enterprising agents of economic growth. This entailed reframing the domestic project of Islamic finance to make it less a marker of identity and more a means of inculcating entrepreneurial values. In so doing, Islamic finance would be deployed to elicit risk-managing and risk-calculating subjects.

In its initial phase, Islamic finance had been part of a broader Malaysian state strategy of creating a modern Islamic identity commensurate with the state's project of capitalist development. To achieve this goal, Islamic finance needed to be Islamic in form only, whereas its religious content was largely left implicit. Islamic financial institutions and the contracts and products they used were given Arabic names. These same firms might offer their customers prizes and promotions identifiable with Islam, such as hajj and *umroh*[3] trips to visit venerated religious sites in Saudi

Arabia. Marketing materials would emphasize women in headscarves and men in identifiably religious dress.

The use of Islamic finance to cultivate an Islamic identity was evident in a story recounted to me by Ramanathan, a senior civil servant in an influential Malaysian ministry. Although he was not Muslim, he had signed up for a credit card through HSBC Amanah, the Islamic arm of the global banking giant. He was traveling for work in the Middle East, and while he was in Dubai, he was purchasing a bottle of wine to give as a gift to some friends at a dinner party. Late to the festivities and in a hurry to complete the transaction, Ramanathan inadvertently used an HSBC Islamic credit card, which he had signed up for due to a promotion. There was a delay in completing the transaction, and while he was waiting at the counter, suddenly he realized that the Emirati religious police had been summoned for his arrest. As they prepared to detain him, Ramanathan appealed for permission to call the Malaysian embassy. Because Ramanathan was a government employee, a consular official was quickly dispatched and explained the misunderstanding to the police. Since Ramanathan was not Muslim, he was released, but he was warned that it would only be possible one time—if he tried to purchase alcohol using an Islamic credit card again, they would not be able to help. Ramanathan was surprised by the incident, noting to me that in Malaysia if one attempted to buy alcohol with an Islamic credit card, the transaction would just be declined, but one would not be threatened with imprisonment. The irony is that the contract that undergirded the credit card was a bai al inah, the sale-based contract that had come under fire from Gulf-based reformers and critics of Islamic finance. Thus the credit card could be used to police the actions of the holder by denying him or her the ability to purchase goods considered haram, in spite of the fact that the religious authenticity of the contract on which the card was based was considered suspect by religious authorities where the card was used!

While in the 1980s and 1990s Islamic finance had been more of an identity-building project, in its substance Islamic finance was then, more or less, conventional finance concealed by a shariah-compliant veneer. Even industry professionals were quick to acknowledge this fact. Some practitioners acknowledged the interpretive gymnastics that had gone in to making Islamic finance shariah compliant. For the most part, Islamic finance in Malaysia was practiced by conventional bankers and financiers who had "converted." They understood conventional debt-based finance with interest as its central feature. Thus the contracts that were deployed might make use of an Islamic name and involve the sale of a physical asset (at least on paper), but for the most part the objective of these transactions was simply to replicate conventional finance. ·

Questions regarding the religious authenticity of Islamic finance could not be papered over indefinitely. This was especially the case as the industry began to move toward global integration during the 2000s. Having achieved a vibrant national Islamic financial system, branches of the Malaysian state such as the Ministry of Finance, Bank Negara, and the Securities Commission began to envision Kuala Lumpur as a central node in the global network of Islamic finance. However, moves toward integration immediately raised the question of the difference with which Islamic finance was practiced in different jurisdictions. There are two main centers for Islamic finance: Malaysia and the countries of the GCC, most prominently Bahrain.[4] Bahrain had been an established banking center in the Middle East since the political troubles in Lebanon that started in the 1970s.[5] Attacks against Malaysia's perceived permissive approach by experts from the Gulf might have been written off as resentment, given that by the 2000s it was clear that Malaysia had the most well-developed infrastructure for Islamic finance in the world. As one former executive of an Islamic bank recalled:

> There was a growing animosity at this time between the Arab world and Malaysia. Malaysia was seen as a bit of an upstart. [The Arab world thought,] "They're doing Islamic finance . . . [but we] should be doing it, so what's Malaysia doing?" The world looked at the Arabs because the world thinks that the Arabs own the Islamic franchise . . . so the Arabs started throwing grenades at Malaysia, saying, "Your shariah is weak, or that and the other." I think that's changed now, but that was a defense mechanism as well. . . . The reality was that they had a sort of conscience about the fact that they should have done more, but they didn't want to admit it openly.

However, given the ambitions of planners and state strategists in Malaysia to make the country a global hub for Islamic finance, the opprobrium blowing bitterly across the Indian Ocean from the Gulf could not simply be dismissed by Malaysian planners. This predicament inspired reflection among experts in Malaysia about what sort of alternative Malaysian Islamic finance indeed offered compared to its conventional counterpart.

It was at this juncture that planners began also to rethink the position of Islamic finance within the broader constellation of the Malaysian modernity project. Given the success of the project of financial inclusion, the push for global integration of Islamic finance, and visceral denunciation from those in the Middle East proclaiming authority over Islamic tradition, whither Islamic finance? Islamic finance was increasingly mobilized to achieve developmental goals, as state economic growth strategies shifted from a project of creating a Malay middle class to the creation of entrepreneurs skilled in not only evaluating risk but also assuming it. Some felt that the earlier project, of which financial inclusion was a key plank, had created a sense of entitlement among Malay Muslims. For example, as the Malaysian authors of a study addressing the new Malay middle class reported, "Some would argue that the reason for their complacency is the over-reliance on government contracts, funding and support. Recognizing this fact, there have been some moves by the UMNO leadership to change the attitudes of bumiputeras so as to be less reliant on the government" (Ariff and Abubakar 2002, 19). This was due to a common representation that bumiputra "as a whole, did not have a tradition of entrepreneurship. Rather, they were used to being either employed in the government service, or self-employed as agricultural farmers or smallholders" (Ariff and Abubakar 2002, 4).

Strategies to change attitudes and encourage entrepreneurial behavior can be seen in various initiatives that the state introduced toward this objective. Patricia Sloane-White has described how promoting Malay entrepreneurship was a concern in Malaysia dating to the New Economic Policy of the 1970s (Sloane 1999). Takashi Torii has written that more recently "under the leadership of Prime Minister Mahathir bin Mohamad, the task of creating the middle classes turned to the promotion of bumiputera middle-class entrepreneurs" (Torii 2003, 223). In an increasing effort to shift bumiputra away from relying on the state for economic support to a more entrepreneurial orientation, in 1995 the government established a distinct government ministry, the Ministry of Entrepreneur Development, which was charged with "the task of formulating the concepts for bumiputera middle-class entrepreneurs or new-middle-class entrepreneurs" (Torii 2003, 235). Sloane-White shows how the emphasis on entrepreneurship was a distinctive feature of the NEP. As Milne has explained, after the NEP it was "*government* in the form of 'bureaucratic entrepreneurs,' which now perform[ed] the entrepreneurial function" (Milne 1976, 249; italics orignal). Indeed, Sloane-White shows how "successful Malay businessmen" were often perceived to have "benefitted from UMNO patronage or had an NEP 'subsidy mentality'" (Sloane-White 2014, 23). Further, she shows how the younger generation of bumiputra elites have rejected Malayness as the "source of their identity" and instead turned to an "Islam that can justify and sacralize their beliefs" (Sloane-White 2014, 33, 34). Thus entrepreneurship and risk taking has become an abiding preoccupation of those who seek to shed the trappings of ethnic privilege, citizens and state planners alike.

Eliciting Entrepreneurs

The state's focus on fostering entrepreneurship, especially among Malay Muslims, accelerated during the 2000s in part by deploying a specific device: the mudaraba contract. Mudaraba contracts play a critical but perhaps not immediately obvious role in the project of creating Malay entrepreneurs in Malaysia today. This is because they presume a subject well attuned to the nuances of entrepreneurship and risk management. In this respect, they could be understood as devices designed to elicit practices of risk calculation. These contracts can be used as the basis for a wide range of instruments in Islamic finance, from deposit accounts to project financing to Islamic bonds.

Efforts to deploy mudaraba contracts to create risk-taking entrepreneurs is evident in government planning documents. For example, the Tenth Malaysia Plan, published in 2010 by the Economic Planning Unit of the prime minister's office, makes multiple references to cultivating entrepreneurship in the country. The document contains sections titled "Supporting the Creation of an Entrepreneurial Culture" and "Strengthening Bumiputera Entrepreneurship to Create Competitive Businesses in High-Impact Sectors" (Economic Planning Unit 2010, 97, 165). With regard to the former, the report notes that the "government is committed to investing in creativity by stimulating entrepreneurship" (Economic Planning Unit 2010, 97). Consistent with the arguments of Ariff and Abubakar cited above, the report connects entrepreneurship to race politics in Malaysia by claiming that the goal is to facilitate "the bumiputera entrepreneur's ability to become independent of Government assistance" (Economic Planning Unit 2010, 168).

Perhaps most illuminating is that the plan explicitly connects the problem of entrepreneurial development to Islamic finance by developing a program for fostering entrepreneurship based on a particular Islamic finance contract, the mudaraba. According to the document, under "the Tenth Plan, the

Government is committed to investing in creativity, including efforts such as stimulating entrepreneurship . . . and promoting availability of risk capital. The Government will provide a larger pool of funds for venture capital, especially on a mudaraba basis (risk sharing) through co-investment with private sector funds" (Economic Planning Unit 2010, 16). Thus, the plan lays out a scheme to use mudaraba contracts to facilitate entrepreneurship:

> During the Plan period the risk capital industry will be strengthened to increase access to funding for innovative start-ups. New funding modes for public venture companies will be introduced to better match investment risk profiles and promote greater private sector participation and risk-taking. Government funding to public venture companies . . . will shift from the current lending model to an equity structure. A Mudharabah[6] Innovation Fund (MIF), with an allocation of RM500 million, will also be introduced to provide risk capital to government-backed venture companies. The MIF will offer enhanced risk return profile to investors and thus attract greater private risk capital to co-invest, and gradually reduce dependence on public funds. (Economic Planning Unit 2010, 86)

Key here is the way in which entrepreneurship, risk, and equity financing are linked together. It makes explicit how the state sees Islamic finance, especially the way in which action premised on risk is represented as a key feature of Islamic finance. The governor of the Central Bank, Zeti Aziz, succinctly captured this assemblage in an address she gave on receiving her prize from the Islamic Development Bank. She said, "In a risk and profit sharing model with participatory or equity-based contracts that support ventures involving entrepreneurship endeavors, savers and fund providers stand to bear the losses in such ventures, similarly to gaining profits from such ventures" (Aziz 2013). The plan and Zeti's remarks both highlight the centrality of the mudaraba contract in the project of creating entrepreneurial subjects adroit at calculating and managing risk. Indeed, much of the conviction that experts place in the superiority of Islamic finance stems from their conviction that it does a better job of eliciting values conducive to innovation, entrepreneurship, and individual economic autonomy.

The risk-calculating features that mudaraba are expected to foster become apparent if a deposit account based on a mudaraba is compared to a conventional interest-bearing savings account. Hamza, the CEO who likened the problems of Islamic finance to that of sustainable poultry rearing, illustrated the features of equity-based contracts that made them conducive to entrepreneurship, in contrast to debt-based contracts, which he saw as more disposed toward rent seeking. In so doing, he explained the rationale behind the split between deposit accounts and investment accounts that had been written into the 2013 IFSA law. In a typical account at a conventional bank, he told me, the account holder receives both a guaranteed interest payment and a promise that the funds can always be withdrawn. Experts such as Hamza argued that the guarantees inherent in conventional bank accounts make them risk free. He further invoked the federal insurance on banking deposits that has formed a key pillar of the American banking system since the Great Depression as evidence of the fact that conventional banking did not require account holders to calculate risk. Hamza told me that deposit insurance creates irresponsible behavior because it discourages customers from evaluating risk and "doing their due diligence." Referring primarily to the American banking system, he argued that in conventional banking deposit insurance guarantees deposits and therefore customers do not "read the financial statements" of banks. He calmly remarked that consumers "don't ensure that the bank is acting responsibly with their money." Rather, they simply rely on the external authority of the state to ensure the credibility of the banks through mechanisms such as licensing and deposit insurance.

In contrast, Islamic accounts based on the mudaraba contract would contain important differences. First, the profit paid to the account holder would be based on the variable returns that the bank generated from the business ventures in which the bank invested the account holder's funds. Second, the principle amount would not be guaranteed: if the bank lost money on the investment, the account holder would have to bear the losses. Finally, Hamza said that Islamic banking instruments based on mudaraba could not be subject to deposit insurance due to the principle that there is "no reward without risk" and that "making profit requires taking risks."

Given the heightened risk to which a depositor's funds would be subject, Hamza suggested that under the mudaraba-based deposit scheme, to which the industry was transitioning following the passage of IFSA, depositors would have to spend more time monitoring the activities in which their banks were engaged. Hamza explained:

> At a conventional bank you just put your money in and you get a guaranteed return. With deposit insurance you don't need to worry about the possibility of a bank's failure. But interest and deposit insurance don't exist in the Islamic system—you may profit off the investment the bank makes with your deposit. But you might lose your money as well!

He further argued that deposit insurance serves as a de facto subsidy because it enables banks to pay out low interest rates on deposits and then subsequently charge low interest rates on loans. In his eyes this was due to the fact that the actual interest rate did not really matter to a bank's balance sheet: its profit comes from the margin between rates. According to Hamza, the deposit insurance subsidy created a "moral hazard" in which consumers "did not monitor" the actions of their banks because they had "faith" that the government was insuring the system.

Hamza claimed that the mudaraba model of banking would encourage banking customers to more accurately "price and distribute" risk. If people were dependent on profit sharing rather than guaranteed interest income from their banking deposits, and if they faced the possibility of losing a portion or all of their initial deposit, they would be more diligent about researching banks and would demand higher rates of return due to the higher risk entailed.

Hamza then distinguished deposit accounts from investment accounts and said that customers should be free to choose which kind of account better suited them. Those with no appetite for risk would use the deposit accounts, which would have "100 percent risk weightage," meaning that funds on deposits would be held in full by the bank. This model would entail an end to the fractional reserve system whereby banks create money. Hamza noted that under the Basel Committee's banking regulations, banks were "required to hold only 8 percent of their funds on deposit in liquid form."[7] In contrast, the investment accounts would be profit generating. A customer would choose what kind of risk they wanted and then select a corresponding account. Low-risk accounts would be based on real estate investments, and high-risk accounts would be based on financing for instruments like credit cards. The returns from each investment would match the risk profile, unlike the current system, which, he argued had become distorted due to the subsidy granted through deposit insurance and "the lender of last resort" dictum, in which the state essentially underwrites firms that are designated "too big to fail." According to this scheme, depositing money in the bank would be more akin to investing in the stock market and would require the same kind of research.

The invocation of mudaraba contracts and risk sharing demonstrates how Islamic finance was mobilized in the state project of entrepreneurialization of the Malays. In the new regime, Malay citizens would no longer be conferred benefits solely by virtue of their ethnic and religious identification. Rather, the state would deploy Islamic finance to instill within

Malays the principles of Islamic economic action as represented in the contracts used historically in Islam (of course seen through the lens of contemporary neoliberal economics). The early affirmative action policies created an entitled, complacent Malay subject who acted in compliance with the will of the state. In this new configuration the state would operationalize the economic ethics that it identifies as intrinsic to Islam to elicit agentive entrepreneurs, rather than what Milne called "bureaucratic entrepreneurs." In its initial iteration, Islamic finance was framed by the affirmative action prerogatives of the postcolonial state. The goal of financial inclusion was part and parcel of the state's objective of creating a middle class of productive Muslims who are still reliant on the state. The goal of entrepreneurialization is more radical in that it seeks to inculcate capitalist values of risk calculation and innovation in subjects who act independently of the state (Atia 2012; Matza 2009; Rose 1999, 139–144; Rudnyckyj 2010). Although some scholars have argued that Islamic finance is best understood within the context of "post-neoliberal world order," addressing the increasing emphasis on equity in Malaysian Islamic finance broadly resonates with neoliberalism understood not so much as "a de-regulated, global free market" (Mohamad and Saravanamuttu 2015, 200) but as a practical technology for forming human beings.

The reconfiguration of Islamic finance from a project of financial inclusion to one of entrepreneurialization reveals the ethos of experimentation common in contemporary Islamic finance. In its initial iteration in Malaysia Islamic finance was an ideological project, but today it has been reinvented as an ethical one. In the 1980s and 1990s, UMNO, the leading party in the ruling coalition, sought to seize the mantel of Islam from the opposition PAS party and foreclose the latter's claims that the state under Mahathir was insufficiently Muslim. Developing an Islamic financial infrastructure was a key part of the state's pretensions to upholding Islamic values, even if the infrastructure that was developed largely replicated conventional finance rather than providing a genuine alternative. This project was ideological in that the goal was to achieve something that fulfilled the formal prescriptions of Islam and could be deployed to make Malays feel as if their economic practices were in conformity with religious ideals. The problem that Islamic finance was in part intended to address was how to create subjects that act in conformity with Islamic norms.

Today, criticism of mainstream Islamic finance and acknowledgment of the tendency toward replication has precipitated reflection on the actual practices of Islamic finance. In response Bank Negara has sought to tighten up regulation on certain disputed contracts, such as bai al inah, and to emphasize the use of more authentic contracts, such as mudaraba. However, these moves are not merely intended to appease Middle Eastern critics. They also fulfilled the state's agenda of creating Malay entrepreneurs in a more competitive regional and global economy. The effort to reform Islamic finance today converges with efforts to create entrepreneurial subjects who are capable of evaluating risk and seizing the financial opportunities afforded through taking risk. In sum, the problem of Islamic finance in Malaysia is no longer bringing Malays into the economy. Today it seeks to economize them by endowing them with certain qualities, such as risk management and risk calculation, that are conducive to neoliberal development in a global economy.

CONCLUSION

An Emergent Geoeconomics

If the primary frame of international action in the twentieth century fell under the rubric of geopolitics, in the twenty-first the frame may turn out to be geoeconomic instead. In Asia today emerging configurations illustrate new economic alignments evident in phenomena such as the emergence of China as an economic superpower and its "Belt and Road" strategy, the fitful integration of nation-states into economic zones such as the Association of Southeast Asian Nations, and efforts to create a global network of Islamic finance. Aware of these changes, the Malaysian state is aggressively seeking to position itself as a hub in at least one of these new configurations. These efforts build on thirty years of developing Islamic finance during which the country first sought to construct a domestic Islamic financial system and then to become a key node in the emerging global network of Islamic finance. In so doing, it has created a knowledge infrastructure that offers the space for contemplating and devising alternatives to conventional finance. In centralizing equity, as opposed to debt, these experiments propose a solution to the crises that have plagued conventional, debt-based finance in North America and Europe. Efforts to become a key node in the emerging field of Islamic financial services are a response to threats to Malaysia's economic competitiveness and continued development success. Emerging economies in East and Southeast Asia, such as China, Indonesia, and Thailand, are increasingly attractive to transnational corporations seeking to offshore industrial production due to their lower wages. Thus the Malaysian state sees Islamic financial services as a distinctive niche in which its well-educated and devout population and growing middle classes can produce value and maintain the country's development success.

In this context, creating an Islamic global city is a calculated strategy and one that proponents of Islamic finance hope will remake the geoeconomic network of contemporary capitalism. Malaysian planners astutely realize that the country's geographical position between the Middle East and East Asia offers a distinct advantage to its Islamic finance project. Given the country's historical ties to both regions and the fact that the majority of its population shares a common religion with the oil-endowed countries of the Arabian Gulf, Malaysian planners wager that Kuala Lumpur will become a pivotal intermediary between the world's greatest source of surplus capital, the Arabian Peninsula, on the one hand, and the world's greatest site of industrial production, East Asia, on the other. As an Islamic global city, Kuala Lumpur has the potential to bridge these two areas of growth as the geoeconomic map of the twenty-first century is remade.

Furthermore, it is a poorly kept secret that oil-rich countries such as Saudi Arabia, Kuwait, Qatar, and the United Arab Emirates have billions of dollars invested in conventional, debt-based instruments in the financial capitals of the West. The dream of many Islamic finance professionals in Malaysia is that once the citizens of these countries wake up to the hypocrisy of Gulf leaders who espouse puritanical, *Salafi*[1] piety but rely on the haram financial services of Citibank, Goldman Sachs, and Barclays, among others, they will demand changes to the ways in which the capital in these countries is managed. Indeed their hope is that the massive sovereign wealth funds held by these countries will be withdrawn from the conventional financial system and instead be invested in financial instruments that do not violate the counterdebt ethos of Islam and its stringent prohibitions on the collection or payment of interest.

In a certain sense, Malaysian planners are following a path already well worn by the country's neighbor and erstwhile competitor, Singapore. During the past thirty years, the city-state has become a global city in its own right. It has achieved one of the world's highest per capita incomes in part by becoming a major financial services hub. However, rather than merely mimic the Singaporean model and attempt to compete against their neighbor's massive head start, Malaysian planners astutely pursue an alternative geoeconomic future in which historical centers of economic and political power in Europe and North America are decentered in favor of new centers in the Muslim world.

Malaysian planners in the Central Bank, the Securities Commission, and other state offices have pioneered an Islamic global city, in no small measure due to economic imperatives. Although it possesses some high-quality oil fields, the country is not blessed with the vast petroleum wealth of many of its Gulf counterparts. Many Malaysian experts were conscious of this deficit and saw Islamic financial services as a means of overcoming its disadvantages. Shamsul, an Islamic finance professional, told me that the Saudi government has a laissez-faire attitude to Islamic banking because "they have too much money." In contrast, he said that Malaysia has "to develop something to attract FDI [foreign direct investment]." Shamsul said that attracting foreign capital was behind efforts to make Malaysia a center for sukuk origination. In his view, Islamic finance represented a renewed effort in Malaysia to attract investment following efforts to set up zones for industrial assembly in the 1970s and 1980s. He said, "If you look at the way we attracted FDI initially, it was based on the Look East Policy. . . . But now the move is more toward the Middle East. We are looking for Middle East funds. . . . The need for Islamic finance is greater. . . . The focus of the government has shifted from 'look east' to 'look to the Middle East.'" Then he invoked the efforts to cultivate a knowledge infrastructure for Islamic finance, stating, "We know that these [Gulf] countries are rich, but they have little knowledge. That's why we push for knowledge first." He continued this theme:

> They have the [basic] knowledge about Islamic finance, but they don't know how to apply it in the current world. . . . We know that it is stated in the Qur'an, for example, that you cannot do riba, but how can you *not* do riba in the current world? So that is why we come up with a lot of innovative products and services, just to cater to them. On the Middle East side they know that we cannot do riba, but they don't come up with innovative ideas on how to address those issues. So . . . that's why we took up Islamic finance.

He saw the formation of the Islamic global city as pioneering in the Muslim world and a strategy that could enable Malaysia to continue its remarkable development success.

The sentiment that there was surplus capital in the Middle East looking for religiously permissible investment opportunities was widespread. In 2013 I attended a public presentation in Singapore in which Abdul, an Islamic finance professional representing an Islamic investment fund, gleefully invoked then-soaring oil prices as an incentive to get involved in Islamic finance. He opened his remarks by rhetorically asking, "Why are we talking about Islamic banking and finance today? The West is, for lack of a better word, sick" due to the "devastating financial crisis" in which investment capital had all dried up. In the meantime, he continued, "oil prices have gone from 35 dollars a barrel in the early 2000s to today hovering around

125 dollars a barrel or so. So you find a whole new wave of money has gone into Middle Eastern countries . . . which is new capital and this capital is looking for investment opportunities! So the rest of the world is repositioning itself and trying to get a piece of the action." For the audience of Islamic finance professionals, the message was clear: Southeast Asian countries should seek to position themselves as the strategic financial intermediary between the capital-rich Middle East and investment-hungry East Asia.

Nevertheless, in spite of the emerging geoeconomic network of Islamic finance and the boosterism of those such as Abdul, Islamic finance was at a decidedly experimental moment. By the time the 2008 financial crisis erupted, the Islamic financial industry had reached a scale by which it could be imagined as a geoeconomic alternative to conventional finance. Simultaneously, however, an acrimonious debate was raging over the extent to which Islamic finance adequately conformed to shariah principles for economic action. These debates largely entailed a binary opposition between two types of Islamic finance. On the one hand, there was the existing system described as shariah compliant, debt based, and characterized by risk transfer. On the other hand, there was the future system that critics and reformers sought to bring into being, one described as shariah based, equity-based, and characterized by risk sharing.

While Islamic finance in Malaysia since its inception in the early 1980s had been dependent on so-called debt-based contracts, thirty years later these contracts were being profoundly questioned. Contracts such as the bai al inah were initially preferred since they could be structured to essentially replicate the function, if not the precise form, of the interest-bearing loan contracts with which the conventional bankers who migrated to Islamic finance were familiar. Two factors precipitated the reaction against debt, which I conclude characterizes contemporary Islamic finance. First was the fact that debt-based contracts such as the bai al inah were not "universally valid," attracting particular skepticism in the countries of the Arabian Gulf, where scholars deemed them impermissible. Malaysian planners realized that if they were to become a global hub for Islamic finance, they would have to use contracts that shariah scholars from around the world found permissible. Second was the global financial crisis, which many Islamic finance experts viewed as a sign of divine reckoning. Indeed, they represented it as heavenly retribution for the metastasizing debt economy that had become a global norm but was decidedly contrary to Qur'anic injunction. ·

While moving fully from a debt-based financial system to one based on investment and equity may appear far-fetched, over the five years that

I conducted fieldwork on this project there was a subtle but clear shift in this direction. Indeed, when I started fieldwork in 2010 there was a profound sense of frustration with the Islamic authenticity of the industry, but by the time my fieldwork came to a close, there was already a sense that concerns regarding religious probity were being taken seriously. Although those seeking to reform the industry still had a long list of grievances about the activities in which nominally Islamic financial institutions were engaged, activities still too derivative of their conventional counterparts, there was a sense of guarded optimism that Islamic finance was headed in the right direction.

One afternoon I was chatting with Saif, a North African–born shariah scholar. He said that, with the prodding of Bank Negara, the industry was "moving toward greater shariah compliance." I found his perspective valuable, as he seemed capable of seeing the Malaysian experiment in the context of Islamic finance as a whole, noting that Malaysia would not become a global hub "without a shariah infrastructure that was valid around the world." In his view, four recent revisions described previously in this book suggested that Malaysia was moving in this direction: the new stock screening methodology implemented by the Securities Commission; Bank Negara's revisions requiring the removal of the interconditionality clause; the legally mandated penalties for shariah noncompliance of up to eight years in prison and a fine of as much as 25 million ringgit; and revisions to the way that mudaraba contracts could be used with the creation of PSIAs. According to Saif, these demonstrated that the Malaysian state was taking the problem of shariah noncompliance seriously and seeking to more clearly differentiate the industry from its conventional counterpart. Moreover, he expressed optimism that a shift from debt to equity as the central mechanism for the provision of capital would make Malaysia even more appealing to potential clients from the Middle East who were skeptical of the religious credentials of Islamic finance in Malaysia.

Other critics drew inspiration from a different set of changes. For example, Mustafa, the Islamic economist, pointed to the increasingly vocal and organized role that shariah scholars were taking to lead the industry toward something that was more readily distinguishable from conventional finance. As evidence of this, he invoked the Kuala Lumpur and Jeddah declarations from 2012 and 2013, in which some of the world's most influential shariah scholars had asserted that the global financial crisis was the direct effect of a surfeit of debt and leverage and called for a shift away from debt financing and toward equity financing. Whereas shariah scholars had been criticized in the past for failing to push the industry away from a standard of shariah compliance and instead toward a shariah-based system, Mustafa saw their recent collective action as a sign that change was coming.

The anxieties over debt in Islamic finance reflected in perhaps more pragmatic fashion the extensive academic critique of debt that has blossomed in recent years. Indeed, the problem of debt and how to remedy it has generated a veritable slew of publications in recent years (Bonner and Wiggin 2009; Han 2012; Lazzarato 2015; Mian and Sufi 2015; Turner 2016). And for good reason: fueled in part by the great debt-fueled crises of our time, social scientists have rightfully latched on to credit as one of the foundational economic arrangements of capitalist economic organization and sought to challenge some of the underlying moral principles on which it is premised (Bear 2015; Joseph 2014; Karim 2011; Peebles 2013). In so doing, some have adopted the venerable anthropological strategy of making the familiar strange by questioning the moral logic that naturalizes debt and the social relationships it precipitates (Graeber 2011). By looking to the past, this work has emphasized the historical contingency of debt relationships and showed that, far from being universal principles, they are in fact the outcome of social production. This has conveyed an important lesson: the moral logic that undergirds our view of debt is not based on universal principles but is itself subject to historical change. Nonetheless, while this work has usefully questioned the judgments attached to debt relationships, it has accomplished little in terms of actually presenting an alternative to the centrality of debt in our economic practices. If anything, it seems resigned to the view that debt is an inevitable and inescapable feature of modern existence only to be resolved by bankruptcy, forgiveness, or periodic jubilees in which the arrears of the indebted are wiped clean through the authority of sovereign power.

This book has sought to show how the problem of contriving an alternative to conventional finance and its reliance on debt is a central preoccupation of Islamic finance. Rather than looking to the past to understand how debt has come to be a foundational feature of economic life, it seeks to identify a contemporary alternative to the pervasiveness of debt. This entails a different kind of anthropology. Rather than seeking to make the familiar strange, I have sought to show how Islamic finance experts are engaged in a range of profoundly anthropological experiments (Holmes 2014). Thus I have shown how debates in Islamic finance over its present and future practices reveal a challenge to the assumed practices of conventional finance. This is most evident in efforts to formulate a financial system that provincializes debt and the leverage it creates in favor of investment and equity. Reformers and critics take Qur'anic injunctions against the payment and collection of interest as a general critique of debt and as an effort to foster risk sharing as opposed risk transfer.

My interlocutors were convinced that the promise of equity-based financial arrangements lay in the limits they placed on leverage. Debt-based finance fosters the ability to invest with borrowed funds. This can lead to extraordinary profits, but it also can precipitate equally sheer losses. Indeed, as postmortems on the most recent financial crises have shown, leverage was perhaps the pivotal factor in casting the global economy into turmoil. In contrast, an equity-based financial system places much tighter limits on speculation: one simply cannot invest capital that one has not already generated.

Efforts by Islamic finance experts to remake finance around equity rather than debt reveal that the financial principles by which most of the world lives today are not the only ones possible, nor are they natural. Debt has largely become taken for granted as an intrinsic feature of contemporary economic life and social relations. A colleague was once startled when I described Islamic finance, exclaiming that "without debt, we wouldn't have banks!" In our time and place this seems to be accurate. Indeed, some Islamic financial institutions even refuse to call themselves banks, raising the question of what kind of language is adequate to contemporary finance (Appadurai 2016). One of the most visible foreign entries on Malaysia's Islamic financial scene self-consciously calls itself Kuwait Finance House. However, debt should no more be taken for granted as a foundation of finance than gold once was. Whereas scholarly work has shown how debt is the historically contingent effect of financial experimentation, I have shown how those seeking to reform Islamic finance today challenge the epistemology of debt by positing equity and investment as antidotes to debt-based finance. In this sense, Islamic finance is a kind of practical anthropology. Just as anthropology as a discipline has inspired reflection on the values and ways of being that we take for granted as natural and universal, Islamic finance demands that we question the unstated assumptions of our financial organization. The lesson that we might take from Islamic finance as practical anthropology is that how we choose to organize our economic lives is limited only by the imagination of what we take to be moral.

Acknowledgments

Writing a book inevitably incurs many debts, and when the subject of the book is debt, gratitude for generosity received can never be a mere platitude. But perhaps those who have assisted and advised me on this project over the past decade will consider their contributions an investment rather than a loan, and maybe this book and the conversations I hope that it will spawn will yield some sort of shared profit rather than a mere interested return.

Most of all, I thank the vast number of exceedingly busy professionals in Malaysia who patiently helped me with this work: making introductions, taking the time to explain Islamic finance, and, most important, recounting their vision of Islamic finance and its alternative potential. The former deputy governor responsible for Islamic finance, Dato' Muhammad Razif, passed away while I was conducting research, but given his support for the project, I hope that the book can in some way be considered a small part of his legacy. I made contact with INCEIF on an early visit to Malaysia in 2010, and its leadership and staff made both intellectual and practical contributions to my fieldwork. Daud Vicary Abdullah was the president and CEO of INCEIF during the time I conducted most of the fieldwork, and he enthusiastically supported the project, both through the institutional capacity of INCEIF and through the time that he took out of his extremely busy travel schedule to discuss Islamic finance in Malaysia with me. I hope that this book can do some justice to the support he offered me. A number of other INCEIF faculty served as extremely valuable resources for this project, and I am deeply grateful to all of them. I would be remiss not to specifically mention the contributions of the following faculty members: Ahcene Lahsasna, Yusuf Saleem, Syed Othman Alhabshi, Abbas Mirakhor, and Mohamad Pisal Zainal. The list of friends and colleagues in Malaysia who supported this research is long, and their contributions are legion. I regret that I am not able to mention them all by name, but I extend my most sincere thanks to them.

I could not have completed this book were it not for generous material support that I received from a number of institutions. Fieldwork in and travel to Malaysia were primarily supported by an Insight Development Grant and a Standard Research Grant, both from the Social Sciences and Humanities Research Council of Canada. A fellowship from the American Council of Learned Societies provided me with leave from teaching to enable overseas fieldwork on this project during the 2013–2014 academic year.

As I was writing this book, I joined the Department of Anthropology at the University of Victoria. The department provided a collegial environment that facilitated completion of the book. I am grateful for the conversations about this material I have had with my new colleagues. A number of friends and colleagues have helped me to think through the material as I was preparing the book manuscript, including Neilesh Bose, Leslie Butt, Emile Fromet de Rosnay, Lincoln Shlensky, and Scott Watson among others. Paul Schure helped me to clarify some of the economic and financial terms that I use in the book, especially in my discussions of leverage and mortgage financing. The Centre for Studies in Religion and Society at the University of Victoria provided a faculty fellowship that enabled me to complete the manuscript. I would especially like to thank the center's director, Paul Bramadat, for his enthusiasm and support for this project. I am grateful to the University of Victoria's Office of Research Services for providing a subvention to support publication of this book.

Colleagues both wiser and more generous than I provided valuable input on this project. There are far too many to name them all, but I would like to recognize a few who were particularly helpful. Both Johan Lindquist and Anke Schwittay read through an entire draft of the manuscript and provided exceedingly generous feedback. Johan gave me his feedback at the Stockholm Cultural Center as the long late-autumn afternoon shadows crept across the Sergels Torg, and Anke provided hers by post in hasty marginal scratches from the other side of the Atlantic. Many thanks to you both. A number of other colleagues read various slices of the book, but I would be remiss not to thank Ilana Gershon, Zeynep Gürsel, Douglas Holmes, Tamir Mustafa, and Michael Peletz, who all provided detailed feedback. I would like to recognize both Basit Karim Iqbal, who gave me excellent editorial feedback, and Maya Cowan, who composed the index. Various pieces of the book were presented at Binghamton University, Cornell University, Heidelberg University, Seoul National University, the University of Chicago, University College London, the University of Hong Kong, the University of Sussex, and the University of Victoria. I am grateful to interlocutors at those institutions for their generous comments and constructive criticism. Any outstanding errors of fact or interpretation are mine alone.

Priya Nelson, my editor at University of Chicago Press, saw the promise in this project from the moment I described it to her and has been an exceedingly generous interlocutor. I am also grateful for the comments and insights of three anonymous reviewers for the press, whose suggestions for revising the manuscript have immeasurably improved the final product. Many thanks are due to Jos Sances for his splendid design work on the graphics for the book. Last, but far from least, I am profoundly grateful to my family for sustaining me throughout this work. Max and Amira persevered through my extended absences while I was away conducting fieldwork but were always full of exuberance and joy when I returned home. Without Anissa's love and support it would never have happened at all, and it is for those reasons, although not those reasons alone, that I dedicate this book to her.

Methodological Notes

The methods for this book draw extensively on an earlier study of Islam and globalization that I conducted in Malaysia's neighboring country, Indonesia, between 2002 and 2008 (Rudnyckyj 2010). That study examined human resources training programs premised on the principle that enhanced Islamic practice was conducive to commercial success and personal growth. These programs created an assemblage of Islamic history, popular psychology, Qur'anic passages, self-help literature, and human resources management theories in arguing that Islamic piety was indispensable for Indonesian competitiveness in an increasingly integrated global economy (Rudnyckyj 2014a). While conducting that study I became interested in other ways in which Islam was being reinterpreted and deployed to be compatible with capitalism and modernity, which led to an interest in Islamic banking and finance. Although my initial explorations into the feasibility of an ethnographic study of Islamic finance started in Indonesia, colleagues there suggested that I would be better advised to conduct research on the other side of the Strait of Malacca, since there was a much more active and vibrant industry in Malaysia.

The advice of my Indonesian interlocutors proved sage. Malaysia is perhaps the best site in the world to understand contemporary Islamic finance, given the extensive state support for it and the sheer volume of educational, legal, and commercial activity. Furthermore, while there had been some important ethnographic and anthropological work on Islamic finance in the United States, the United Kingdom, and Indonesia (Maurer 2005, 2006), there was as yet no comprehensive empirical study of Islamic finance from the perspective of one of the industry's emerging hubs.

As ethnographers increasingly take up modern forms of knowledge and power as objects of analysis, we find ourselves confronted by new

methodological challenges. While the anthropological fiction of total knowledge through an exhaustive survey of a confined social milieu was ex-
ploded over thirty years ago (Clifford 1986), many anthropologists struggle with how to conduct ethnographic work in complex modern societies.
When I was discussing this project with an eminent senior anthropologist
as I was beginning fieldwork, he said to me blankly, "I just don't get it.
Back when I did [village-based fieldwork] everything was public, out in
the open. I don't know how this type of project could work." Indeed my
fieldwork with Islamic finance experts had to largely conform to the hectic
schedules of my interlocutors in Malaysia, who were, for the most part,
busy professionals. This meant that, by and large, my interactions with
them were limited to previously scheduled exchanges or only slightly less
constrained interactions during conferences and workshops. There was
little of the "deep hanging out" that James Clifford predicted in the late
1990s would increasingly characterize anthropological fieldwork (Clifford
1997, 90). Islamic bankers, given the demands on their time, did not really do much hanging out. Ultimately, collecting data for this project was
subject to scheduled interviews and chance encounters and took place in
a variety of physical settings, most of which were in and around Kuala
Lumpur. These sites included university classrooms, hotel ballrooms, res-
taurants, conference centers, taxicabs, gyms, office buildings, and other
sites that would appear neither foreign nor exotic to most European or
North American professionals. Nonetheless, it has yielded a study that
might inspire financialized subjects (which, after all, include most of us)
to reflect critically on some of the core economic truths we so take for
granted that we hardly ever pause to reconsider them.

Fieldwork among expert communities demands innovation in ethnographic methods. Although fieldwork for this project maintained some
consistency with conventional anthropological methods, my ethnographic
objectives differed from classic approaches. While I spent a great deal of
time in Malaysia with the various constituencies described in this book,
my goal was neither to discern the "native's point of view" (Malinowski
[1922] 2002, 19), as if there ever was a single one, nor to deploy "thick
description" to reveal "a stratified hierarchy of meaningful structures"
(Geertz 1973, 7). Rather, I sought to identify the specific problems for
which Islamic finance experts sought solutions. In so doing, I drew on
Foucault's notion of "problematization," which refers to the ways in which
subjects reflect on and question specific practices (Rabinow 2002; Rudnyckyj 2014b; Schwittay 2014). Foucault wrote that a problematization

"does not mean the representation of a persistent object nor the creation through discourse of an object that did not exist. It is the ensemble of discursive and nondiscursive practices that make something enter into the play of true and false and constitute it as an object of thought (whether in the form of moral reflection, scientific knowledge, political analysis, etc.)" (quoted in Rabinow 2003, 18). Building on this formulation, I approach the authenticity and alternative potential of Islamic finance as recurring and persistent objects of thought and reflection among Islamic finance experts.

Due to professional and personal obligations, I was unable to confine my ethnographic work in Malaysia to a single, long-term visit. Nonetheless, I was able to recreate the long-term immersive nature of ethnographic fieldwork through a number of visits over an extended period of time. Fieldwork in Malaysia for this project entailed eight trips over a period of five years, between 2010 and 2015, for stints ranging between three weeks and five months. I also attended a number of international conferences, such as the biannual Harvard Islamic Finance Forum in Cambridge, Massachusetts, and the Eighth International Conference on Islamic Economics and Finance in Doha, Qatar. During my time in Malaysia I was affiliated with the International Centre for Education in Islamic Finance. INCEIF provided tremendous support for this project by obtaining my research visa, hosting me as a visiting researcher, providing office space, sharing contacts, and offering access to libraries, archives, events, and meetings focusing on Islamic finance. During my longest continuous set of stays in Malaysia in 2013 and 2014 I had hoped to work as a researcher at Malaysia's Central Bank. Although I met with several senior officials to discuss this possibility, ultimately we were unable to find a mutually beneficial capacity in which I could do so. Nevertheless, over five years of fieldwork I developed an extensive network of contacts who facilitated access to a variety of meetings, workshops, and discussions where critical issues in Islamic finance were debated, many of which were inaccessible to the general public. This network also enabled me to arrange interviews with a number of influential figures in Islamic finance at regulatory institutions and private banks.

Ultimately, the majority of the information compiled in this book was drawn from formal and informal interviews; observation of and participation in workshops, conferences, and other expert meetings; and reading a diverse array of published materials pertaining to Islamic finance. Over thirty formal research interviews and scores of informal conversations

were conducted with members of the four main groups of experts working in Islamic finance and described in chapter 2 (Islamic finance professionals, regulators, Islamic economists, and shariah scholars). I also interviewed and discussed Islamic finance with a number of other figures,
including lawyers, academics, activists, businesspeople, students, and government officers. In most cases, to comply with protocols for the protec-
tion of human subjects, I have given pseudonyms to individuals quoted
as well as the institutions with which they were affiliated. In some cases I
have had to change identifying details for certain individuals to fulfill my
guarantee of anonymity. In cases where events I observed were described
in other published sources, such as newsletters, magazines, or books, I have
used the details in the published versions as empirical evidence rather than
my own field notes, recordings, and transcripts.

Although I am fluent in the Malaysian language, having conducted
a previous research project in Indonesia where the national language is
closely related to Malaysian, the vast majority of my fieldwork was conducted in English. This is due to three factors. First, due to its status as
a former British colony, English is widely spoken in Malaysia, especially
in urban areas. Every Islamic finance professional I encountered spoke
fluent English. Second, the international language of Islamic finance is
English. Although Arabic would appear to be a more likely choice, most
Islamic finance professionals outside the Middle East do not speak Arabic, but virtually all of them are conversant if not fluent in English. Therefore, English serves as the de facto lingua franca of contemporary Islamic
finance. Third, Malaysia has sought to attract Islamic finance expertise
from around the world, and therefore a substantial number of the Islamic
finance experts with whom I engaged were expatriates living in Malaysia
and did not speak Malay in their professional or personal lives.

Recently anthropologists have called for explicit attention to meetings as critical sites where expert knowledge is articulated and debated
(Brown, Reed, and Yarrow 2017; Deeb and Marcus 2011; Garsten and
Sörbom 2016; Sandler and Thedvall 2017). In concert with these insights,
another central facet of my methodology was observation and, where
possible, participation in meetings and events where experts discussed,
debated, and reflected on Islamic finance and its devices. These included
dozens of conferences and larger forums, public lectures, small private
workshops, and other meetings consisting of multiple participants. I also
had the good fortune to meet an Islamic financier who allowed me to
accompany him in a series of negotiations, described in chapter 4, as he

sought to find a backer in Malaysia for a $500 million sukuk. I found observing these events especially useful in distilling the central problems facing experts in Islamic finance as they saw them. Through observation of meetings, conferences, workshops, and so forth I was able to identify the problems posed by experts in Islamic finance in a way that did not require the direct intervention of the analyst. Thus I was able to collect discourse and observe practices "in the wild" and in ways not explicitly framed for my research project (Callon and Rabeharisoa 2003). Oftentimes formal and informal interviews would involve discussing a topic or a question that had been raised at a meeting.

I also took advantage of my affiliation with INCEIF to sit in on classes offered at the university. During the period of my fieldwork I audited three courses: Islamic jurisprudence (*fiqh muamalat*), Islamic law (shariah), and Islamic economics. These courses afforded me an opportunity to understand some of the technical problems in Islamic finance and the practical challenge of bridging Islam and capitalism. Several faculty members at INCEIF served as shariah scholars on the shariah advisory boards of Islamic financial institutions or identified as Islamic economists. As a result, auditing courses proved an excellent way of understanding practical problems in Islamic finance. Furthermore, INCEIF served as an important training ground for Islamic finance professionals. Research participants I first met when they were students in 2010 were, by the time I returned between 2013 and 2015, working in the industry. During the time I spent there I found an experimental ethos common at the institution characterized by a pervasive sense that the norms and forms of Islamic finance were still in formation. Students and professors regularly debated the practices of the industry and conducted research that sought to improve existing instruments and fabricate new ones. The university was a key site where the practices of Islamic finance were reflected on and problematized and where experiments in Islamic finance were devised and executed. Both faculty members and students were simultaneously enthusiastic about the future potential of Islamic finance and critical of its existing operations and practices.

Glossary of Islamic Financial Terms

bai al inah: A contract in which one party sells an asset to a second party on a deferred payment basis and then buys it back from the second party at a lower price in cash. This contract effectively replicates an interest-bearing loan.

faedah: Interest or benefit. At one point this term was used in Malaysian Islamic banking instead of riba, such as in the 1990s-era Skim Perbankan Tanpa Faedah (Interest-Free Banking Scheme). However, by the 2010s this term was virtually never used.

fatwa: An Islamic legal opinion arrived at by a religious authority knowledgeable of shariah.

fiqh: Islamic jurisprudence. Evident in human efforts to put divine injunctions, as revealed in the Qur'an and the sunnah, into practice.

gharar: Excessive uncertainty. One of three fundamental prohibitions in Islamic finance, the other two being riba and maysir. "Gharar" refers to excessive uncertainty in a contract, transaction, or other commercial arrangement. Often used to describe situations in which a party to a contract stands to be deceived through ignorance of an essential element of the exchange. Gambling is considered gharar because a gambler is uncertain of the outcome of a wager.

hadith: From the Arabic word for "report" or "account." Hadiths refer to recorded words and actions of the prophet Muhammad. These serve as an important basis for shariah.

hajj: Pilgrimage to Mecca. One of the five pillars of Islam, it is required once of every Muslim who is not restricted from traveling due to financial or physical limitations.

halal: Lawful or permissible. In Islam there are activities, contracts, and transactions that are explicitly prohibited (haram) by the Quran. Anything not explicitly prohibited is deemed permissible.

Hanafi: One of four major Sunni fiqh schools of thought (mazhab). The prevailing fiqh school in Central and South Asia and parts of the Middle East, including Turkey, Egypt, and the Levant.

Hanbali: One of four major Sunni fiqh schools of thought, this is the predominate fiqh school in most of Saudi Arabia, Qatar, and the United Arab Emirates.

hibah: A gift or a contract in which one party voluntarily transfers ownership to another without the expectation of compensation.

hiyal: A legal stratagem. A mode of reasoning that achieves shariah compliance through contrivance and possibly even subterfuge while formally conforming to the letter of the law. For example, many Islamic finance experts consider the deployment of two sales in a bai al inah contract (to replicate an interest-bearing loan) to be hiyal.

ijara: Leasing. A contract in which the use of an asset (manfa'ah) is transferred but not the ownership of the corpus of the asset.

ijazah: A grant of permission to indicate that one has been authorized to transmit Islamic knowledge.

istisna': A contract in which a manufacturer agrees to produce an object for future delivery at a specific time to a second party at a fixed price and according to the buyer's specifications.

kafalah: A guarantee of the repayment of a debt or other liability to a creditor.

mal: Property, capital, or, more generally, wealth.

Maliki: One of four major Sunni fiqh schools of thought and the prevailing one in most of North Africa.

manfa'ah: The usufruct or benefit from a property or object. Sometimes referred to as "beneficial ownership." Manfa'ah is generally distinguished from outright ownership, especially in lease arrangements. In a lease for commercial real estate, for example, manfa'ah might be used to describe the benefit that the lessee derives from the use of the property during the lease in contrast to the actual ownership of the property.

maysir: Gambling or overly speculative activity. One of three fundamental prohibitions in Islamic finance (the other two being riba and gharar), it literally means profiting too easily.

mudaraba: A profit-sharing contract in which one party provides capital (rabb al mal) and the other provides labor and/or management (mudarib). Losses are borne by the capital provider unless they are due to the mudarib's misconduct, negligence, or breach of contractual terms.

mudarib: An entrepreneur who contributes labor and management to a partnership but typically does not invest any of his or her own capital. In return for their efforts, the mudarib receives a share of the profits.

mufti: An Islamic scholar qualified to give legal opinions or fatwa.

murabaha: A contract in which one party sells a commodity to another party at a marked-up price on a deferred payment basis. The increase is not considered interest but profit.

musharaka: Joint venture. A profit-sharing contract in which two or more parties agree to pool their assets and labor for the purpose of making a profit. Losses are borne by both parties at an agreed ratio.

musharaka mutanaqisah: A diminishing partnership in which both partners provide initial funds, but one of the partners promises to gradually buy out the equity of the other until she or he has assumed complete ownership.

qard al hasan: A benevolent loan, permitted in Islamic finance because there is no riba in the arrangement. The funds repaid must be exactly equivalent to the amount of the initial loan.

rabb al maal: Capital provider in a mudaraba contract. Sometimes referred to as a "sleeping partner" because she or he does not take an active role in managing the partnership but rather invests in the concern and receives a prearranged share of the profits.

riba: One of three fundamental prohibitions in Islamic finance (the other two being gharar and maysir), literally meaning "increase." Used in Islamic finance to refer to interest paid or owed on a debt. In Islamic finance any risk-free or guaranteed rate of return on a loan or investment is considered riba.

Shafi'i: One of four major Sunni fiqh schools of thought (mazhab). The predominate school in Southeast Asia, it is also widespread in East Africa and parts of the Middle East.

shariah: Islamic law ordained by Allah and derived from three main sources: the Qur'an, the hadith, and the sunnah. In contemporary Islamic finance, a central question is whether a standard of "shariah-compliance" is sufficient or whether an instrument should be "shariah-based." Shariah-compliance refers to a standard in which an instrument or device does not violate the formal conventions in the Qur'an, hadith, or sunnah. In contrast, a shariah-based instrument has a substantive historical and/or textual foundation in those sources.

sukuk: Financial instruments used by corporations and governments to raise capital for activities such as business expansion and infrastructure development. They are often referred to as "Islamic bonds" in media coverage about Islamic finance.

sunnah: The practices and traditions of the prophet Muhammad. Related to hadiths, the sunnah also serves as a basis for shariah.

takaful: Islamic mutual insurance based on the principle of reciprocal assistance.

tawarruq: Reverse murabaha. A contract in which one party purchases an asset from another party on credit with a deferred payment and then sells the asset to a third party with an immediate payment.

ummah: The global community of Muslims.

umroh: Widely known as the "the lesser hajj," a religious pilgrimage to the Arabian Peninsula that takes place outside the hajj season. Unlike the hajj, umroh is not obligatory for Muslims and is typically of shorter duration than the hajj.

wa'd: Promise. A commitment made by one person to another to undertake an action beneficial to a second party.

wadiah: Safekeeping. A contract in which one party leaves belongings with another for safekeeping.

wakalah: Agency. A contract in which one party delegates another party to act on its behalf.

waqf: A charitable foundation established for a social or religious purpose by benefactors.

zakat: Alms that every Muslim is required to pay to benefit his or her community. One of the five pillars of Islam, zakat is an obligatory tax on wealth required of every Muslim. According to custom, zakat is 2.5 percent of one's total wealth above a threshold minimum.

Notes

Introduction

1. The ummah refers to the global community of Muslims.

2. https://www.flickr.com/photos/occupyamsterdam/6247968168, accessed February 14, 2018.

3. I thank Paul Schure for helping me to clarify this discussion of leverage.

4. CIMB developed what its former CEO Badlisyah Abdul Ghani called a "dual banking leverage model," in which it used its existing conventional infrastructure to grow the Islamic side of its business. This involved opening an Islamic bank and a conventional bank in the same physical branch space but using two separate clearing and handling codes and profit and loss sheets for each branch, ensuring that they were virtually separate. Bank Rakyat's claims of "100% Islamic banking" was an attempt to assert its authenticity in the face of dominant competitors in the market, such as CIMB.

5. These plans were dramatically altered by the 1MDB scandal that ensnared the administration of the Malaysian prime minister Najib Razak in 2015 and 2016, while this book was being written.

6. "Halal" refers to food that is permissible for Muslims to eat. Pork is always impermissible, and other animals must be slaughtered according to prescribed rituals to be fit for consumption.

Chapter One

1. In so doing, they invoked a metaphor for slumbering capital that is familiar in non-Islamic contexts as well (D'Avella 2014, 184; Peebles 2008, 235).

2. Alatas was a vice chancellor of the University of Malaya and the author of the landmark study *The Myth of the Lazy Native*, a critique of Orientalist representations that anticipated the subsequent interventions of Edward Said (Alatas 1977).

3. Bursa Malaysia is Malaysia's main stock exchange and is located in Kuala Lumpur.

4. Mohamad and Saravanamuttu interpret this stipulation as an effort to divest Malaysian civil courts of authority in Islamic finance and provide more control for bankers (Mohamad and Saravanamuttu 2015, 206).

5. For example, there are over twenty universities in the United Kingdom offering degrees in Islamic finance.

6. RM is the symbol for the Malaysian ringgit, the national currency of Malaysia. During the period of research for this book the exchange rate between the ringgit and the US dollar oscillated between three and three and a half ringgit per dollar.

7. A murabaha is a sale contract in which one party sells a commodity to another party at a marked-up price on a deferred payment basis.

8. The most frequently invoked scriptural justification for the prohibition of money for money is what Abdullah Saeed calls the "six commodities hadith," which reads, "The prophet said: Gold for gold, silver for silver, wheat for wheat, barley for barley, dates for dates, and salt for salt should be exchanged like for like, equal for equal and hand-to-hand. . . . If the types of the exchanged commodities are different, then sell them as you wish, if they are exchanged on the basis of a hand-to-hand transaction" (Saeed 1996, 31).

Chapter Two

1. The roundtable is discussed in detail below.

2. A measure of the public esteem for Zeti was that in 2015 her office was tasked with a politically contentious investigation of alleged fiscal improprieties by 1MDB, a state fund established by Malaysia's prime minister, Najib Abdul Razak. Her office was seen as one of the few credible institutions in the country capable of conducting such an investigation.

3. As Andrea Muehlebach points out, formulations of liberalism by none other than Adam Smith did not exclusively emphasize individual self-interest. In his lesser-known work *The Theory of Moral Sentiments*, Smith "spends dozens of pages fretting over the question of balance and proportion in moral and emotional life, and over how a perfect equilibrium between self-love and fellow-feeling can be achieved" (Muehlebach 2012, 29).

4. The Gulf Cooperation Council consists of Bahrain, Kuwait, Oman, Qatar, Saudi Arabia, and the United Arab Emirates.

5. Established in 1990 and based in Bahrain, AAOIFI is an international organization that prepares accounting, auditing, governance, ethics and shariah standards for Islamic financial institutions and the industry. Whereas AAOIFI focuses more on religious standards for Islamic finance, the IFSB focuses more on issuing practical standards used in the actual operation of Islamic finance on an everyday basis.

6. "Najmah" means "star" in Arabic. Many global banks that have Islamic subsidiaries brand the subsidiaries with an Arabic term that has a religious referent.

NOTES TO PAGES 69–91

For example, HSBC calls its subsidiary HSBC Amanah ("trustworthy"), and Standard Chartered calls its subsidiary Standard Chartered Saadiq ("truthful").

7. "Tawhid" refers to the oneness of God and the attempt to comprehend the absolute truth represented by monotheism. "Tasawwuf" essentially refers to Sufism and could be loosely glossed as "spirituality."

8. Indonesian and Malay are closely related, mutually intelligible languages.

9. This was equivalent to between about $750 and $3,000 at the time.

10. The Al-Haram mosque is the largest mosque in the world and one of the most important pilgrimage sites during the hajj. Recently the Saudi Arabian government has authorized several controversial development projects on historical sites adjacent to the mosque to facilitate the construction of luxury hotels, condominiums, and other buildings for wealthy hajj pilgrims and other elites.

11. The Kaaba lies at the center of the Al-Haram mosque and is one of the most sacred shrines in Islam. It is the center of the circumambulation that takes place during the hajj.

12. This amount was equivalent to approximately $76,000 at the time.

13. Abdul Ghani resigned as CEO of CIMB Islamic in July 2015 after posting controversial Facebook comments critical of the *Wall Street Journal*'s investigative reporting of the state investment fund, 1MDB, which had been started by Prime Minister Najib Razak.

14. While the crisis was commonly attributed to subprime loans in the United States, Malaysia, and elsewhere, recent research suggests that wealthy and middle-class house "flippers" were as responsible for the crisis as were subprime borrowers, if not more so (Adelino, Schoar, and Severino 2016).

15. A musharaka contract is a profit-sharing contract in which two or more parties agree to pool their assets and labor for the purpose of making a profit. Losses are borne by both parties at an agreed ratio.

16. "Mu'amalah" means "commercial transaction."

17. This amount was equivalent to roughly $7.6 million at the time.

Chapter Three

1. "Riba" is literally translated as "increase" but is commonly understood to refer to usury or interest. This is discussed further below.

2. John Bowen provides an excellent synopsis of debates over whether Muslims living as minorities in Europe are permitted to participate in contracts that require the payment of interest (Bowen 2010, 137–149). As he notes, these debates are often framed by the absence of any alternatives to interest-based financing in Europe.

3. Other interpreters attribute the prohibition of riba to different rationales. Historians have argued that riba was prohibited because interest rates during the time of the prophet were exorbitantly high and led to debtors being required to

pay many times the amount of their original loans to settle debts. Some analysts have attributed the prohibition of interest to the moral principle, dating at least to Aristotle, that money should not be attributed the power of living things in being able to beget more money (Taussig 1980, 129–133).

4. Giddens contrasts the modern conception of the future in terms of risk with premodern conceptions of the future in terms of fate (Giddens 1990).

5. As David Graeber has noted, Smith appears to have borrowed his famous example of the division of labor in a pin factory from the works of the eleventh-century Islamic scholar al-Ghazali (Graeber 2011, 279).

6. Jubilee 2000 was an international coalition that called for the cancellation of debt held by countries in the Global South by the year 2000.

7. Rahim's analysis of the immorality of interest-bearing debt resonated with Tomas Piketty's recent arguments that inequality in contemporary capitalism is a result of the fact that the rate of capital return in developed countries is persistently greater than the rate of economic growth. Those with surplus capital to invest in securities, like stocks, bonds, or real estate, do better financially than those whose income is derived from solely from contracting their labor (Piketty 2014).

8. In these discussions, equity refers to an ownership stake or shares that carry no fixed interest. Equity thus entitles the owner to the profits of a business, which are subject to the vagaries of the market and thus are neither guaranteed nor fixed. This usage of equity differs from that of Maurer and Martin, who describe it as the "use of substantive principles of fairness and justice that are meant to mitigate the formal strictures of law" (Maurer and Martin 2012, 531).

Chapter Four

1. Maurer defines sukuk as "Islamic bond structures that securitize leases (ijara) as well as other Islamic financing contracts such as murabaha (sale with markup), musharaka (partnership based on the mingling of capital contributions and proportionate profit and loss-sharing), and mudaraba (profit and loss-sharing partnership based on funds provision by one source and effort by another source)" (Maurer 2010, 32).

2. Cash waqfs are cash endowments, the proceeds from which can be used for charitable purposes. Waqfs are described in detail in chapter 5.

3. Most international Islamic financial transactions were denominated in US dollars, and that was the currency on which Uzair had based his proposal.

4. Bill Maurer provides an account of the debates kindled by mortgage-backed securities, with a special focus on the Guidance product (Maurer 2006, 85–92).

5. A sovereign bond is a debt instrument issued by a nation-state that entails a promise to make periodic interest payments and repay the full face value of the bond to its holders on the maturity date.

Chapter Five

1. According to Article 3 of the Federal Constitution of Malaysia, each Malaysian state is authorized to regulate Islamic religious practice in that state (Whiting 2008, 230). In states with a sultan, the sultan is the "Head of the religion of Islam in his State" (Federal Constitution of Malaysia 2013, 3:2). Each state also has a state Islamic Religious Council (Majlis Agama Islam) "to advise the ruler on Islamic religious matters and Malay customs. Consisting mainly of *ulamak* [religious scholars] who were appointed by the Sultan, chief *kadi* [judges] and senior government officers, the Majlis is responsible for determining those Islamic principles and laws that are going to be administered in the state" (Hassan and Cederroth 1997, 49). These religious councils have jurisdiction over Muslim personal law, including matters of marriage, divorce, waqf, and inheritance.

2. Because the profit rate is indexed to rental prices rather than interest rates, the version of diminishing musharaka championed by Idris was more akin to another, less popular contract used in Islamic finance in the United States, an ijara (Maurer 2006, 45–47). Maurer writes that the ijara, which is essentially a lease-to-own contract, "seems on the surface to be more shariah-compliant" because it "more closely seems to adhere to the prohibition of interest" (Maurer 2006, 3).

3. There are two further categories of financial contracts used in Malaysia: lease-based contracts such as the ijara and fee-based ones, such as *wakalah*. However, these are less commonly used in Malaysian Islamic finance than the equity-based and debt-based ones described here.

Chapter Six

1. Al-Azhar University is located in Cairo and is one of the most famous, oldest, and well-respected universities in the Islamic world.

2. Syed Muhammad Naquib al-Attas was a prominent Malay intellectual who helped to found the National University of Malaysia. He is also a cousin of the founding figure of Islamic finance in Malaysia, Ungku Abdul Aziz, who formulated the first plan for Tabung Haji (Pilgrim's Savings Fund).

Chapter Seven

1. A mufti is an Islamic scholar qualified to give legal opinions or fatwa.

2. Penang, Selangor, Perak, and Perlis are all Malaysian states. Nuraini was remarking on the fact that the chief Islamic authorities from each of these four states were all in attendance at the transaction.

3. This is a daily interest rate and is analogous to LIBOR.

4. A balance sheet is a common financial device that reflects the assets and liabilities held by a financial institution.

5. The Banking Regulation and Supervision Agency is the agency responsible for regulating commercial banks in Turkey and is analogous to the Office for the Superintendent of Financial Institutions in Canada or the Prudential Regulatory Authority in the United Kingdom. In these jurisdictions these agencies act autonomously from the country's central bank.

6. Unrestricted PSIAs are accounts in which the bank is authorized to invest the account holder's funds in any manner with no restrictions as to where, how, or for what purpose the funds should be invested.

7. I thank Paul Schure for helping me to clarify this definition.

Chapter Eight

1. These prayers are religious rites performed by Muslims at sunset.

2. Other scholars have likewise drawn attention to the rise of religiously marked consumption elsewhere in the Muslim world (Jones 2010; Meneley 2007; Rouse and Hoskins 2004).

3. Umroh, also called "the lesser hajj," is a religious pilgrimage to the Arabian Peninsula that takes place outside the official "hajj season." Unlike the hajj, umroh is not obligatory for Muslims and is typically of shorter duration than the hajj.

4. London is also making a push to become a hub of Islamic finance.

5. Following the Arab Spring and the recurring political instability that has afflicted Bahrain, Dubai has usurped its position as the Gulf's capital of Islamic finance. This follows a coordinated effort by Dubai's prime minister, Sheikh Al Makhtoum, to make the emirate the capital of the global Islamic economy.

6. In Malaysia there are at least three different common spellings of this word: mudaraba, mudarabah, and mudharabah. They all refer to the same Islamic finance device. For the sake of consistency and to avoid confusion with the murabaha contract, I have used mudaraba.

7. The Basel Committee's banking regulations were under revision at the time of our conversation. The Third Basel Accord is scheduled to be implemented by 2019.

Conclusion

1. "Salafism" refers to the puritanical, reformist version of Islam developed on the Arabian Peninsula in the eighteenth century and still holds sway in most of the countries of the GCC.

References

Abdalla Khiyar, Khiyar. 2005. *The Rise and Development of Interest-Free Banking.* New Delhi: Institute of Objective Studies.

Abdul Ghani, Badlisyah. 2009. "Is AAOIFI Ban on Musharaka Sukuk Justified?" *Islamic Banker* 160–161: 10–16.

Abdul Hamid, Ahmad Fauzi. 2005. "The Strategy of Islamic Education in Malaysia: An Islamic Movement's Experience." In *Islamic Education in South and Southeast Asia: Diversity, Problems, and Strategy*, edited by S. Yunanto, Abdul Wasik, Badrudin Haurn, Farhan Effendy, Sri Nuryanti, and Syahrul Hidayat, 171–204. Jakarta: Ridep Institute and Friedrich Ebert Stiftung.

Abdullah, Taufik. 1986. "The Pesantren in Historical Perspective." In *Islam and Society in Southeast Asia*, edited by Taufik Abdullah and Sharon Siddique, 80–107. Singapore: Institute of Southeast Asian Studies.

Adam, Nathif J., and Abdulkader Thomas. 2004. *Islamic Bonds: Your Guide to Issuing, Structuring and Investing in Sukuk*. London: Euromoney Books.

Adelino, Manuel, Antoinette Schoar, and Felipe Severino. 2016. "Loan Originations and Defaults in the Mortgage Crisis: The Role of the Middle Class." *Review of Financial Studies* 29 (7): 1635–1670.

Agamben, Giorgio. 1998. *Homo Sacer: Sovereign Power and Bare Life*. Stanford, CA: Stanford University Press.

Al-Attas, Muhammad Naquib. 1978. *Islam and Secularism*. Kuala Lumpur: Muslim Youth Movement of Malaysia.

Alatas, Syed Hussein. 1977. *The Myth of the Lazy Native*. London: F. Cass.

Alim, Emmy Abdul. 2013. *Global Leaders in Islamic Finance: Industry Milestones and Reflections*. Singapore: John Wiley and Sons.

Appadurai, Arjun. 2011. "The Ghost in the Financial Machine." *Public Culture* 23 (3): 517–539.

———. 2016. *Banking on Words: The Failure of Language in the Age of Derivative Finance*. Chicago: University of Chicago Press.

Appel, Hannah. 2014. "Occupy Wall Street and the Economic Imagination." *Cultural Anthropology* 29 (4): 602–625.

Ariff, Mohamed, and Syarisa Yanti Abubakar. 2002. "Strengthening Entrepreneurship in Malaysia." Accessed February 21, 2018. http://www.mansfieldfdn .org/backup/programs/program_pdfs/ent_malaysia.pdf.

Asad, Talal. 1986. *The Idea of an Anthropology of Islam.* Washington, DC: Center for Contemporary Arab Studies, Georgetown University.

———. 1993. *Genealogies of Religion: Discipline and Reasons of Power in Christianity and Islam.* Baltimore: Johns Hopkins University Press.

———. 2003. *Formations of the Secular: Christianity, Islam, Modernity.* Stanford, CA: Stanford University Press.

Asutay, Mehmet. 2012. "Conceptualising and Locating the Social Failure of Islamic Finance: Aspirations of Islamic Moral Economy versus the Realities of Islamic Finance." *Asian and African Area Studies* 11 (2): 93–113.

Atia, Mona. 2012. "'A Way to Paradise': Pious Neoliberalism, Islam, and Faith-Based Development." *Annals of the Association of American Geographers* 102 (4): 808–827.

Atkinson, Jane M., and Shelly Errington. 1990. *Power and Difference: Gender in Island Southeast Asia.* Stanford, CA: Stanford University Press.

Aziz, Zeti Akhtar. 2013. "Financial Stability, Economic Growth and Development." Islamic Development Bank Prize Lecture, November 27, Jeddah, Saudi Arabia.

Bank Negara Malaysia. 2010. *Shariah Resolutions in Islamic Finance.* Kuala Lumpur: Bank Negara Malaysia.

———. 2015. "Sasana Kijang and Lanai Kijang." Accessed May 19, 2015. http://www .bnm.gov.my/index.php?ch=en_about&pg=en_thebank&ac=1110&lang=en.

Barker, Joshua, and Johan Lindquist. 2009. "Figures of Indonesian Modernity." *Indonesia* 87: 35–38.

Barry, Andrew, Thomas Osborne, and Nikolas S. Rose. 1996. *Foucault and Political Reason: Liberalism, Neo-Liberalism and Rationalities of Government.* Chicago: University of Chicago Press.

Bassens, David, Ben Derudder, and Frank Witlox. 2011. "Setting Shari'a Standards: On the Role, Power and Spatialities of Interlocking Shari'a Boards in Islamic Financial Services." *Geoforum* 42 (1): 94–103.

———. 2012. "'Gatekeepers' of Islamic Financial Circuits: Analysing Urban Geographies of the Global Shari'a Elite." *Entrepreneurship & Regional Development* 24 (5–6): 337–355.

Bassens, David, Ewald Engelen, Ben Derudder, and Frank Witlox. 2013. "Securitization across Borders: Organizational Mimicry in Islamic Finance." *Journal of Economic Geography* 13 (1): 85–106.

Baxstrom, Richard. 2008. *Houses in Motion: The Experience of Place and the Problem of Belief in Urban Malaysia.* Stanford, CA: Stanford University Press.

Bear, Laura. 2015. *Navigating Austerity: Currents of Debt along a South Asian River*. Stanford, CA: Stanford University Press.

Beck, Ulrich. 1992. *Risk Society: Towards a New Modernity*. London: Sage.

Benes, Jaromir, and Michael Kumhof. 2012. "The Chicago Plan Revisited." *IMF Working Paper*. Accessed May 12, 2014. https://www.imf.org/external/pubs/ft/wp/2012/wp12202.pdf.

Boholm, Åsa. 2003. "The Cultural Nature of Risk: Can There Be an Anthropology of Uncertainty?" *Ethnos* 68 (2): 159–178.

Bonner, William, and Addison Wiggin. 2009. *The New Empire of Debt: The Rise and Fall of an Epic Financial Bubble*. Hoboken, NJ: Wiley.

Bosworth, Derek L., and Elizabeth Webster. 2006. *The Management of Intellectual Property*. Cheltenham: Edward Elgar.

Bowen, John R. 2010. *Can Islam Be French? Pluralism and Pragmatism in a Secularist State*. Princeton, NJ: Princeton University Press.

———. 2012. *A New Anthropology of Islam*. Cambridge: Cambridge University Press.

Brenner, Suzanne. 1995. "Why Women Rule the Roost: Rethinking Javanese Ideologies of Gender and Self-Control." In *Bewitching Women, Pious Men: Gender and Body Politics in Southeast Asia*, edited by Aihwa Ong and Michael Peletz, 19–50. Berkeley: University of California Press.

Brown, Hannah, Adam Reed, and Thomas Yarrow. 2017. "Introduction: Towards an Ethnography of Meeting." *Journal of the Royal Anthropological Institute* 23 (S1): 10–26.

Brown, Wendy. 2011. "The End of Educated Democracy." *Representations* 116 (1): 19–41.

Buckley, Susan L. 2000. *Teachings on Usury in Judaism, Christianity and Islam*. Lewiston, NY: Edwin Mellen.

Bunnell, Tim. 2004. *Malaysia, Modernity and the Multimedia Super Corridor: A Critical Geography of Intelligent Landscapes*. London: RoutledgeCurzon.

Callon, Michel. 1998. *The Laws of the Markets*. Malden: Blackwell.

Callon, Michel, and Vololona Rabeharisoa. 2003. "Research 'in the Wild' and the Shaping of New Social Identities." *Technology in Society* 25 (2): 193–204.

Chakrabarty, Dipesh. 2000. *Provincializing Europe: Postcolonial Thought and Historical Difference*. Princeton, NJ: Princeton University Press.

Chapra, Mohammad Umar. 1996. *What Is Islamic Economics?* Jeddah: Islamic Development Bank.

Chin, Christine. 1998. *In Service and Servitude: Foreign Female Domestic Workers and the Malaysian "Modernity" Project*. New York: Columbia University Press.

Çizakça, Murat. 2011. *Islamic Capitalism and Finance: Origins, Evolution and the Future*. Cheltenham: Edward Elgar.

Clifford, James. 1986. "Introduction: Partial Truths." In *Writing Culture: The Poetics and Politics of Ethnography*, edited by James Clifford and George E. Marcus, 1–26. Berkeley: University of California Press.

———. 1997. *Routes: Travel and Translation in the Late Twentieth Century.* Cambridge, MA: Harvard University Press.

Cohn, Bernard S. 1996. *Colonialism and Its Forms of Knowledge: The British in India.* Princeton, NJ: Princeton University Press.

Comaroff, Jean, and John Comaroff. 2000. "Millennial Capitalism: First Thoughts on a Second Coming." *Public Culture* 12 (2): 291–343.

Crouch, Harold. 1996. *Government and Society in Malaysia.* Ithaca, NY: Cornell University Press.

D'Avella, Nicholas. 2014. "Ecologies of Investment: Crisis Histories and Brick Futures in Argentina." *Cultural Anthropology* 29 (1): 173–199.

Davis, Elizabeth A. 2013. "'It Wasn't Written for Me': Law, Debt, and Therapeutic Contracts in Greek Psychiatry." *Political and Legal Anthropology Review* 36 (1): 4–34.

Deeb, Hadi Nicholas, and George Marcus. 2011. "In the Green Room: An Experiment in Ethnographic Method at the WTO." *Political and Legal Anthropology Review* 34 (1): 51–76.

Department of Statistics Malaysia. 2017. "Population and Housing Census." Accessed August 1, 2017. https://www.dosm.gov.my/v1/index.php?r=column/cthemeByCat&cat=117&bul_id=MDMxdHZjWTk1SjFzTzNkRXYzcVZjdz09&menu_id=L0pheU43NWJwRWVSZklWdzQ4TlhUUT09.

Dhofier, Zamakhsyari. 1999. *The Pesantren Tradition: A Study of the Role of the Kyai in the Maintenance of the Traditional Ideology of Islam in Java.* Tempe: Arizona State University Southeast Asian Studies Monograph Series.

Dusuki, Asyraf Wajdi. 2010. *Can Bursa Malaysia's Suq Al-Sila' (Commodity Murabahah House) Resolve the Controversy over Tawarruq?* Kuala Lumpur: International Shari'ah Research Academy for Islamic Finance.

———, ed. 2012. *Islamic Financial System: Principles & Operation.* Kuala Lumpur: International Shari'ah Research Academy for Islamic Finance.

Economic Planning Unit. 2010. *Tenth Malaysia Plan, 2011–2015.* Putra Jaya: Economic Planning Unit.

Economist. 1997. "Mahathir, Soros and the Currency Markets." September 25. Accessed February 21, 2018. http://www.economist.com/node/101043.

———. 2015. "Graduate Stock." August 20. Accessed July 31, 2017. http://www.economist.com/news/finance-and-economics/21661678-funding-students-equity-rather-debt-appealing-it-not.

El-Gamal, Mahmoud. 2006. *Islamic Finance: Law, Economics, and Practice.* Cambridge: Cambridge University Press.

———. 2007. "Mutuality as an Antidote to Rent-Seeking Shariah Arbitrage in Islamic Finance." *Thunderbird International Business Review* 49 (2): 187–202.

Escobar, Arturo. 1995. *Encountering Development: The Making and Unmaking of the Third World.* Princeton, NJ: Princeton University Press.

Esposito, John L. 1998. *Islam and Politics.* Syracuse, NY: Syracuse University Press.

Evers, Hans-Dieter. 2003. "Transition Towards a Knowledge Society: Malaysia and Indonesia in Comparative Perspective." *Comparative Sociology* 2 (2): 355–373.

Federal Constitution of Malaysia. 2013. Petaling Jaya: International Law Book Services.

Fernando, Mayanthi. 2014. *The Republic Unsettled: Muslim French and the Contradictions of Secularism.* Durham, NC: Duke University Press.

Fischer, Johan. 2008. *Proper Islamic Consumption: Shopping among the Malays in Modern Malaysia.* Copenhagen: NIAS.

———. 2011. *The Halal Frontier: Muslim Consumers in a Globalized Market.* New York: Palgrave Macmillan.

Fischer, Michael M. J. 1980. *Iran: From Religious Dispute to Revolution.* Cambridge, MA: Harvard University Press.

Fisher, Melissa S. 2012. *Wall Street Women.* Durham, NC: Duke University Press.

Foucault, Michel. 1991. "Governmentality." In *The Foucault Effect*, edited by Graham Burchell, Colin Gordon, and Peter Miller, 87–104. Chicago: University of Chicago Press.

———. 2008. *The Birth of Biopolitics: Lectures at the College de France, 1978–1979.* Houndmills: Palgrave Macmillan.

Friedman, Milton. 1955. "The Role of Government in Education." In *Economics and the Public Interest*, edited by Robert A. Solo, 123–144. New Brunswick, NJ: Rutgers University Press.

Furnivall, John S. 1948. *Colonial Policy and Practice: A Comparative Study of Burma and Netherlands India.* Cambridge: Cambridge University Press.

Gade, Anna M. 2004. *Perfection Makes Practice: Learning, Emotion, and the Recited Qur'an in Indonesia.* Honolulu: University of Hawai'i Press.

Garsten, Christina, and Anna Hasselström. 2003. "Risky Business: Discourses of Risk and (Ir) responsibility in Globalizing Markets." *Ethnos* 68 (2): 249–270.

Garsten, Christina, and Adrienne Sörbom. 2016. "Magical Formulae for Market Futures: Tales from the World Economic Forum Meeting in Davos." *Anthropology Today* 32 (6): 18–21.

Gaunaurd, Pierre M., Hdeel Abdelhady, and Nabil A. Issa. 2011. "Islamic Finance." *International Lawyer* 45 (1): 271–285.

Geertz, Clifford. 1973. "Thick Description: Toward an Interpretive Theory of Culture." In *The Interpretation of Cultures: Selected Essays*, 3–30. New York: Basic Books.

Geisst, Charles R. 2013. *Beggar Thy Neighbor: A History of Usury and Debt.* Philadelphia: University of Pennsylvania Press.

Giddens, Anthony. 1990. *The Consequences of Modernity.* Stanford, CA: Stanford University Press.

Goodale, Mark, and Nancy Postero. 2013. *Neoliberalism, Interrupted: Social Change and Contested Governance in Contemporary Latin America.* Stanford, CA: Stanford University Press.

Graeber, David. 2004. *Fragments of an Anarchist Anthropology*. Chicago: Prickly Paradigm.

————. 2011. *Debt: The First 5,000 Years*. Brooklyn, NY: Melville House.

————. 2012. "On Social Currencies and Human Economies: Some Notes on the Violence of Equivalence." *Social Anthropology* 20 (4): 411–428.

Gürsel, Zeynep. 2012. "The Politics of Wire Service Photography: Infrastructures of Representation in a Digital Newsroom." *American Ethnologist* 39 (1): 71–89.

Guyer, Jane. 2004. *Marginal Gains: Monetary Transactions in Atlantic Africa*. Chicago: University of Chicago Press.

Hallaq, Wael B. 2009. *Sharīʿa: Theory, Practice, Transformations*. Cambridge: Cambridge University Press.

Hammoudi, Abdellah. 2006. *A Season in Mecca: Narrative of a Pilgrimage*. New York: Hill and Wang.

Han, Clara. 2012. *Life in Debt: Times of Care and Violence in Neoliberal Chile*. Berkeley: University of California Press.

Haneef, Rafe. 2009. "From 'Asset-Backed' to 'Asset-Light' Structures: The Intricate History of Sukuk." *ISRA International Journal of Islamic Finance* 1 (1): 103–126.

Harvey, Penny, and Hannah Knox. 2015. *Roads: An Anthropology of Infrastructure and Expertise*. Ithaca, NY: Cornell University Press.

Hasan, Aznan. 2011. *Fundamentals of Shariah in Islamic Finance*. Kuala Lumpur: Institute of Islamic Banking and Finance Malaysia.

Hasan, Zubair. 2016. "Risk-Sharing: The Sole Basis of Islamic Finance? It Is Time for a Serious Rethink." *Journal of King Abdulaziz University-Islamic Economics* 29 (2): 23–36.

Hasan, Zulkifli, and Mehmet Asutay. 2011. "An Analysis of the Court's Decisions on Islamic Finance Disputes." *ISRA International Journal of Islamic Finance* 3 (2): 41–71.

Hassan, Sharifah Zaleha Syed, and Sven Cederroth. 1997. *Managing Marital Disputes in Malaysia: Islamic Mediators and Conflict Resolution in the Syariah Courts*. Richmond: RoutledgeCurzon.

Hayden, Cori. 2003. "From Market to Market: Bioprospecting's Idioms of Inclusion." *American Ethnologist* 30 (3): 359–371.

Hertz, Ellen. 1998. *The Trading Crowd: An Ethnography of the Shanghai Stock Market*. Cambridge: Cambridge University Press.

Hirschman, Charles. 1987. "The Meaning and Measurement of Ethnicity in Malaysia: An Analysis of Census Classifications." *Journal of Asian Studies* 46: 555–582.

Ho, Karen. 2009. *Liquidated: An Ethnography of Wall Street*. Durham, NC: Duke University Press.

Hoesterey, James. 2016. *Rebranding Islam: Piety, Prosperity, and a Self-Help Guru*. Stanford, CA: Stanford University Press.

Holmes, Douglas R. 2014. *Economy of Words: Communicative Imperatives in Central Banks*. Chicago: University of Chicago Press.

Holmes, Douglas R., and George Marcus. 2005. "Cultures of Expertise and the Management of Globalization: Toward the Re-Functioning of Ethnography." In *Global Assemblages: Technology, Politics, and Ethics as Anthropological Problems*, edited by Aihwa Ong and Stephen Collier, 235–252. Malden: Blackwell.

IFSB. 2009. *Capital Adequacy Requirements for Sukuk, Securitisations and Real Estate Investment*. Kuala Lumpur: Islamic Financial Services Board.

———. 2011. *Guidance Note in Connection with the IFSB Capital Adequacy Standard: The Determination of Alpha in the Capital Adequacy Ration for Institutions (Other Than Insurance Institutions) Offering Only Islamic Financial Services*. Kuala Lumpur: Islamic Financial Services Board.

———. 2017. *Islamic Financial Services Industry Stability Report*. Kuala Lumpur: Islamic Financial Services Board.

International Accounting Standards Board. 2004. "International Accounting Standard 38: Intangible Assets." Accessed May 29, 2017. https://www.iasplus.com/en/standards/ias/ias38.

Iqbal, Munawar, and Philip Molyneux. 2005. *Thirty Years of Islamic Banking: History, Performance, and Prospects*. Houndmills: Palgrave Macmillan.

Ishak, Mohamad Shuhaimi. 2011. "Tabung Haji as an Islamic Financial Institution for Sustainable Economic Development." *International Proceedings of Economics Development and Research* 17: 236–240.

Isik, Damla. 2014. "Vakif as Intent and Practice: Charity and Poor Relief in Turkey." *International Journal of Middle East Studies* 46 (2): 307–327.

Islamic Banking and Takaful Department. 2010. *Shariah Governance Framework for Islamic Financial Institutions*. BNM/RH/GL_012_3. Kuala Lumpur: Bank Negara Malaysia.

ISRA. 2013. "Jeddah Roundtable Declaration." International Shari'ah Research Academy for Islamic Finance. Accessed October 4, 2016. http://ifikr.isra.my/documents/10180/16168/Jeddah%20Roundtable%20Declaration.pdf.

ISRA Bulletin. 2009a. "Responsibility Banking." 2: 1–2.

———. 2009b. "Intellectual Discourse with ISRA Council of Scholars." 3: 10–11.

Jacobs, Michael. 1993. *The Green Economy: Environment, Sustainable Development and the Politics of the Future*. Vancouver: UBC Press.

Jomo, Kwame S. 1991. "Whither Malaysia's New Economic Policy?" *Pacific Affairs* 63 (4): 469–499.

Jones, Carla. 2010. "Materializing Piety: Gendered Anxieties about Faithful Consumption in Contemporary Urban Indonesia." *American Ethnologist* 37 (4): 617–637.

Joseph, Miranda. 2014. *Debt to Society: Accounting for Life under Capitalism*. Minneapolis: University of Minnesota Press.

Juris, Jeffrey S. 2012. "Reflections on #Occupy Everywhere: Social Media, Public Space, and Emerging Logics of Aggregation." *American Ethnologist* 39 (2): 259–279.

Kamali, Mohammad Hashim. 1999. "Maqāṣid Al-Sharī'ah: The Objectives of Islamic Law." *Islamic Studies* 38 (2): 193–208.

Kar, Sohini. 2013. "Recovering Debts: Microfinance Loan Officers and the Work of 'Proxy-Creditors' in India." *American Ethnologist* 40 (3): 480–493.

Karim, Lamia. 2011. *Microfinance and Its Discontents: Women in Debt in Bangladesh*. Minneapolis: University of Minnesota Press.

Kassim, Salina. H., M. Shabri Abdul Majid, and Rosylin Mohd Yusof. 2009. "Impact of Monetary Policy Shocks on the Conventional and Islamic Banks in a Dual Banking System: Evidence from Malaysia." *Journal of Economic Cooperation and Development* 30 (1): 41–58.

Klima, Alan. 2004. "Thai Love Thai: Financing Emotion in Post-Crash Thailand." *Ethnos* 69 (4): 445–464.

Kuran, Timur. 1997. "The Genesis of Islamic Economics: A Chapter in the Politics of Muslim Identity." *Social Research* 64 (2): 301–338.

———. 2004. *Islam and Mammon: The Economic Predicaments of Islamism*. Princeton, NJ: Princeton University Press.

Lahsasna, Ahcene. 2014. *Shari'ah Non-Compliance Risk Management and Legal Documentation in Islamic Finance*. Singapore: John Wiley and Sons.

Laldin, Mohamad Akram. 2008. "The Islamic Financial System: The Malaysian Experience and the Way Forward." *Humanomics* 24 (3): 217–238.

Lazzarato, Maurizio. 2012. *The Making of the Indebted Man: An Essay on the Neoliberal Condition*. Los Angeles: Semiotext(e).

———. 2015. *Governing by Debt*. Cambridge, MA: MIT Press.

Leaf, George. 2014. "Equity Is Better Than Debt in Financing Higher Education." *Forbes,* March 26. Accessed May 17, 2017. https://www.forbes.com/sites/georgeleef/2014/03/26/equity-is-better-than-debt-in-financing-higher-education/—f74b3117cf63.

Lee, Benjamin. 2004. *Financial Derivatives and the Globalization of Risk*. Durham, NC: Duke University Press.

Lee, Shi-ian. 2014. "I Have Failed as Malays Know No Shame, Says Dr M." *Malaysian Insider,* September 11. Accessed August 1, 2017. https://sg.news.yahoo.com/failed-malays-know-no-shame-says-dr-m-094017568.html.

Legal Research Board. 2011. *Islamic Banking Act* 1983. Act 276. Petaling Jaya: International Law Book Services.

———. 2013. *Islamic Financial Services Act* 2013. Act 759. Petaling Jaya: International Law Book Services.

Lepinay, Vincent 2011. *Codes of Finance: Engineering Derivatives in a Global Bank*. Princeton, NJ: Princeton University Press.

Lévi-Strauss, Claude. 1969. *The Raw and the Cooked*. New York: Harper and Row.

Liow, Joseph. 2009. *Piety and Politics: Islamism in Contemporary Malaysia*. Oxford: Oxford University Press.

MacKenzie, Donald A., Fabian Muniesa, and Lucia Siu. 2008. *Do Economists Make Markets? On the Performativity of Economics*. Princeton, NJ: Princeton University Press.

Mains, Daniel. 2012. "Blackouts and Progress: Privatization, Infrastructure, and a Developmentalist State in Jimma, Ethiopia." *Cultural Anthropology* 27 (1): 3–27.

Makdisi, George. 1989. "Scholasticism and Humanism in Classical Islam and the Christian West." *Journal of the American Oriental Society* 109 (2): 175–182.

Malik, Muhammad Shaukat, Ali Malik, and Waqas Mustafa. 2011. "Controversies That Make Islamic Banking Controversial: An Analysis of Issues and Challenges." *American Journal of Social and Management Sciences* 2 (1): 41–46.

Malinowski, Bronislaw. (1922) 2002. *Argonauts of the Western Pacific: An Account of Native Enterprise and Adventure in the Archipelagoes of Melanesian New Guinea*. London: Routledge.

Marcus, George E., and Michael M. J. Fischer. 1986. *Anthropology as Cultural Critique: An Experimental Moment in the Human Sciences*. Chicago: University of Chicago Press.

Masud, Muhammad Khalid, Brinkley Messick, and David Powers. 1996. *Islamic Legal Interpretation: Muftis and Their Fatwas*. Cambridge, MA: Harvard University Press.

Matza, Tomas. 2009. "Moscow's Echo: Technologies of the Self, Publics, and Politics on the Russian Talk Show." *Cultural Anthropology* 24 (3): 489–522.

Maurer, Bill. 1999. "Forget Locke? From Proprietor to Risk-Bearer in New Logics of Finance." *Public Culture* 11 (2): 365–385.

———. 2005. *Mutual Life, Limited: Islamic Banking, Alternative Currencies, Lateral Reason*. Princeton, NJ: Princeton University Press.

———. 2006. *Pious Property: Islamic Mortgages in the United States*. New York: Russell Sage Foundation.

———. 2010. "Form versus Substance: AAOIFI Projects and Islamic Fundamentals in the Case of Sukuk." *Journal of Islamic Accounting and Business Research* 1 (1): 32–41.

———. 2015. *How Would You Like to Pay? How Technology Is Changing the Future of Money*. Durham, NC: Duke University Press.

Maurer, Bill, and Sylvia J. Martin. 2012. "Accidents of Equity and the Aesthetics of Chinese Offshore Incorporation." *American Ethnologist* 39 (3): 527–544.

Mauss, Marcel. (1925) 1990. *The Gift: The Form and Reason for Exchange in Archaic Societies*. London: Routledge.

McKee, Yates. 2013. "Debt: Occupy, Postcontemporary Art, and the Aesthetics of Debt Resistance." *South Atlantic Quarterly* 112 (4): 784–803.

Meneley, Anne. 2007. "Fashions and Fundamentalisms in Fin-de-Siecle Yemen: Chador Barbie and Islamic Socks." *Cultural Anthropology* 22 (2): 214–243.

Mian, Atif, and Amir Sufi. 2015. *House of Debt: How They (and You) Caused the Great Recession, and How We Can Prevent It from Happening Again*. Chicago: University of Chicago Press.

Milne, R. Stephen. 1976. "The Politics of Malaysia's New Economic Policy." *Pacific Affairs* 49 (2): 235–262.

Milne, R. Stephen, and Diane Mauzy. 1999. *Malaysian Politics under Mahathir*. London: Routledge.

Mirakhor, Abbas, and Wang Yong Bao. 2013. "Epistemological Foundation of Finance: Islamic and Conventional." In *Economic Development and Islamic Finance*, edited by Zamir Iqbal and Abbas Mirakhor, 25–66. Washington, DC: World Bank.

Miyazaki, Hirokazu. 2013. *Arbitraging Japan: Dreams of Capitalism at the End of Finance.* Berkeley: University of California Press.

Mohamad, Maznah, and Johan Saravanamuttu. 2015. "Islamic Banking and Finance: Sacred Alignment, Strategic Alliances." *Pacific Affairs* 88 (2): 193–213.

Moors, Annelies, and Emma Tarlo. 2013. *Islamic Fashion and Anti-Fashion: New Perspectives from Europe and North America*. London: Bloomington.

Muehlebach, Andrea. 2012. *The Moral Neoliberal: Welfare and Citizenship in Italy*. Chicago: University of Chicago Press.

Muniesa, Fabian, Yuval Millo, and Michel Callon. 2007. "An Introduction to Market Devices." *Sociological Review* 55 (S2): 1–12.

Mutalib, Hussin. 2008. *Islam in Southeast Asia*. Singapore: Institute of Southeast Asian Studies.

Nagaoka, Shinsuke. 2012. "Critical Overview of the History of Islamic Economics: Formation, Transformation, and New Horizons." *Asian and African Area Studies* 11 (2): 114–136.

Nagata, Judith A. 1984. *The Reflowering of Malaysian Islam: Modern Religious Radicals and Their Roots*. Vancouver: UBC Press.

Nakissa, Aria. 2014. "An Epistemic Shift in Islamic Law: Educational Reform at al-Azhar and Dār al-ʿUlūm." *Islamic Law and Society* 21 (3): 209–251.

Nash, June C. 1979. *We Eat the Mines and the Mines Eat Us: Dependency and Exploitation in Bolivian Tin Mines*. New York: Columbia University Press.

Nelson, Benjamin. 1949. *The Idea of Usury: From Tribal Brotherhood to Universal Otherhood*. Princeton, NJ: Princeton University Press.

Ng, Adam, Abbas Mirakhor, and Mansor H. Ibrahim. 2015. *Social Capital and Risk Sharing: An Islamic Finance Paradigm*. New York: Palgrave Macmillan.

Ong, Aihwa. 1987. *Spirits of Resistance and Capitalist Discipline: Factory Women in Malaysia*. Albany: State University of New York Press.

———. 1990. "State versus Islam: Malay Families, Women's Bodies, and the Body Politic in Malaysia." *American Ethnologist* 17 (2): 258–276.

———. 1999. *Flexible Citizenship: The Cultural Logics of Transnationality*. Durham, NC: Duke University Press.

———. 2006. *Neoliberalism as Exception: Mutations in Citizenship and Sovereignty*. Durham, NC: Duke University Press.

———. 2011. "Introduction: Worlding Cities, or the Art of Being Global." In *Worlding Cities: Asian Experiments and the Art of Being Global*, edited by Ananya Roy and Aihwa Ong, 1–26. Malden, MA: Wiley-Blackwell.

Ortner, Sherry. 1972. "Is Female to Male as Nature Is to Culture?" *Feminist Studies* 1 (2): 5–31.

Osman, Salim. 2013. "Bumiputra Plan a Step Backward for Najib." *Straits Times,* September 23. Accessed August 1, 2017. http://www.asiaone.com/malaysia/bumi putera-plan-step-backwards-najib.

Patail, Abudul Wahab. 2006. "Affin Bank Bhd vs. Zulkifli Abdullah." *Current Law Journal* 1: 438–456.

Peebles, Gustav. 2008. "Inverting the Panopticon: Money and the Nationalization of the Future." *Public Culture* 20 (2): 233–265.

———. 2010. "The Anthropology of Credit and Debt." *Annual Review of Anthropology* 39: 225–240.

———. 2013. "Washing Away the Sins of Debt: The Nineteenth-Century Eradication of the Debtors' Prison." *Comparative Studies in Society and History* 55 (3): 701–724.

Peletz, Michael G. 1996. *Reason and Passion: Representations of Gender in a Malay Society.* Berkeley: University of California Press.

———. 2002. *Islamic Modern: Religious Courts and Cultural Politics in Malaysia.* Princeton, NJ: Princeton University Press.

Pietz, William. 2002. "Material Considerations: On the Historical Forensics of Contract." *Theory, Culture & Society* 19 (5): 35–50.

Piketty, Thomas. 2014. *Capital in the Twenty-First Century.* Cambridge, MA: Belknap Press of Harvard University Press.

Pitluck, Aaron. 2008. "Moral Behavior in Stock Markets: Islamic Finance and Socially Responsible Investment." In *Economics and Morality: Anthropological Approaches,* edited by Katherine Browne and Lynne Milgram, 233–255. Lanham, MD: AltaMira.

———. 2013. "Islamic Banking and Finance: Alternative or Façade?" In *The Oxford Handbook of the Sociology of Finance,* edited by Karin Knorr Cetina and Alex Preda, 431–449. Oxford: Oxford University Press.

Polanyi, Karl. 1944. *The Great Transformation.* New York: Farrar and Rinehart.

Pollard, Jane, and Michael Samers. 2007. "Islamic Banking and Finance: Postcolonial Political Economy and the Decentring of Economic Geography." *Transactions of the Institute of British Geographers* 32 (3): 313–330.

———. 2013. "Governing Islamic Finance: Territory, Agency, and the Making of Cosmopolitan Financial Geographies." *Annals of the Association of American Geographers* 103 (3): 710–726.

Poon, Martha. 2009. "From New Deal Institutions to Capital Markets: Commercial Consumer Risk Scores and the Making of Subprime Mortgage Finance." *Accounting, Organization and Society* 34 (5): 654–674.

Power, Michael. 2007. *Organized Uncertainty: Designing a World of Risk Management.* Oxford: Oxford University Press.

Prakash, Gyan. 1999. *Another Reason: Science and the Imagination of Modern India.* Princeton, NJ: Princeton University Press.

Rabinow, Paul. 1977. *Reflections on Fieldwork in Morocco*. Berkeley: University of California Press.

———. 1996. "Artificiality and Enlightenment: From Sociobiology to Biosociality." In *Essays on the Anthropology of Reason*, 91–111. Princeton, NJ: Princeton University Press.

———. 2002. "Midst Anthropology's Problems." *Cultural Anthropology* 17 (2): 135–149.

———. 2003. *Anthropos Today: Reflections on Modern Equipment*. Princeton, NJ: Princeton University Press.

Reid, Anthony. 1969. "The Kuala Lumpur Riots and the Malaysian Political System." *Australian Outlook* 23 (3): 258–278.

———. 1988. *Southeast Asia in the Age of Commerce, 1450–1680*. New Haven, CT: Yale University Press.

Reinhart, Carmen, and Kenneth Rogoff. 2009. *This Time Is Different: Eight Centuries of Financial Folly*. Princeton, NJ: Princeton University Press.

Rethel, Lena. 2011. "Whose Legitimacy? Islamic Finance and the Global Financial Order." *Review of International Political Economy* 18 (1): 75–98.

Riles, Annelise. 2010. "Collateral Expertise: Legal Knowledge in the Global Financial Markets." *Current Anthropology* 51 (6): 795–806.

———. 2011. *Collateral Knowledge: Legal Reasoning in the Global Financial Markets*. Chicago: University of Chicago Press.

Rodgers, Susan. 2012. "On Exhibiting Transnational Mobilities: Museum Display Decisions in 'Gold Cloths of Sumatra.'" *Museum Anthropology* 35 (2): 115–135.

Rogoff, Kenneth. 1999. "International Institutions for Reducing Global Financial Instability." *Journal of Economic Perspectives* 13 (4): 21–42.

Roitman, Janet. 2003. "Unsanctioned Wealth; or, the Productivity of Debt in Northern Cameroon." *Public Culture* 15 (2): 211–237.

———. 2014. *Anti-Crisis*. Durham, NC: Duke University Press.

Rose, Nikolas S. 1999. *Powers of Freedom: Reframing Political Thought*. Cambridge: Cambridge University Press.

Rosly, Saiful Azhar. 2005. *Critical Issues on Islamic Banking and Financial Markets: Islamic Economics, Banking and Finance, Investments, Takaful and Financial Planning*. Kuala Lumpur: Dinamas.

Ross, Andrew. 2014. *Creditocracy and the Case for Debt Refusal*. New York: OR Books.

Rouse, Carolyn, and Janet Hoskins. 2004. "Purity, Soul Food, and Sunni Islam: Explorations at the Intersection of Consumption and Resistance." *Cultural Anthropology* 19 (2): 226–249.

Rudnyckyj, Daromir. 2004. "Technologies of Servitude: Governmentality and Indonesian Transnational Labor Migration." *Anthropological Quarterly* 77 (3): 407–434.

———. 2009. "Spiritual Economies: Islam and Neoliberalism in Contemporary Indonesia." *Cultural Anthropology* 24 (1): 104–141.

————. 2010. *Spiritual Economies: Islam, Globalization, and the Afterlife of Development*. Ithaca, NY: Cornell University Press.

————. 2014a. "Regimes of Self-Improvement: Globalization and the Will to Work." *Social Text* 32 (3): 109–127.

————. 2014b. "Economy in Practice: Islamic Finance and the Problem of Market Reason." *American Ethnologist* 41 (1): 110–127.

————. 2016. "Objectifying Economies: Contemporary Themes in the Anthropology of Economic Knowledge and Practice." In *Routledge Companion to Contemporary Anthropology*, edited by Simon Coleman, Susan B. Hyatt, and Ann Kingsolver, 244–264. London: Routledge.

————. 2017a. "Assembling Islam and Liberalism: Market Freedom and the Moral Project of Islamic Finance." In *Religion and the Morality of the Market*, edited by Daromir Rudnyckyj and Filippo Osella, 160–176. Cambridge: Cambridge University Press.

————. 2017b. "Subjects of Debt: Financial Subjectification and Collaborative Risk in Malaysian Islamic Finance." *American Anthropologist* 119 (2): 269–283.

Rudnyckyj, Daromir, and Filippo Osella, eds. 2017. *Religion and the Morality of the Market*. Cambridge: Cambridge University Press.

Saeed, Abdullah. 1996. *Islamic Banking and Interest: A Study of the Prohibition of Riba and Its Contemporary Interpretation*. Leiden: Brill.

Sandler, Jen, and Renita Thedvall. 2017. *Meeting Ethnography: Meetings as Key Technologies of Contemporary Governance, Development, and Resistance*. New York: Routledge.

Sassen, Saskia. 1991. *The Global City: New York, London, Tokyo*. Princeton, NJ: Princeton University Press.

Schmitt, Carl. (1922) 2005. *Political Theology: Four Chapters on the Concept of Sovereignty*. Chicago: University of Chicago Press.

Schuster, Caroline E. 2014. "The Social Unit of Debt: Gender and Creditworthiness in Paraguayan Microfinance." *American Ethnologist* 41 (3): 563–578.

Schwittay, Anke. 2011. "The Marketization of Poverty." *Current Anthropology* 52 (S3): 71–82.

————. 2014. *New Media and International Development: Representation and Affect in Microfinance*. New York: Routledge.

Scott, James C. 1976. *The Moral Economy of the Peasant: Rebellion and Subsistence in Southeast Asia*. New Haven, CT: Yale University Press.

Securities Commission Malaysia. 2010. *Proceedings of SC-OCIS Roundtable and Forum 2010*. Kuala Lumpur: Securities Commission.

Sedgwick, Mark. 2010. *Makers of the Muslim World: Muhammad Abduh*. London: Oneworld.

Shamsul, Amri B. 2001. "A History of an Identity, an Identity of a History: The Idea and Practice of 'Malayness' in Malaysia Reconsidered." *Journal of Southeast Asian Studies* 32 (3): 355–366.

Shatzmiller, Maya. 2001. "Islamic Institutions and Property Rights: The Case of the 'Public Good' Waqf." *Journal of the Economic and Social History of the Orient* 44 (1): 44–74.

Siegel, James T. 1969. *The Rope of God*. Berkeley: University of California Press.

Silverstein, Brian. 2011. *Islam and Modernity in Turkey*. New York: Palgrave Macmillan.

Skovgaard-Petersen, Jakob. 1997. *Defining Islam for the Egyptian State: Muftis and Fatwas of the Dar Al-Iftā*. Leiden: Brill.

Sloane, Patricia. 1999. *Islam, Modernity, and Entrepreneurship among the Malays*. New York: St. Martin's.

Sloane-White, Patricia. 2014. "Interrogating 'Malayness': Islamic Transformations among the Malay College Kuala Kangsar (MCKK) Cohort." *Journal of the Malaysian Branch of the Royal Asiatic Society* 87 (1): 21–36.

Smeltzer, Sandra. 2008. "The Message Is the Market: Selling Biotechnology and Nation in Malaysia." In *Taking Southeast Asia to Market: Commodities, Nature, and People in a Neoliberal Age*, edited by Joseph Nevins and Nancy Lee Peluso, 191–205. Ithaca, NY: Cornell University Press.

Smith, Wilfred Cantwell. 1957. *Islam in Modern History*. Princeton, NJ: Princeton University Press.

Sorkin, Andrew Ross. 2009. *Too Big to Fail: The Inside Story of How Wall Street and Washington Fought to Save the Financial System from Crisis—and Themselves*. New York: Viking.

Star Online. 2012. "Axiata Plans Airtime Sukuk." August 3. Accessed July 31, 2017. http://www.thestar.com.my/business/business-news/2012/08/03/axiata-plans-airtime-sukuk/.

Stein, Jerome L. 2010. "Greenspan's Retrospective of Financial Crisis and Stochastic Optimal Control." *European Financial Management* 16: 858–871.

Stoler, Ann. 1985. *Capitalism and Confrontation in Sumatra's Plantation Belt, 1870–1979*. New Haven, CT: Yale University Press.

Stout, Noelle. 2016. "#Indebted: Disciplining the Moral Valence of Mortgage Debt Online." *Cultural Anthropology* 31 (1): 82–106.

Tagliacozzo, Eric. 2013. *The Longest Journey: Southeast Asians and the Pilgrimage to Mecca*. New York: Oxford University Press.

Taussig, Michael T. 1980. *The Devil and Commodity Fetishism in South America*. Chapel Hill: University of North Carolina Press.

Tobin, Sarah A. 2016. *Everyday Piety: Islam and Economy in Jordan*. Ithaca, NY: Cornell University Press.

Torii, Takashi. 2003. "The Mechanism for State-Led Creation of Malaysia's Middle Classes." *Developing Economies* 41: 221–242.

Totaro, Lorenzo. 2009. "Vatican Says Islamic Finance May Help Western Banks in Crisis." *Bloomberg News*, March 4. Accessed April 10, 2012. http://www

.bloomberg.com/apps/news?pid=20601092&sid=aOsOLE8uiNOg&refer
=italy.

Tripp, Charles. 2006. *Islam and the Moral Economy: The Challenge of Capitalism*. Cambridge: Cambridge University Press.

Turner, Adair. 2016. *Between Debt and the Devil: Money, Credit, and Fixing Global Finance*. Princeton, NJ: Princeton University Press.

Udovitch, Abraham L. 1970. *Partnership and Profit in Medieval Islam*. Princeton, NJ: Princeton University Press.

Usmani, Taqi. 2008. "Sukuk and Their Contemporary Applications." Accessed July 31, 2017. http://www.kantakji.com/media/7747/f148.pdf.

Venardos, Angelo M. 2006. *Islamic Banking and Finance in South-East Asia: Its Development and Future*. Hackensack: World Scientific.

Walton, Jeremy F. 2017. *Muslim Civil Society and the Politics of Religious Freedom in Turkey*. Oxford: Oxford University Press.

Warde, Ibrahim. 2010. *Islamic Finance in the Global Economy*. Edinburgh: Edinburgh University Press.

Weber, Max. (1920) 2001. *The Protestant Ethic and the Spirit of Capitalism*. London: Routledge.

Weiss, Hadas. 2014. "Homeownership in Israel: The Social Costs of Middle-Class Debt." *Cultural Anthropology* 29 (1): 128–149.

Whiting, Amanda. 2008. "Desecularising Malaysian Law?" In *Examining Practice, Interrogating Theory: Comparative Legal Studies in Asia*, edited by Sarah Biddulph and Penelope Nicholson, 223–266. Leiden: Martinus Nijhoff.

Wicks, Robert Sigfrid. 1992. *Money, Markets, and Trade in Early Southeast Asia: The Development of Indigenous Monetary Systems to A.D. 1400*. Ithaca, NY: Southeast Asia Program, Cornell University.

Wilson, Rodney. 2004. "The Development of Islamic Economics: Theory and Practice." In *Islamic Thought in the Twentieth Century*, edited by Suha Taji-Farouki and Basheer M. Nafi, 195–222. London: I. B. Tauris.

Wolf, Eric R. 1982. *Europe and the People without History*. Berkeley: University of California Press.

World Bank. 2016. "Upper Middle Income Countries." Accessed June 6 2016. http://data.worldbank.org/income-level/UMC.

Xiang, Biao, and Johan Lindquist. 2014. "Migration Infrastructure." *International Migration Review* 48 (S1): 122–148.

Yaacob, Hakimah. 2011. "Analysis of Legal Disputes in Islamic Finance and the Way Forward: With Special Reference to a Study Conducted at Muamalat Court, Kuala Lumpur, Malaysia." *ISRA Research Paper* 25. Kuala Lumpur: International Shariah Research Academy for Islamic Finance.

Yehambaram, John. 2012. "Political Technologies and Multiculturalism in Malaysia." Master's thesis, University of Victoria.

Zahraa, Mahdi, and Shafaai Mahmor. 2002. "The Validity of Contracts When the

Goods Are Not Yet in Existence in the Islamic Law of Sale of Goods." *Arab Law Quarterly* 17 (4): 379–397.

Zaloom, Caitlin. 2004. "The Productive Life of Risk." *Cultural Anthropology* 19 (3): 365–391.

———. 2006. *Out of the Pits: Trading and Technology from Chicago to London.* Chicago: University of Chicago Press.

Index

Page numbers in italics refer to figures.